New Age Economics
By Clarissa Wilson Pine & D.A. Hewlett

Dedicated to Dad

Table of Contents

New Age Economics

Introduction

Greetings Gentle Reader. Welcome back and thank you for your continued interest in my helpful writing. I hope you are receiving some useful insights and your mental outlook is comfortable and improving, or in the state you find most desirable. Also welcome to the first time reader. If you like this book I have two others you may find enjoyable. In fact, you will probably find reading those first two books helpful to fully understanding this one.

As you may know from reading my earlier efforts I came into author Dom as a last resort. After years in the job market behaving in accordance with general rules and policy, I found that the label of uncontrollable was part of my character baggage. I was controllable by the rules which I naively thought applied equally to all, but I was out of control of popular networks and their personal interests. In addition, with technology creating job cuts across the board and globalization sending jobs overseas, my status as a single person relatively unfettered by financial and familial obligations made me the natural choice for dismissal. I suppose it was assumed that my work ethic would ensure an endless fount of employment while neglecting the damage being done to my character appearance otherwise.

Every so often I see my situation skillfully portrayed in media as when watching the PBS mystery series called "Foyle's War" where the main detective character is repeatedly referred to as out of control by his superiors, underlings and others usually breaking the law. In my usual TV watching fashion I was sitting there shaking my fist at the screen saying only moderately loudly that "Foyle is not out of control you fools. You're the ones not following any of the decency guidelines, much less the rules. Give me a *fudging* (the G rated version) break!"

Of course one of the reasons I enjoyed watching this particular program was because the virtuous depiction of Foyle's crime fighting team reassured me that I was not absolutely adrift in the middle of the modern cosmic consciousness that anything goes if it feels right. It made me feel good and secure, that is until I remembered that it is set during WWII whose background details are habitually grizzly, and that the time frame took place 70 years ago when the threats of overpopulation had not fully given the educated, the influential, and leadership the bright idea of confusing everyone about what constitutes desirable methods of feeling good while also dismantling government aid institutions.

Anyway, I kept being dismissed from jobs or heavily harassed until I took the clearly shouted hint by harassment actions to please leave. Finally I stopped meekly leaving and started putting up more of a fight which then rendered me completely unemployable. As I saw it my choice was to become a slave to whichever network had absorbed me on a probationary basis, or to follow the carefully arrived at rules and policy for an organization designed to apply and keep everyone happy and productive, an ideal of general equality. In my opinion there was no contest between the options. It was not as if people were not granted sick days, vacation time, personal days, holidays, healthcare, and a variety of other benefits, it was just that the general ordinary person was feeling a lack of control in their lives and sought remedy outside of the control provided by the rules and policy.

Why does everyone feel a lack of control in their lives? Is it the close quarters of society which encourages everyone to compete and compare themselves with others? A person always finding that there is someone out there presenting a vastly different option there is no competing with, or worst case scenario, someone smarter, more athletic, talented, and resourceful as judged by a person socially approved to pass such judgments leaves the poorly judged person feeling dissatisfied.

Would he feel so dissatisfied if he was not constantly made aware of his short comings perceived by others and thus pushed to engage in controlling competitive behavior? Minus critique he would reward himself for accomplishing various milestones in his journey to gain supporting skills which allow him to participate in society usefully in a manner desirable to both society and himself.

Maybe people feel out of control because they made decisions very early in life before they had all the facts regarding the environment to hand and now find they are married with a house full of children and the life style is extremely uncomfortable. Some of these early settlers may feel they have missed out in some way, not appreciating the benefits which accrue to those who get on board with the most rewarded and favored lifestyle early on in life.

In some cases the early settlers may fully appreciate the rewards to their lifestyle decisions and in an attempt to reap even more benefits, adopt a dissatisfied demeanor to help keep others off balance and in eternal consideration of their apparent disappointed condition. All sorts of possibilities exist.

Generally, however, a population of people covered for food, shelter, and other basic necessities would seem to be beyond the absolute need to compete. Why do those with a lovely home, pool, cars and other paraphernalia still feel the need to get more? Is it greed or is it something else? Gentle reader, if you have read my other two books you know my viewpoint is that it is something else which prods people on in the face of mental and physical devastation to try and accomplish one more senseless goal like getting a golf course in addition to a tennis court and pool.

In some cases money accrues according to economic formulas so fast that once a person has a certain surplus amount of it invested wisely, they cannot help but acquire more by no more conscious effort than sitting back in a chair in the sun and living within the comfortable means of the money accruing from their investments at a steadily increasing rate. For others less mathematically savvy and adventurous, if they want more prestige items and lifestyle, they must find a way to get paid for work to acquire those items. In a nutshell, to not publically demonstrate an insatiable desire to have bigger and better things ear marks a person as unambitious, out of control, and questionable good citizenship material, believe it or not.

A low income person may not have the focus and stamina to have a better paying job, but he should at least be wise enough to say he wishes he could have one, whether he really wants one or not. Additionally, a person suffering from lack of ambition and hence immune to overbearing societal control must be willing to engage in networked dirty work as a demonstration of support for the ambitious.

Without the internal mechanism making a person feel low self-esteem and a yearning emptiness due to odious comparisons and the survival fear triggered by these damaging appraisals, a person might happily direct his life and free time after fulfilling his ample contribution to supporting society's need for efficient acquisition and distribution of resources, the idealistic model for society based on equality under decent, realistic standards and rules applied to all.

Because of the presence of the social hierarchy and these comparisons, most feel a lack of control and security regarding ongoing survival. Hence, the world is engulfed in an atmosphere which makes almost all feel the need to act outside the scope of rules and policy regardless of their level of fair play and careful attempts to act as a safety net. When the crafty implementation of rules and standards is designed to support the appearance of a hierarchy of goodness where such an actual hierarchy does not exist in nature, or is only manufactured by creating the appearance of inherent worthiness in chosen peoples (also referred to as approved bigotry) people acting out of a sense of survival interest engage in activities to gain security they may not be altogether proud to admit in the harsh glare of the light of day.

Admittedly, whenever the character Detective Chief Superintendent Christopher Foyle would let loose with some comment about how a particular black marketer or other such scoundrel was destined to hang for his crime due to the war back drop to his nefarious actions, I lost a wee bit of respect for the old sleuth, but then again, no one is perfect. I suppose on occasion, in the privacy of my own home I have gleefully entertained the occurrence of some dismal prospect for a person who I feel has dealt me a pretty raw deal, but in real life I do not want punishment justice, revenge, or the rich satisfaction of telling a person off for a too short lived moment because these deeds only add to the problem in the long run, not improving the situation for even a tiny second or lightening the ongoing load for myself in any appreciable measure.

Thus, as a result of my hyper rational attitude, rather than joining the network fray and trying to place as many warm bodies beneath my heels as possible, I have come to the present dilemma of general lack of employability and taking up the writing quill/computer to earn my keep by helping others to see the world accurately and hopefully healthily. So, gentle reader, what is this book going to be about? Well, I don't expect to stray too far from my earlier themes of thinking for you, support for the equality ideal, embracing the emotion of love as much as possible without making a sacrifice of yourself, and defining current modern problems correctly.

Obviously I need a new theme to center my various practical homilies around. Previously I was able to use my lifetime romantic search to help demonstrate the impact of the surrounding social environment on that particular dream. In my second book I used my lifetime experience with cats and my use of popular religions and philosophies to help keep a relatively calm energetic upbeat outlook, permitting me to see the surrounding environment more clearly rather than obfuscated by a personal fog of self-loathing and assumed individual failure. Since I felt my life experience was thoroughly informed on these topics, I thought I brought the necessary credentials to be able to "write what I knew" to the table. So what else do I know a lot about? Hmm.

Some might say I was deluding myself in writing those first two books and I don't know anything at all, period. Although I was writing about the romantic search, cats, and popular religions/philosophies, what I was also writing was encouragement for the reader to adopt a mental habit of thinking for himself as much as possible to add quality of life.

4

Thinking for you is extremely important to overall happiness in the absence of some generous caretaker who foresees and takes care of your survival needs, and the needs for personal growth which arrive after one has locked down a survival niche. Many will tell you that God is the generous caretaker who will foresee all needs and all that is required by the individual is humility, faith, obedience, gratitude and prayer. That list seems pretty short, simple, clear and easy to achieve, but like so many attractive propositions, the actual delivery of the goods is suspect, mostly because human beings are making these promises for God without really knowing much about this unknowable entity.

What the authors of popular religions do know is that leadership in civilization, under ideal laboratory conditions, would like to take care of everyone's needs and personal fulfillment goals, but to be able to arrive at the plum laboratory ideal conditions, the general populace must adopt a demeanor of humility, faith, obedience, gratitude, and patient request. Well, this idealism presents a lovely picture of life to be enjoyed as a gift from a munificent creator, and personally, this picture has inspired most of my life activity to date. Even while I have been thinking for myself, I have dared to continue to hope for this breathtaking vista of possibility for my own life and for everyone else.

I suppose some might rightly accuse me of selfishly populating other people's life with my hoped for ideal, so with that in mind, some time ago I modified my dream for everyone else to be under each individual's own personal particular direction. I believe it is this realistic accusation which seems to throw a monkey wrench into the workings of the sanitized laboratory conditions.

The divergence of idealism goals I feel results from the fact that the world is a large place, even with technology making it smaller in a virtual sense every day and the presence of a social hierarchy impacting the distribution of survival resources which separates individuals into climate and mental outlook cubicles or in some cases actual prisons. I doubt too many people were dreaming of prison as their ultimate ideal, but nonetheless, that is what they got.

In any event, once the world is visibly occupied by persons enjoying varying levels of comfort and rich variety of life experience, you set the laboratory stage to commence at a point distant from the ideal sanitized condition, making the meek demeanor no longer a definite ticket to rewards, unless it is accompanied by a generous portion of thinking clearly on your own. In essence, the meek demeanor works if you are fortunately placed within a powerful network ably taking care of the network membership in a manner which clears your conscience's goal posts easily, allowing for calm mental equilibrium. Difficulties may arise if at lunch break every day the bottom five least productive/useful people are dismissed one way or another.

In the above example voicing shock and dismay with the company policy to daily winnow the staff will no doubt land a person in a least productive slot sooner than later, so keeping a meek demeanor in this case is vital to ongoing survival. For some, however, rationally keeping mum does not feel like a life worth continuing while watching five panic stricken victims being lead to the door. Perhaps these impulsive loudmouths are envisioning the day at some point in the future when their turn will arrive for departure and are unable to muster the calm patient fortitude to push the dismal specter out of mind until absolutely necessary. Perhaps they just cannot stand to watch the horrifying spectacle day in and day out, maybe it is a combination of the two. It could be that they have been beguiled by a stronger personality who wants to use a persuaded victim's warm body to block the inevitable selection of their own conniving person for as long as possible.

Whatever the case, meekness is dependent on a person being at peace with environmental stimulus, be it generous paychecks or panic inducing fears. How does a person arrive at this state of meekness, this cool detached adjustment to otherwise panic provoking circumstances, this Zen like clarity of feeling like you are standing on a mountaintop able to perceive the whole world and nodding sagely in informed agreement with the spectrum of appalling goings on?

Well, let's see. There are always mind altering drugs, not personally recommended. There are other forms of legal and socially sanctioned escapism, immersion in work, a hobby, media entertainment, or role playing games. And last but not least, there is thinking for you. Some might also call this meekness road another form of escapism, but I feel for this method to be a true strengthening aid, a person will have to do their best to absorb the whole environment, warts, wars and all.

So is this book going to be about meekness? Loving meekness? Informed meekness? Meditative meekness? All of the above? None? Hmmmmph. Although I cannot categorically endorse all sources of meekness, specifically drugs and extreme physical limit pushing, I do feel the gentle reader will benefit from, at the very least, a passing acquaintanceship with the internal state of meekness and to that end, I am going to write this book in part about the obstacles to meekness and happiness with an examination of economics compared to religion.

No doubt there is a large group of people out there who is going to disagree with my pairing of meekness with happiness, feeling that

6

boldness, competitiveness, strife, challenges, and domination more certainly lead to happiness, and to those habitual conflict seekers, I say read my second book about security in survival resources and the journey of life which is an acknowledged worldwide metaphor for the general unfolding of the life experience for all mankind. Maybe a book about meekness and happiness is not for the merry battle chaser, but perhaps a conflict hunter can still enjoy this book by doing the very thing he does best, by disagreeing with it as much and as loudly as he pleases, and then destroying it utterly in the fashion he relishes the most within the bounds of humanity and the law.

Meekness 101

Meek (adj) 1)Exhibiting humility and patience: GENTLE. 2) Easily imposed on: SUBMISSIVE. From Webster's II New Riverside University Dictionary.

Synonyms for meek: patient, humble, timid, docile, modest, compliant, mild, quiet, lowly, weak, cowed, fearful, tame, yielding, unassuming, orderly, manageable, forbearing, long-suffering

Antonyms for meek: assertive, overbearing, bold, arrogant, irritable, proud, high-spirited

The above summary of meekness demonstrates its spectrum of description within the English Language. On the one hand there are the words "patient, modest, mild, quiet, unassuming, orderly, manageable, and forbearing" all of which have a positive connotation standing alone. Any of the previously listed positive words, however, can take on a disparaging negative vibe when in the mouth of a wit dispensing with a sense of compassion when creating a bon mot or quotable quote.

For example: Patience: a minor form of despair, disguised as a virtue –Bierce. In this saying Bierce is clearly in the camp of conflict and fighting since he views patience as despair of winning a battle and hence parades as a virtue rather than being properly labeled as cowardice.

Perhaps Bierce is envisioning a person who should be standing up to an oppressive authority but instead is patiently tolerating an authority the person is unequal to engaging meaningfully in battle. Is a person a coward for wisely avoiding a wasteful situation, or is he virtuous for patiently enduring the situation without creating the strife which will impact innocent bystanders?

These situations are difficult to sift through for right and wrong answers and hence require the ability to patiently address complicated matters, waiting quietly and mildly for additional information. Naturally the downside exists also. One can become so patient that a person dulls

7

their sensitivities and exhausts themselves, becoming unable to recognize a real need to step up and run, or fight if hopelessly cornered.

By itself the dictionary is a compendium of words and meanings. For any given language the emotional importance of certain items is evident by the number of words present to use in discussion and description. Meekness has nineteen synonyms in the English language which I was able to locate from a variety of sources, perhaps there are more.

My analysis of positive connotations and negative connotations will differ from others performing the same task, but the main point is that you can view meekness as a positive thing or a negative thing and the surrounding environment, as I never tire of emphasizing, will be a great aid in the pointing out the direction for personal truth. What is a necessary battle for one person is a moment for gathering further information, patiently, for another.

In any given situation the facts may reveal an actual attitude of cowardice behind heroic actions, or as is most often the case, the facts of any given moment are hard to pin down and write in stone as self-interest colors away at the presentation of perceptions. So any complete discussion of mild meekness will also necessarily include considerations of bravery, boldness, arrogance and so forth. Really more like two sides of the same coin, as it were, than true opposites if enough speculative delving into the illuminating details is accomplished.

As a personal example, I believe people often mistake me for brave, when actually I am more accurately described as fun loving in most instances of label application. This initial inaccurate label application came up when I was out dancing or when I was wearing spectacle creating attire. I did and do consider myself to fall within the range of a mild, meek personality, but many pointed to my dancing and attire choices and said I was deluding myself. If I wanted to fall within the popularly accepted category of meek personality I needed to become ten degrees more invisible and much, much quieter in cases where I insisted on at least putting my opinion on the record once.

I believe the divergence of opinion in this case is a result of my internal state when I am dancing and wearing garish clothing or engaging in the anxiety release of getting my opinion on record. As far as I am concerned, the actual experienced internal state as reported by the person doing the feeling and experiencing more reliably relates the emotional experience rather than a blanket of emotions being assigned to any given set of actions universally by a person or persons competitively trying to win the appearance game. Back in the 1990's I noticed a definite trend amongst some of my couples dancing acquaintances to equate dancing skill with fighting skill, hence, one fellow in particular who recognized my ability to dance well with almost any partner constantly suggested I should take up the martial arts.

To my way of thinking a social couple's dance performed to enjoyable music in no way resembles hand to hand combat. What was that fool thinking? In addition to the dance activity I also enjoyed making my own fancy clothes and wearing them, basking in the chivalrous compliments from my dance partners. What would be the counterpart in judo to this part of the dance activity? Being complimented on my fraying white belt as my opponent strangled me with it? Nonetheless because I was very bold in my dance moves, my willingness to wear eye catching attire, and openness to welcoming first time dancers into the community, I witlessly earned a reputation for bravery I think still haunts me to this day.

From the labelers' point of view, many women in the dance community wore more professional style attire and did not attempt any personal embellishment to the standard dance moves taught in class. From the perspective of not standing out in a crowd and the safety in numbers experienced in the herd, this type of behavior is cautiously conservative, but not necessarily meek. Many of the ladies did have a professional career and wearing their casual clothes which reflected this status was more competitive than otherwise in my book.

Another loss to competition is diversity in behavior which does not lead to some kind of competition advantage. Swinging hips rhythmically, energetic step bounces, hip circles, rib cage accents and other embellishments I brought to line dancing and couples dancing from my Belly Dancing repertoire were all rejected by the other ladies, for the most part, although the fellows certainly enjoyed my dance style.

In my unique, non-confrontational way I was competing in the meekest manner possible by not directly coming into conflict with the other ladies. Rather than competing for executing west coast swing sidekicks with the most precision, I simply performed the move in an entirely new and different way which avoided competition and comparison altogether or so I thought.

Only later did I realize completely that no matter what you do, the competitive will still compete with you whether you are actively and consciously competing with them or not. Also, they will also make sure you suffer some sort of losing consequences to make sure they enjoy a win. Even though these ladies were clearly better looking than me, better employed than me, and better liked by the men than me for having these advantages, it was not enough of a pride buzz when I was prancing about being entertaining in my own humble style.

Looking at the above description of female styles, my placement of adjectives differs from how someone else might "spin" the yarn of dance participants. Really, no matter what you talk about, there is always plenty of this type of wiggle room to place controlling labels and adjectives. Probably the most important distinction to notice is the offensive placing of labels and defensive placing of labels. Frankly, left up to my own devices, I do not place labels at all, but if called upon to do so defensively, than I will make an attempt if absolutely necessary, or if possible, avoid the conversation altogether.

Given enough time for reflection I can come up with a defense, as I have done here, but on the spur of the moment the often repeated remarks about my trying to outdo or outperform others were met with my intention of having a good time, naturally, using skills I developed over the past twenty years before I was even aware of a couples dancing community. I was not insisting all the ladies with better chest endowments (all of them) wear less revealing cloths or get breast reductions so that I would not have to fail miserably in that competition/comparison.

Why couldn't they let me enjoy the vagaries of blind luck which afforded me a slight and meaningless advantage of presenting a visually engaging dance? Although the men enjoyed dancing with me, none of them were going to take a risk on a wild card like me with uncertain employment, not to mention that most considered me too old when many younger options were readily available.

Right alongside of word spinning is actual spinning during the dance. One of the aids to spinning in dance technique is focusing, while spinning, on one point by moving your head as needed to keep the one sighting spot in the field of vision at all times during the spin. By performing this spinning spotting a dancer avoids becoming dizzy and staggering, perhaps completely collapsing to the ground, when the spin ends because their internal concentration on one spot does not change for the entire fifteen or more rotations. Otherwise, taking in all the changing scenery during the spin leaves the brain unable to keep up and not be sure where the body is located at the end of the visually riveting whirl.

One of the pieces of advice given to religion and philosophy students is the value of picking one religion or philosophy for starters and really getting a firm grip on this one belief system before diverging into attempting to understand how other popular creeds support a particular culture. The firm foundation helps in recognizing similar points of belief while also making the differences clearer and easier to detect. When

10

pondering the differences from the original religion or philosophy of investigation, one could speculate about historical events, climate impact, and government type on the differing emphasis of various religions. Thus, while trying to sift through all the spins of differing religions and philosophies, a person would have their own inner focus on an earlier predetermined chosen spot.

On a more personal note, I have done quite a bit of dance spinning throughout the years. I was likened by some generous enraptured audience members (it is truly wonderful when people recognize the willingness to entertain and share behind even amateur dance performances) to a figure skater in my speed and sustainment of a spin. Skating spinning, although I have never dance skated, I imagine is different from the type of dance spinning previously described, and when I have watched professionals and Olympic skaters, they are spinning so fast it is impossible for their head to whip around in a determined attempt to keep their eyes focused on one spot on one of four walls. How do they do it? More importantly, how did I do it?

Although these dance feats took place some time ago, I do still remember how I did it even if I cannot do it equally well anymore. The trick is to keep your focus on an outstretched hand, like whirling dervishes, or to follow that hand with your eyes if you attempt something more spectacular like bending forward or back during a spin. Like grasping the views of religions, you have to work up to the really long sustained spins.

At first, you may not feel like you look good because your legs are sort of stumbling about, your feet are not necessarily doing exactly what you want them to do, and your other hand is doing something, but you cannot be sure exactly what. Eventually, though, strength through habit will come to those feet and legs, and a dancer can throw in a rhythmic head toss with their spin to really wow the spectators. As it happens, these tosses can feel very elating when matched up properly to the music.

Other feet, knee, and leg strengtheners are walking, jogging, jump roping, yoga and weight lifting, all of which I have done at one time or another. By engaging in a little bit of cross training a person can be surprised at the new ability to be in touch with various parts of the body they did not have so much direct control over previously. Give it a try. Trust me, you will be surprised.

Likewise, if you want to cross train in your ability to spin words to create a meekness/boldness identity which will act as a shield against others lobbing in identity cement to restrict your ability to participate in the gifts of life everyone has a right to partake of, I suggest that the previously specified exercise options will also be a terrific aid to these verbal and mental skills as well. Body and soul, body and brain, body and mind, body and spirit, body and _____ (fill in the blank), whatever your choice for describing the activity which runs a person's life experience, the physical and the non-physical component are permanently connected in real time. By neglecting one a person is also neglecting the other.

A couple of exercise options which are noticeably missing from the above list are any kind of competitive sports activity, hunting sport or participation in extreme sport activity. Since I am using my own personal experience in compiling what I am hoping will be widely useful and helpful information, I cannot personally speak to extreme sport activity since I have never tried it. It is just one of those things I have never felt the irresistible pull toward so I cannot say one way or the other if jumping off a bridge attached to a bungee cord will make you humbler, or braver, or how others will perceive you, or attempt to label you. I suspect it is safe to say onlookers will be momentarily impressed, thus I would caution the bungee jumper not to let this brief and probably fickle presence of awe go to their head in a prideful manner or a cynical one. Brief moments of mob awe on such occasions are quite natural, but fleeting.

Actual spinning in bungee jumping may occur as a person dangles helplessly from the end of his cord until the moment he is able to help himself. No doubt spinning takes place in some of the other extreme activities, but it may be the presence of spinning is not consciously initiated or desirable since it is usually a precursor to crashing or drowning. I suppose heart stopping excitement can strengthen the heart and circulatory system as well as bring a calmer resting level to general day to day activity. It may be these types of benefits an extreme sports aficionado can look forward to from his activities. More than that, I can offer no comment.

As for hunting and fishing, likewise, these activities hold no allure for me and might most accurately be termed as actually repulsive to me. This being the case, I cannot say if lying in wait with a deadly weapon for some hapless and environmentally strained creature to wander across your path so you can shoot him is helpful to the type of mental abilities which allow a person to see the world clearly. If I was going to submit a guess, I would say not, especially if a person is coupling alcohol consumption with these activities as the likelihood for self-inflicted injury causing blinding agony is present as a statistically meaningful probability.

In the interest of fairness and completeness, a hunting enthusiast might characterize the activity as careful planning and alertness to face the vagaries of nature and hence full of opportunity to exercise both physical and mental apparatus. Forgive me, but I can be no more flattering than that on the subject, although I am sure it is possible to do so for some. We all have our own little mental prisons of outlook. Again, spinning in these situations seems to not be indicated.

Lastly, there are competitive sports. In my youth I was attracted to a young man who played tennis and I was informed (incorrectly) he returned my interest. Despite my lack of overall competitiveness and killer instinct, I took up tennis to impress this young lad. While I was able to make contact with the tennis ball using my racquet, develop some skill at placement, spin, and speed, my heart simply was not in vanquishing my opponent. I had my most engaging tennis moments hitting the ball around in a friendly fashion with what I erroneously hoped would soon be my publically acclaimed young fella.

All the rest of my tennis activity might rightly be described as practice so I could bring the best rallying expertise to my sessions with him. Well, needless to say, that is not really the attitude you want to bring to the game, although, I did manage to win a tournament with this mindset when I was first starting out. I don't think killer instinct won the day, but more beginners luck and visions of my increased ability to captivate my chosen love. Of course it may have just been a consequence of inexperience, youth, and lack of competitive drive, but I can't say my overall mental or even physical ability improved much as a result of this competitive activity. Frankly, I found my long distance running activity much more helpful and less stressful, bringing an assortment of benefits to my character and life experience.

If I had been a more competitive person naturally, I suspect I would have benefitted more from competitive sports activity. Why are some people competitive while others prefer to compete with themselves to gage improvement? Is competitiveness the result of parental instruction? Since my mother was the person who erroneously informed me the boy next door had a crush on me, and most likely knew she was telling a bit of a fib, I suspect she thought she was doing her maternal duty in trying to get me to engage in activity which would make me more alert to opportunities, and to some degree, how to make opportunities for myself via competition.

Well, if that was the lesson, I wish she would have just said so. As it was my own internal compass and interpreter took over and the lessons became what types of tennis outfits were most comfortable and highlighted my bean pole physique best (an ongoing lifetime theme), what types of rallies were most pleasurable, and how to direct the tennis ball without too much reflection on what constituted winning strategy.

It may be I am reading too much into my Mother's motives. Perhaps all that was really occurring was her attempt to make me competitive as she herself was, and that hopefully I would accrue the same happy life advantages she had achieved through her competitive zeal. There may have been some element of a darker appearance game present, as my mother did think in these terms I was later to learn from watching her political career as President of various nonprofit organizations flourish. Therefore, on a slightly darker note, she may have been trying to ensure the public visibility of her discharging of maternal responsibilities in properly preparing me to engage in battle effectively, and enjoyably.

Since she rightly recognized this tendency was not going to develop naturally on its own, she used my attraction to the boy next door to get me competitively involved for my teen years, after which my adulthood would be my own affair. Also, as a fairly helpful extra, by directing my love life in an indefinitely fruitless direction, she was sparing herself the teenage journey of love/sexual growing pains. The journey was put off into the future distance for quite some time with this strategy of carefully dropped hints and encouragements to the meek, docile, and eager to please youth that I was.

The point is you can try to develop a competitive nature, but not to be surprised if you find it difficult to maintain this hard edge when it does not materialize as a result of environmental stimulus internally and naturally. Additionally, I suspect my mother did not fully realize the meekness and docility messages she was also sending me trying to ensure a relatively trouble free child rearing experience which effectively countered the competitive monster she may have hoped to unleash for adult success.

"If only she could have gotten the timing right!" she may now be criticizing herself. Oh well, you can't have it all. By the time I became negatively labeled and other people in the environment had a stake in my character appearance, I was pretty much a confirmed pacifist with all the backing religion and philosophy to maintain that demeanor for a life time, thanks entirely to my father, who loved me enough to foresee the oncoming train wreck with reality and gave me the necessary tools to survive without becoming mentally deranged.

Whether a person chooses a competitive identity or a meek one, having a central philosophy, like looking at your hand during speed and endurance spins, will help a person from feeling schizophrenic with his choices when outside competitors' interests coincide with keeping this person off balance, unable to spin his life story to himself or anyone else when necessary. I would be willing to bet that most women with children interested in seeing their offspring able and independent would at least understand my own mother's viewpoint, even if they themselves opted for some other child rearing style.

In fact, for the noncompetitive, keeping the limited neutral territory available to those who do not care for the competitive drama requires that some portion of the populace *must* engage in the win/lose game so that others do not have to. At present, for the historical past, and for the indefinite future until the bell curve to society is changed for a modest horizontal line, gradations of good and bad guys are deemed necessary to create the bell curve shape which can support an area of plateau at the summit whose size depends on overpopulation concerns. Whatever your external social label, remember, you can always think of yourself just as you please as long as you keep the mental tools in good shape to do so.

Although I know I sound a little judgmental about my mother, I too appreciate her position. If I would not have made the choice to attempt creating a competitive child or a sexually stunted one which a parent need never fear competition from through comparison at some future date, I also would not want to sentence the competitive to exhausting competition indefinitely, including my mother. I can tell that the competitive have gotten tired because they graciously bow out in many cases leaving the playing field to the younger generation, not even wishing to address opponents with their own same physical age induced disadvantages.

At some point I am pretty certain early zealous competitors look back, recognize the innocence and rose colored glasses which armored their competitive adventure in the first place, and maturely decide they have done their part already, time for others to step up and do their part. In this particular instance I am referring to the non-winners or losers of competitions. The losers, having participated in competition under false pretenses and now fully informed and aware of the senselessness of hierarchical rankings, are somewhat intolerant of those who bowed out from the very beginning, not doing their part when young and presumably able. With genuine cause for concern, these losing competitors may rightly feel their position within the hierarchy may suffer from their apparent losing tendencies, and to dispel the effect of this losing stink, point to the lack of participation in competition by some neutral group altogether who are depicted as shirking competitive duty, much like shirking military duty.

The above intolerant, in some respects, may be preferable to those who carry on competing as a life style for an entire life span using whatever tricks and strategy will garner a win. At this point they too may have suffered some disillusionment, but instead of accepting less of a rewarded lifestyle, wish to continue competing and winning to the end of maintaining perks.

In another similar instance you have my mother competing to the end of her days with her children. She has not managed to simply enjoy activity for the activities sake, unable to muster mental health giving ambivalence toward the presence or lack of presence of a win. Rather, in addition to exterior rewards loss, she shuns failure in her internal comparison with anyone else in her circle with which she or others might compare her. Having others attribute a pitying subpar appraisal might impact her internal state negatively simply because she never got her philosophy patter down solid.

In a nutshell, she is eternally mentally insecure, and as such deserves sympathy from those she is not actively destroying in competition. Naturally some of that sympathy should be addressed to her victims as well. As one of her victims, while I do not blame her, desiring some kind of personal justice, nonetheless, I must admit I do not hate myself enough to wish her continued unqualified success.

Lastly, the predominantly ongoing winners do not generally suffer disillusionment and are always in a position to relish their memories and behave as good sports to all others as long as the others are losing with good graces as well. Alas, not everyone wins forever. The old saying "The bigger they are the harder they fall" applies here where the ongoing winners underwent some pains and sacrifices to win.

For them the winning was all and they really did not have a particularly good time other than receiving public acclaim for the grueling trek of continuous success. When the first place trophy does finally land on someone else's efforts, this type of ongoing winner will need to do some rapid and thorough philosophizing or have someone on hand to help him mentally adjust to prevent causing too much physical devastation when engaged in substance abuse to help dampen the shock.

Basically, meekness or competitiveness is often a topic for discussion by others who may or may not have real first-hand experience, may be unsure how to accurately label any given inner state, or have appearance game goals for misinforming others. All of these sources of information can be incomplete or riddled with error purposely or accidentally.

Given the current priority of competitive behavior as the cosmic order of the universe on the one hand, or on the other hand, the gift of the earth to the meek by god with a general folk wisdom nod to the humble salt of the earth people being the bedrock of society, I personally feel an understanding of these states is important. As has always been emphasized in my previous two books, and will continue to be emphasized in this one, sharpening up one's internal compass of understanding is highly recommended as the best sifter and actual source of wisdom.

Going for a long run will help get a person grounded into their body and emotional feelings. After a certain amount of physical endurance is achieved, running is one of the best times for sorting out problems, or maybe a long walk can be a useful substitute for a run for the less physically active. Some prefer listening to music when running, which I also enjoy. Jogging to moving music can really get a person into performance physical shape, but be aware that when the music is not there you may find you feel lethargic and unmotivated.

While this type of workout achieves the physical benefits of getting the heart rate up and muscles deeply used, I personally found I tended to dwell in the heavily euphoric emotional realm of joy and exhilaration, which is good and definitely has a place when moving beyond depression, but these emotional states, like panic, do not yield the optimum capacity for clear thinking and empathy. Another way of putting it is, the person is completely physically overwhelmed by the musical experience and closes down the openness to other sources of input during those particular moments of racing passionately to a favorite song.

There is nothing wrong with getting in shape this way and achieving a general improved resting point of calm from the before getting in shape journey, just be aware that other physical options exist for adding emotional and mental content to overall comprehension which will be very helpful in navigating the life journey. For instance, I have found dancing to different types of music helpful for getting in touch with different emotional outlooks. Knowing the words to the music is helpful since the words communicate the message the song writer is trying to share, although I have often been surprised by the explanations offered by some song writers long after I had come up with my interpretation of a song.

Additionally, there has been no shortage of occasions when I came up with one set of lyrics only to discover later that the words were totally different and that the song no longer made sense to me, or that while I still liked the musical melody, I was not so in love with the actual language message as previously. As a minor caution, knowing the documented words may be the safest course before declaring an affinity for a piece of music. Even one tiny word difference can completely change an emotional tone and before you know it you are declaring love for a paean about possessiveness and jealousy, rather than an ode to physical constancy. Take for example these words which totally tripped me up and gave easy ammunition to already over advantaged competitors at work:

What I heard: I don't think I can stand to have another hand upon me; all I know is that I should.

Actual lyrics: I don't think I can stand to have another hand upon you; all I know is that I should.

One little word, me instead of you, and suddenly I had become a raging stalker. What a mess. Oh well, I did a lot of healing to that song in my version, and then once I witnessed others' reaction to my enjoyment of the song I dug up the words. I can't say I really enjoyed that song the same way again, but I did really like my version.

Of course, for the song to make sense after the correct "you" gets exchanged in for the incorrect "me" meant that I had a few of the other words garbled as well, but the one word inaccuracy that counted for labeling me as a crazy, frothing nutcase was that mistaken "me" instead of "you". Be warned! You may enjoy a version of a song according to lessons you have already done the learning for predisposing you to error, but you will not receive the benefit of what is actually being said in the song if you do not get the real lyrics to mull over.

With time, I have found the pieces you personally choose as interesting, listened to regularly, eventually yield music which starts speaking to you. Like any built up skill, you have got to stick with it. Generally I listen to music during dancing, aerobics, jump roping, yoga, and weight lifting. Walking and jogging, I may or may not listen to music or the radio. As often as not I just hit the road when I have some pressing concern on my mind or just need to get out and move around a bit. Personal taste and needs should be your compass.

So when engaged in all this flurry of activity with or without music do I feel meek? Do I feel happy? Do I feel competitive? Well, I would have to say, accurately reported, the sensation is meekness. But who knows for sure? One thing I can say, it is not competitiveness. When arriving at the meekness conclusion I am to a degree using mental reasoning, but I do know that I am feeling an overall gentleness I feel all the time rather than a desire to be rough and destructive.

Feeling the usual calm gentleness and patience with exercises does not prevent me from feeling good when listening to music, does it? Meekness does not prevent me from thinking about what the point of a particular song or a particular daily event means, in my opinion. Humbleness is indicated as part of the definition and feeling range as well. How does humbleness fit in? Perhaps recognizing my lapses in general knowledge which leads me to gather more information is the source of humbleness, which again, is present regularly or always.

Some might insist I am flying in the face of meekness and humility when supposing I have any tools for answering my questions. Meekness and humility means asking the questions, but not answering them. These fussy meek and humble folks would deny me the right to direct my own life!! Who are these people?!!! These pig headed life deniers who want to answer MY questions for ME?!!!!

If you will notice what happened there, I stopped being meek and hit the road running as an enraged, domineering, controlling, insecure competitor. The switch can happen just as quickly as that, and I sent myself into a tail spin panic all on my own. Not really, just kidding, sort of. I needed a spot of humor there. More in keeping with my general character, I would simply say I have to disagree; I can answer my own question if I want to. I suppose it is safe (sage?) to say that words and definitions are one thing, and interpretations are quite another, as evidenced in the many versions and interpretations of the Bible and other sacred works.

As for being submissive and imposed upon during any part of the day, or especially while I am exercising, pretty much living within the confines of some civilization automatically involves submission for everyone, the competitive and the meek alike. I am not sure conscious awareness of submission is an indisputable element of meekness. Like any emotion, for example anger, people lost in throes of an angry seizure often deny the presence of any emotional impression. Hence, the psychological term "denial". So, where are we at the end of our Meekness 101 lecture? Absolutely nowhere. Exactly where we would expect to be having embraced meekness and no expectations.

Meekness Expectations

Obviously, being meek does not mean a person is forbidden to entertain dreams and expectations. The previous declaration was included to demonstrate a point of view I do not condone, but want to address to help the gentle reader when some self-interested individual determines your meekness stance is weak and open to foisting their views of meekness upon you. Given the earlier definition of meek indicating a predisposition to be put upon, I am really muddying the waters right here.

Character strength is not monopolized by the competitive. In fact, the competitive, in choosing the rigors of a competitive lifestyle, are bringing a certain amount of absolute submission to themselves and others by legitimizing comparisons into the life assessment process through this decision. More importantly, a person can choose meekness out of strength, rather than weakness.

For me personally, if I ever find myself going over to the ruthless camp of competitiveness it will be out of meek resignation of not being able to live a healthy life of kindness and love. Truthfully, there may be some question as to whether I really submitted or not. I will never be able to mentally trick myself into buying into cosmic comparisons and rankings after all the coercion and blackmail I have been through. In order to get mental and complete behavioral compliance to my competitiveness I will have to suffer some kind of devastating head trauma which destroys a portion of my brain or outright kills me. Then perhaps I can be correctly meekly competitive.

Perhaps most accurately, at some point of informed life experience a person simply cannot mentally retreat into some sort of hierarchy system. Physical strength, mental strength and character strength have nothing to do with it. A person is just meek. No more to be said. Prior to attaining this mental state through experience, a person can tenaciously cling to their hopes and dreams for a kind and loving atmosphere to civilization using resistance strength or willpower, which has minor differences to competitive strength when achieving domination.

The problem with willpower is that like patience or trust even, it can get used up. A more useful aid to resistance is maintaining your kindness by ready empathy and understanding of others which will prevent a person from taking hurtful actions when they do not want to witness or be responsible for resultant pain and senseless destruction. Not desiring to engage in competition does not mean a person is unable to create a point and meaning to their life experience. The people who have trouble figuring out what the point to life is are the ones who feel they cannot win and that love and kindness do not really exist, like Santa, the Easter Bunny, and the Tooth Fairy.

If the people who so desperately long for a win could actually win regularly, they might find their life mission in competition after all. Not having that choice, and also not having the choice of loving kindness, the life meaning deniers feel stuck up a creek without a paddle, and they don't care, the one positive point to making this mental state endurable.

Does their lack of caring make them gentle and meek? Do they have a lingering whiff of competitiveness about them since the only reason they are choosing not to compete is because they do not feel like losing? In recognizing that the rules do not allow them to win, these folks have chosen not to care. If only they could go that one tiny step further on the path and see the rules are changing all the time and don't have much to do with who wins anyway.

These people are so close to being empathetic and loving without fully understanding the promising brink they are teetering on. Perhaps they do know but cannot talk themselves into taking that last tiny step of faith and just choosing to live life in recognition of the flawed hierarchy environment and trying to make things better. For the life meaning deniers to embrace this lifestyle would mean conceding defeat to the hierarchy currently in place whose rules have been judged unfair, inadequate, and dishonestly applied, in other words, helping out the enemy who stole all their original personal source of meaning in the first place.

In the catalog of personality traits these people are no longer competitive in the traditional sense, but instead of head on competition with the current hierarchy a la political system and political parties, go the road of undermining the warm and fuzzy values of love and kindness which help keep everything running smoothly when providing a meaning foundation where few people get to be acclaimed winners.

These are the people who will try to convince the meek that they have no right to dreams and expectations if they are a supportive part to the corrupt state of affairs currently suffocating life forms on the planet, but especially those with defeated dreams of winning. The life meaning deniers are actually still competing within the current hierarchy system, they are just doing it from behind the safe shield of warm bodies comprised of civilization supporters. Cowards. Weak, lowly, yellow bellied snakes. Well, look at that, they are coming very close to being meek according to Webster, same as me.

I suppose a moment of clarification is necessary here so that when the gentle reader takes away my lesson of tolerance they do not also take away a lesson of blindness to dangers. For example, a person can be meek with all people placed above him in the hierarchy in a position to visit life changing devastation into his life, while being domineering and competitive with anyone not so advantageously placed, in order to secure more benefits, resources, and the possibility that someday the conditionally meek themselves will be better positioned with still more people below protecting them from an uncomfortable fate. In these cases, a person is temporarily meek, not genuinely meek as an ongoing character trait.

When the above person fails to elevate himself, he can easily become uncaring, switching his competitive energy over to undermining the very hierarchy he hoped to have a superior position in. Either way, as a success, a hopeful for success or a failure of success, this interim meek person is fairly dangerous to all below him. Also, those placed above this wolf in sheep's clothing would be advised not to let him scramble over their heads to find themselves also at this person's conniving mercy. Of course, while wisely shielding yourself from the dangers, be aware that the very structure of hierarchy and institutionalized competitiveness are what creates this person's insecurities and character in the first place.

The genuinely meek may have brief lapses of temporary domineering competitiveness when subjected to panic situations or otherwise ambushed into a rage in some manner. However, this is not really their chosen life style, and the meek are unable to maintain a hardened competitive edge much beyond the stimulus which provokes the uncharacteristic behavior. If sufficiently aggravated in an ongoing manner, an ordinarily meek person may become unhelpful generally or specifically to those responsible for the aggravation, creating an appearance of freeloading idleness.

What with the machine work force and globalization of jobs, the meek are subjected to the panic of job loss or hour cuts regularly, and competition has gotten seriously fierce, regardless of the negligible amount of ruthless calculations any particular competitor started out his career with. It is these goals toward a peaceful world and overpopulation concerns which actually heat up the competitive kitchen, burning the meek and competitive alike. Personally, I like to think that a more direct approach from those pulling the environmental strings would be helpful by legislating laws which equally support and reward other life paths than getting married to a member of the opposite sex and having as many children as you can stand. I was gratified to see that only last week same sex marriages were nationally legalized here in the U.S.A.

I have done an awful lot of thinking and careful explaining here to help the reader have an example of sorting out the problems of adjectives, any adjectives, not just meek or competitive. But really, who has time and energy for all this thinking? Personally, I have set aside time for these exercises because the severities of my job situation (being negatively labeled) required me to be on constant alert for attempts to cement my label by making me believe I had done things which I could prove I had not. Failing that goal it was still important to get the rest of the witnessing workforce to buy the falsehood of subpar employee for me. By establishing the artificial ranking of quality of people, general motivation remains intact and stabilized.

Previous to my red alert mental state, when I was positively labeled or occupying neutral territory, I did not feel an anxious tug to be figuring out all the strange things happening in my work experience because these happenings were simply not there. As a reliable productive member of the work force I was allowed to simply do my job and get on with it to ensure the meeting of deadlines for resource production and distribution. Only after the job cuts due to technology advance and globalization did I become a desirable bad guy due to my single status without dependents or others who would be impacted by my continuous misfortune.

This is a very brief summary of the appearance game which appears more completely explained in my first and second books. Also, in those first two books I have a heavy emphasis on thinking for oneself and using books and media entertainment to help round out an accurate perception of the world environment. I suppose those first two books have enormous encouragement to use thinking and information gathering because those were great tools AFTER I became negatively labeled. Prior to negative labeling I used my feeling senses all the way. Now that I have developed a more complete picture of the environment, I can return to relying on my feelings from visual, audio, and other sensory input, while also keeping an eye on the calculating shenanigans which are portrayed in media entertainment.

The information gathered from books, news, other media, and my own sensory input by themselves, however, are not enough to forming a reliable, objective assessment of the world which allows me to make decisions according to my chosen method of giving meaning to life. All those mental functions need to take place in a healthy, calm body. Without that healthy body providing a solid foundation to mental activity, my picture would be skewed.

Still, I believe it is more than that which my body brings to my life experience. I believe it is the lovely sensations of joy, serenity and wellbeing on the one hand, and anxiety and panic on the other, which colored my impulsive actions both before and after negative labeling, for the good and also for the bad. When I was allowed to be filled with the meaning of doing a good job and being liked for it, I was able to be generous with others sheltered in my own unquestioned security, and my well maintained body only added strength to my good feelings generated from these mental sources.

Later, when I began the journey of sorting out the craziness of my job situation created by the changing work force I no longer had my mental fortress of unquestioned security, but I still had my physical wellbeing which is what carried the day in kindness actions from me. Even though my brain did not work fast enough against all the ambushes and attacks to come up with what was happening right away which would have given me a wise guru like demeanor to meet social interactions, I still felt basically good, if somewhat anxious, and able to be patient and kind with associates, my preferred interaction style.

Although the accumulating years added ongoing anxiety to my mental state, I decided to counteract that anxiety with exercise, comforting reading, and sorting out the intricacies of the environment where previously I had settled for a general summary, like most people busily and happily employed. My main point is, the healthily maintained body can be counted on to produce societally improving actions by the individual without much need for mental reflection when the person in question basically supports the ideals in society, and is not suffering from the harassments of negative labeling. Even when they are suffering such abuses if they started out with a solid core of positive civilization support and take the steps to regain mental adjustment as needed, even if that adjustment requires work, a person will still fairly consistently come up with the attitude and actions which help keep society the kind of place people want to inhabit, rather than tweak, change, or revolutionize in some manner.

For example, consider a person, who has a job, friends, maybe even a mate and lifestyle they are essentially comfortable with. I am not requiring the person have found their god given calling or vocation for a meaningful career, or the ideal mate as depicted in popular media. This example person has found a niche which is comfortable and rewarding and lifetime companions who they enjoy spending time with as much or more than other people of acquaintance, maybe they have even found someone to share intimacy.

I don't think the requirements are impossible accomplishments. Given this starting point a person dwelling in their physical body spends time at work and with companions on a daily basis without stress, strain and competition casting a pall of unpleasant sensations and emotions over simple life choices. Instincts do not have much or any opportunity to get activated, setting a person into panic. Instead, these people get to grow in depth of shared experience, or in other words, love.

Detractors to this lifestyle will try to create visions in the mind space imagination of humdrum boredom, but I advise the gentle reader to leave your imagination out of it if you are otherwise happy. Don't take the bait to reflect that you will be sharing your life with the same person for fifty plus years, or engaging in the same day to day career activities for similar lengths of time. Allowing someone else to create mental imagination pictures of this type can only lead to dissatisfaction, and what good is that really to anyone?

Start imagining for yourself, or better, recall your job experience to date. Things don't stay absolutely the same day in and day out. Perhaps the dissatisfaction you were easily seduced into feeling was just as likely a result of the stress of keeping up with constant changes designed to invariably make the work force smaller at some future date to accommodate new technology, making a work attachment/investment seem futile and brief, but not really boring per se.

Similarly, when two people get together to test the possibility for an intimate relationship, unless love is the basis, mistaking boredom for absence of meaning and reciprocal caring would be easy to make, especially if some disenchanted cowardly competitor is recommending this attitude. If the romantic hopefuls make each other compete for attention with other candidates, it would be quite difficult to imagine enjoying anyone's company who was juggling an intimate relationship with work and 3 other people.

Thinking that some sign in the future would tell you when and with whom to settle down means you do not have an invested responsibility to actively make the relationship full of good feeling. Fate is supposedly arranging all that. Waiting to see who turns out to be the best material package is just as empty emotionally during the span of time set aside to weed out the field.

On the other hand, being involved with one person who basically meets your physical, mental, and spiritual comfort zone, the passage of shared time would tell you when you two had grown together to be able to make shared goals of some type like marriage, children, buying a house, starting a business or taking up a hobby together. It would just begin to feel right and the dialogue could begin.

The only thing which throws a whammy into this natural growth is competition, similar to plants in the garden. Given enough space to grow and no environmental stressors, a plant can be expected to grow until it reaches it genetically determined size and to live for a genetically predetermined space of time. Of course any number of factors can cut a plant's life short, forest fires from droughts, too many competing seedlings, soil becoming infected with fungus from some hapless traveler traipsing down the garden path, or being dug up and transplanted over and over again.

Everyone is entitled to expectations of happiness, equality, liberty and healing justice. Being able to survive is a necessary skill, but unless a survival lifestyle is a person's idea of bliss, than any person has a right to expect the society he is supporting through his efforts, to encompass him within the protection circle. Whether a person is keeping a garden full of plants for the environment, doing volunteer work, simply trying to live peacefully while making some other type of small contribution as allowed, or more fortunately is supportively employed, since society leaves no humane alternative choices to the individual, it must provide a healthy environment for him and everyone else. The modern day consciousness may not agree with this assessment, supposing that there is no order or meaning in the universe and therefore no expectations of order or meaning are valid for life on earth.

In my opinion what is more likely is that the order and meaning are well beyond human understanding at the moment and will remain out of psychic reach indefinitely, but that does not mean we cannot decide for ourselves to embrace a loving atmosphere for society which utilizes an equality civilization structure to provide happiness, love, liberty, and healing justice. Human beings do not need permission from the Universe to make this decision, as already stated here and almost everywhere else, the Universe does not really care.

As for God, apparently most writers delving into the nature of this entity do characterize the Supreme Almighty as indeed caring very much. There may be an additional detailed agenda of God's concerns depending on the particular religion, but I feel the only safe thing to say, if God is there, is He must care, otherwise, why bother? I cannot conceive of a being both powerful enough to create this world and also being abused and abusive.

I am leaving myself open to the accusation of putting words in the Almighty's mouth, a big no no which I have often pointed an accusing finger at others for doing. Also, I may be subjecting God to human criteria. Since God is essentially unknowable, it is possible he would behave as a heartless sociopath; it is possible he could have abandoned this project and is playing in some other part of the universe. Even if God has chosen to go play elsewhere, I doubt he created this whole planet full of beauty and pleasure as a torture device for large parts of the population, animals and other endangered life forms. It just does not scan, compute, or make any sense.

Religion does enjoy a general popular acceptance due to the hope it brings for a better future and by relating stories whose themes intersect with the ongoing realities of the cycles of overpopulation within a hierarchy structured civilization. Hope and some identification with reality are what make religion acceptable to the general populace, in my opinion. If God were supposed to be a devil like presence, how popular and supported would that be? Satan worshippers do exist, but these people fall into the group of meaning deniers I described previously who could not buy into love and the hierarchy supported by hierarchical religion because they feel their life experience would be as a loser and unacceptable.

My guess is if Satan worship could gain popular acceptance, it might receive the nod from the movers and shakers in the environment simply because it does a better job of controlling people and allowing all manner of cruel punishing actions to clear the goal posts. As it is, as long as Satan worshippers do not break the law, or are not stupid enough to get caught, they can get away with quite a bit of morale killing behavior which although ungentlemanly conduct, helps winnow the exploding population numbers.

As the population grows exponentially, who knows, those refusing to be losers, or those refusing to promote a loving equality lifestyle may choose the Satan worshipper network. Like any subversive group, they may humanely be permitted to carry on since the presence of a hierarchy structure creates these emotional states. They will not be allowed however, to grow to the proportions of seriously endangering current leadership based on ideals of happiness, liberty, and justice for all supported by the appearance game which masks the presence of an artificial hierarchy.

When the time is right and the Satan worshippers have been as helpful as possible but start delivering diminishing returns, in economic parlance, their presence will be officially recognized as a menace and their heyday will come to an end by removing some large portion into the official hierarchy where they always wanted to be in the first place, or removed from jeopardizing leadership in some manner which may not tolerate the light of day. The overpopulation cycle will begin once again, and a new group of disenfranchised losers who desperately want to win will grow, predating the meek civilization supporters at will. The practical real life Revelation story from what I can tell.

Either way, the universe will not mind, God has already given his permission, so the only remaining votes to be tallied are the actual people on the planet. Simply in terms of numbers, my guess is that most people will vote for loving equality, but this kind of poll is impossible. Who are the people who will not be voting for equality? Those who feel they have worked much too hard to achieve their lifestyle advantages and do not want to render their life meaning measured by wage/salary accrual to zero by becoming on equal footing with everyone else deemed to be lazy, unproductive, and defective in some manner. Also, anyone who does not have faith in human nature and feels their ability to work the hierarchy to their personal advantage is the best way to get quality of life will not be casting a loving equality vote. Egomaniacs who are convinced of their superiority will probably not vote for equality as well.

Of course, there are others, but these are a good start to defining the problems and investigating how to persuade the non-equality folks. Perhaps their persuasion is not absolutely necessary as long as they feel life is satisfactory, and rationally, why fix something which is not broken to their minds. Agreement may be secured from the non-equality folks simply by the presence of a rich lifestyle full of their favorite things, even if they do not have added ego rushes of dominating the world to achieve their enjoyment.

How can a return to happy meekness and a healthy individual competitiveness be accomplished? Well, as I never tire of reminding everyone, we will all need to be on the same informed page. To determine the content of this informative page we need to come up with a plan to help create the meek laboratory conditions which allow leadership to perform their services to civilization optimally, while leaving enough individual freedoms for those who want to compete in a healthy manner to do so, and allowing the cooperative to go about their business happily unhindered.

Meekness Economics

Economic (adj) 1) Of or relating to the development, production, and management of material wealth, as of a country, household, or business enterprise, 2) Of or relating to economics, 3) Of or relating to matters of finance, 4) Of or relating to the necessities of life: UTILITARIAN. Webster's II New Riverside University Dictionary

Economics (n) The science that deals with the production, distribution, and consumption of commodities. Webster's II New Riverside University Dictionary

More definitions for the gentle reader. Although economics is a science, experimentation is extremely difficult because of complex changing conditions, but also because, at the moment anyway, a small shred of general morality still prevails which frowns upon experimenting with people to gain questionably useful knowledge due to condition one, complex changing conditions which prohibit accurate prediction and the ability to replicate an experiment over and over again. Still, the specter of resource shortages and overpopulation allows many who might notice, to turn a blind eye, permitting some senseless unsavory experimentation to take place.

For the purposes of this book, I will be considering the definition of economics to be the study of providing the necessities of life, which include food, shelter, health, and meaningful life experiences. A person I was in conversation with the other day asked "Have you ever said I have enough, give my raise, unemployment benefits, social security payment, tax refund, whatever, to someone else who needs it?" At the time the question made me a little uncomfortable because of course I would not dream of doing such a thing when resources and survival advantages are so insecure and uncertain in my neck of the woods. Having enough can change in the blink of an eye and a voluntary gambler I am not.

The question has been rooting around in the back of my mind and I feel, to be fair, that the question is very incomplete and does not begin to cover the items it would be useful for a person to decide they have enough of which are unrelated to money, the freedom provider. After all, freedom is almost the breath of life and who wants to monkey with their oxygen supply.

Some of the other commodities it might be useful for people to take a reflective look at to determine if perhaps, for the moment anyway, they have enough would be: 1) daily challenges when the challenges necessitate that other people have to run at an uncomfortable pace so that the challenge can be met providing an accomplishment rush to the whip holder, 2) admiration/status/prestige when many go without due to placement of vast amounts of quality labels onto one person, 3) networked security where a person has unethical access and control over others securing their advantages through information gathering and personnel manipulation, and 4) recognition for service and contributions when others could just as easily contribute, but to maintain the appearances of an artificial hierarchy the majority of recognition goes to a small group of people, or the people whose self-esteem is so compromised that they will give up a portion of life and health to receive societal acceptance and recognition.

Naturally, one can accumulate other things, like a lot of books, as I have done when I had access to free and low cost supplies. I figure I read a lot and the books are otherwise going into the trash. It is not as if I deprived anyone of a book. Over the years I have managed to accumulate a large supply of handmade clothes and hats. It is fun to make things expressly to suit my tastes. If one is going to participate in many traditional work environments one has to have a more mainstream wardrobe, so I have store bought clothes as well.

My making of hats and clothes did not require that anyone else had to run to help me complete my outfits; I did all the work myself. Perhaps I did not spin the cloth, harvest the cotton, or engage in the textile industry to produce fancy fabrics, but I have no say in the management of those concerns. If I have some guilt as a consumer of material, I hope that my writing to promote equality and happiness is granting me some redemption.

Some could point to my participation in retirement plan's investment makes me responsible for whatever human rights violations may be taking place in factories, but again, I feel trying to spin out the lines of responsibility in this manner misses the whole point. The hierarchy structure to civilization is responsible and quite frankly, I have lived my entire life making this point so I for one refuse to take on a further burden of guilt.

Some would argue that the very act of making special attire as entertainment and enjoyment for me makes others feel bad because onlookers feel they fare poorly in a comparison and then follow my bad example of vanity. First off, I'll have to say I do not consider my actions to be a sign of vanity. Once again, it is all in the adjectives. I would describe my actions as a sign of responsible thrift when I wanted to look nice but did not have the money to spend on expensive apparel. If people follow my example of thrift, why is that so bad?

I developed healthy self-esteem at being able to learn and employ a skill; I also developed my ability to learn period. Who wants to argue with that? Believe me there is someone out there saying I have an unhealthy absorption with directing my own energies when I should be helping out more, neglecting the fact that there are much more people than jobs or even volunteer jobs. Must I just sit still until I die?

Economically speaking, I am promoting poor manufacturing processes by consuming more than I actually need. Well, who decides how much a person needs? Do we each get one spoon, fork, knife, plate and so on? Perhaps we get 2 pairs of pants, 2 skirts, 2 dresses, 2 vests and so forth if we are women, but the men get a tuxedo, a business suit, a leisure suit, and a pair of shorts. As far as I know, as of this date, there are no laws on this subject in this country.

Looking at my closet it is plain to see I have more than enough clothes, but the fact is I got almost all of them second hand and rescued some from the landfill. I have to believe that I am not the only person out there who came by their wardrobe this way, so are we second hand Sallies responsible for gross consumerism? Would our refusal to give second hand clothes a home prevent the initial consumer from buying new clothes for each new season? I cannot imagine how that would work.

As you may be able to tell I have been reading economics texts lately. When studying economics and developing theory, one assumes the presence of pure competition will ensure absolute efficiency and the best outcomes. Like many logic based disciplines, economics fails to account for the great energizer of human endeavors, emotions. Many sciences have this failing, the inability to control for emotional influences in experimentation and theorizing, so being unable to develop a hypothesis including this undeniably crucial component to human behavior, the theorizing thinker pushes on as if emotions were not there. Humph, snort, giggle...Fools.

Sciences like Chemistry and Physics are centered on inanimate matter, which does not have emotion based forerunners impacting actions which take place. In these sciences electrical, magnetic, and chemical principles have been developed which are not impacted by any kind of human activity. The science of economics uses the inanimate substances of property, land, and manufactured goods to measure economic events to help create theories.

I knew right away reading that economics text that economics reminded me of something. The feeling continued to nag away until I realized that this introductory economics book reminded me of a Catholic Catechism I read many years ago when trying to understand why so many of the people I felt attracted to as friends were Catholics. Later I realized that being Catholic was not the common denominator but just having a general ongoing sense of decency, or perhaps they were rich and good looking, it is hard to be sure all these many years later. Most likely it was both. I do know that no matter how good looking a person is if they are mean spirited, predatory, callous, or manipulative, I lose interest pretty quickly.

Jesuits are the authors of the catechism along with the Pope. In the Catholic Church Jesuits are a sort of scientific thinker attached to this extremely hierarchical religion, which perhaps helps to explain the similarity between them and economists. With time the label Jesuit has developed a common daily meaning as the word jesuit, a person who applies ethical principles correctly or incorrectly. I have often heard bridge players being referred to as legal or jesuit arguers for their opinions regarding the play and bidding of a hand of cards.

Given the presence of ethical principles as a major jesuit consideration helps explain science's recent expansion into creating meaning via philosophy for the masses. As it turns out the scientists come by this behavior very naturally from reconciling Catholic faith with scientific research in monastic orders of old. One of the very first points made in my economics text is that all resources for securing survival are scarce. Nature does not provide very well for growing human needs. This fundamental truth is the backbone for the economic conclusions which follow, much like original sin casting Adam and Eve out of the bountiful Garden of Eden is the setting for the Christian story here on earth.

Some economic questions to be answered are what and how much to produce to take care of human needs, how to divide people into niches supporting production, what system should be used to reward people for work, and who is responsible for the distribution of resources. Questions posed by religion center around meaning instead of physical survival resources. The questioning, instead of being done by economists trying to plan for the needs for a society, is to be done by the individual yearning for communion with the Supreme Ultimate being. Some of these questions regard the actual presence of a Supreme Being, what the Supreme Being wants for people in general, and what the Supreme Being wants for any one person in particular. Instead of food, shelter, and improved comfort, a person is trying to find a way of life that is acceptable to his Creator and a philosophy which will make this way of life acceptable to the individual as well.

In Catholicism, as with most religions, ideally, once an individual comes to ask these difficult questions, he must continue by questioning his own ability to create meaning for himself and allow an outside popular religion/philosophy to answer these questions as well, that is he must abandon any independent self-confidence which would allow him to recognize that he cannot answer these questions and neither can anyone else, and that is okay. Life on earth can still be meaningful without knowing precisely in absolute detail what the Creator has planned for each and every ones of us.

Why does a person start asking questions about a Supreme Being in the first place? Do his parents encourage this type of questioning, or do the questions come up because he feels anxious about his ability to secure survival resources? In modern times a person might note some group of people who seem to have a much easier time than others. Hopping immediately from anxiety to wish fulfillment a person decides to look into the possibility of a Supreme Being to lighten his load like those other happy, smiling fortunates. Upon investigation the questioner discovers, much to the economist's relief, that if a person accepts God, this person will also have to accept ferreting out God's plan which usually involves enduring manipulation and coercion by humans until the questioner finally comes up with the right answer in compliance with the economist's designs for society.

Those who are brought up in religion may never question the presence of a Supreme Being at all or ever have to be talked into crediting the possibility of his presence. Thus between the people who have never known any other way of thinking and the ones who must be starved to death to create the mental and physical weakness which will produce openness to popularly accepted myths, lays the spectrum of challenges to the scientific economist. Rationally, one would think that the most cooperative people are the ones who had a solid belief in a Supreme Being for as long as they could remember, but the details of a surrounding religion's rules may throw a whammy in the cooperative works by forbidding abortion, medical care, and the above cited independent thinking which aids in learning.

From what I can see, economics is the version of popular religion for those who prefer hard science to faith in an ultimate being. Fiercely independent, the only way a reasoning scientist will find himself in mental support of society is if he can think himself into that position on his own. Although he may be reluctant to admit it, abundant survival resources will act as an aid in his thinking efforts to produce personal support for society, which as a planning economist he can reason into existence for his own personal use.

For others, who support society without resorting to a Supreme Being's presence creating circumstances, societal support comes naturally as a result of a feeling connection to others. In all cases support for society is enhanced by the amount of material support that particular society provides to any given member of the tribe. Primarily based on individual feelings of relaxation and security, those who feel these health giving tonics regularly are able to develop the most fellow feeling and compassion because survival fear is not acting as a block to relating to others.

More emotional blocks to connecting with others depleting useful social cement are feelings of superiority to others, feelings of inferiority to others, feelings of grief and loss, feelings of exclusion, feelings of power to exclude others, feelings of anger, and feelings of euphoria, and the list goes on. Looking at this list of feelings which prevent people from being able to recognize or at least tolerate each other's individual situations may be why there is at present such an emphasis on reason and thinking.

In fact, seeing visually that a person seems upset may require a little mental figuring to determine what kind of upset is being dealt with in the absence of clear indicators like tears or screaming. Additionally it is the presence of thought which will help to bridge the gaps between isolating emotional extremes.

Oddly, though, quite a few of the catalog of previous feelings result from mental compliance with philosophy and religion. For example, in order to entertain feelings of superiority a person must first have determined that some group of people is better than other groups and that he is a member of the elite clan. Similarly, once membership is determined, one has to go that extra step mentally if one wants the additional domineering rush of excluding other people based on questionable criteria. On the other hand feelings of anger, euphoria, grief and other surging emotions of the moment require a person employ some thinking if he wants to avoid or arrange for a more regular experience of these states.

In terms of economics, feelings of the moment which the individual may achieve on his own or through the vagaries of luck are like survival resources of food, shelter, and companionship, the feelings are the baseline of emotional fare available to all. The superiority and exclusion emotions are like luxury goods, only available to a select few. Do the economists plan all this? Believe it or not they have a word which covers mental states called psychic value of a particular good, like a Rolls Royce, in addition to its material value.

Psychic value involves how satisfied a person is by their ownership of a material item or salary. I suppose that once again mental reasoning has as much to do with psychic value as the other emotions which require a supportive foundation in philosophy before a person can engage in them. A homeless person might be quite happy to find a Rolls Royce in his possession in terms of having a larger sheltered place to sleep, other than that, I don't know if such a hobo would take great pride in keeping others out or simply do so to make sure he could continue to access the sheltering vehicle himself as needed.

From my point of view the reading is pretty dense and right from the beginning there are indications of the whole discipline being based largely on shifting sands, evaporating smoke, and the vagaries of fleeting, fast moving bodies of water. In the first fundamentals chapter alone I read statements like:

1) Confirmation of economic ideas is tricky to hopeless.

2) Economic tenets are customarily expressed as expected tendencies after long passages of time, with numerous exclusions and limiting stipulations. (How long? Geologic ages? How many and what stipulations? Ball park figure...go ahead, give it a try. Well, that may mean something solid to somebody, but in my opinion it might just be easier to say anything can happen due to happenstance created by individual interpretations of survival competition, but ideally, in theory, things are supposed to go according to plan.)

3) Testing economic hypotheses is constrained by an active, vibrant, breathing environment where changes of all types occur regularly, many unseen and unknown to scientific observers. The one tiny change being experimentally considered may or may not be utterly lost in the lack of understanding of what in human terms can only be defined as surrounding chaos. If the surrounding chaos could somehow be neutralized, the impact of applied economic principles could be definitively determined. (Neutralized???!!!?!?!? How? Not really a question I have the strength or desire to face right now unless the answer is by creating an equality environment full of survival resources for all.)

4) Various types of statistical math formulas can be employed to help reduce the impact of the surrounding chaos on experimental results, but the findings will actually prove nothing. (Okay.......)

5) Data collection in economic experiments is frequently corrupted and no amount of mathematical magic will correct for data errors. (REALLY, oh my.)

6) Given all of the above, agreements on interpretations to produce ideas and theories can be a nuisance, but evidently, based on the size and number of texts and economists, not one that has disqualified the science altogether.

7) It is the responsibility of those consulting economic information to analyze the supporting documents and claims before accepting the information as a sound basis for truth and proceeding to problem solving. (Perhaps it would be better to skip the publication of all accompanying economic conclusions which might tend to bias a reader of documents, leaving the reader the precious commodity of time to sort out the information for himself since he is being encouraged to do so anyway. A text on sample economic thinking might be an aid in warming up the mind to thoughtful economic consideration.)

8) In order to converse in economic terms a vocabulary is necessary. Due to the loose structural support to this science altogether, it is not surprising that explanations of terms vary to the point of actually being arbitrary. (Arbitrary (adj) Determined by impulse or whim. Based on or subject to individual judgment or discretion. Established by a court or judge rather than by a specific law or statute. Not limited by law: DESPOTIC. Webster's II New Riverside University Dictionary.)

Although I have taken some care to paraphrase these examples, arbitrary is actually the word used to describe economic definitions. The description of terms is then followed by the ability of these terms to communicate precise information. I suppose the implication the gentle reader must always bear in mind is the precise meanings are limited by their occupation within the economic scientific fairytale realm. The economic terms description is similar perhaps to determining the scientific accuracy of a measuring instrument in the harder sciences where decimal points become meaningless as a reflection of accuracy for some devices.

Well, all those statements appeared in the very first introductory chapter. Admittedly my hand in relaying these statements is present via my paraphrasing and some asides, but I do not feel I changed the overall significance of what was being said in my translation of the lingo into more realistic and colorful language for the average non-economist reader. I will give the economics authors their due, they are forthcoming and honest about the foundation of all economic theory, but you have to read an economics text book to get that information. Although anyone could do so, not too many pick up such a book out of curiosity to expand their horizons.

I suppose my main criticism of the scientific community in general at this time is their constant casting of doubt for lack of proof on religion's assertions and ideas, such as the presence of an individual soul, when they themselves do little better in forging their conclusions in economic science. Not that I agree with many religious assertions, especially the claims for a life after death with the detailed accompanying description, it is just I feel the scientific community should own more of their questionable contentions before taking out the source of other desperate people's source of personal power grabs.

Although recognition of the previous truths makes economics appear to be based on the shaky ground of the untried and unknown, what is often used instead of real life experience and documented experimental data are mathematical calculations, some from the lofty realms of calculus. When I was in high school calculus was the highest level of mathematics available and only recently introduced into the general curriculum.

It is a difficult discipline, as are all maths, especially after you get past the basic levels. I myself only took the basic calculus class, but essentially the math language attempts descriptions just like word languages do, except in math, the rules of mathematics cross all borders of nations and verbal languages for easier communication, if not actual agreement, at least in modern times. No ongoing consequences from the tower of Babel creating confusion and barriers to language communication in this subject.

I imagine that the story of the tower of Babel has such far reaching appeal because of the difficulty of math. In the wake of complicated calculations used as a foundation to architectural planning, destruction of monuments to man's ability to create structures of beauty and magnificence might appeal to many by giving the prospect of regained control to be delivered by the avenging Almighty. For those feeling insecure and out of control engaging unhappily in the work force, the empire creating humans who have gotten carried away when leaving the enslaved laborers on 24/7 call, would finally be unable to continue their relentless march of grand triumphs.

Unfortunately, if almost everyone was separated by this instance of the Lord creating communication barriers, the most imminent competitive threats to the Creator's ability to perform miracles of one sort or another were the only ones left with the ability to communicate freely with each other, or if necessary, the ability to employ ingenuity to create a common useful language too complicated to include your average person burdened with survival concerns. It almost seems as if the Almighty was not using enough foresight.

Well, it has always been my interpretation that the Supreme Being could not possibly mean to have condemned such useful knowledge as that generated by science and math to feed and provide for large populations, once the large populations were established as matters of record and fact. There are the parables of Jesus feeding masses of assembled people after all.

Also, it has always been my opinion that more people could enjoy and understand math if freed from the anxiety of competition and survival concerns. In this instance, using focus to gain an understanding of math would be like praying to God to help a person grow in faith and comprehension of the Almighty's capacity, wisdom and wishes.

God, the Universe, or the Cosmic Clown may have been separating men from the ease of trivial conversational communication used in networked empire building, but still allowing the ease of communication of knowledge inspired from nature and love to solve problems creating tragic misery. Employing my limited grasp of calculus, the infinite nature of the universe and matter in nature is utilized to solve complicated mathematical equations by substituting in infinity or zero for variables where deemed applicable. While calculus exhibits an incredible performance beauty and predictability in the hard sciences of chemistry and physics, it breaks down under the influences of human interpretation of rational actions which become more diverse and random as the population grows, branching off into stress relieving brooks and streams from the flooding banks of competitively fed rivers of popularly presumed rational behavior.

In my opinion, the science of economics demonstrates the presence of blind faith in the scientific community. The blind faith present is in the ability of thinking by scientists to thoroughly grasp circumstances, or at any rate, to grasp circumstances better than any other group of people. Other groups of people might employ thinking also, but utilize additionally some amount of personal experience of emotions to interpret the hard data manipulated by the scientific community in their conclusions. Personally, I feel the scientist probably also employs some kind of emotional compass in his thinking calculations, but I have not heard one mention that tool to date. It may be that like many other people, their background emotional state, which is always present casting some influence on actions and thought impacts thought processes invisibly.

The differences which arise from conclusions come from differences in types of acceptable meritorious productive behavior. For some people all types of ruthless destructive behavior are acceptable as long as the destruction is pointed in the right direction, which is not always stated officially. For others, destruction needs to be curtailed in favor of loving cooperation.

Acceptable Meritorious Productive Behavior

Both economics and religion deal with human behavior as the behavior impacts the larger community. Although these two subjects seem to be in irreconcilable disagreement with each other, they both assume as unquestioned fact the natural presence of a hierarchy, much like the general acceptance that the sun will rise and set every day, the sky is above the ground or that some force like gravity anchors matter to the earth. Once the presence of some kind of natural vertical hierarchy is established, all kinds of conclusions follow in both cases.

On the one hand, the Christian religion for example comes up with God, Jesus, Angels, the Devil, Mary the virgin mother of Jesus, Noah, Moses and the Apostles, to name a few of the better known characters which derive from inspired writings, populating the Christian religion hierarchy. Other religions exist with different slots to fill populating the pecking order. As another example, Buddhism has a strict caste system which defines social and economic class.

On the other hand economic model hierarchy slots include labor, consumers, entrepreneurs, merchants, and government. Within those broad categories are opportunities for further breakdown into hierarchical levels. Depending on the economic model, the slots can occupy roughly the same level, the slots can fluctuate or the slots can be carefully arranged one above the other in a rigid order. Sadly, in my opinion, some forms of economic models include a slot for slaves.

One way or another, either by having a preference for scientific endeavor or by having a preference for developing a moral center in harmony with general surroundings, a person immediately finds the presence of a vertical hierarchy being forcibly promoted as absolute truth. Why this intractable attitude about the organization of human beings? My personal belief explained in detail in my first and second books is that a vertical hierarchy is an invaluable aid in population control without expressly declaring the need for numeric population control to the general public, a very scary declaration.

Why not just bite the bullet and own the need for human self-control to prevent more painful consequences? Just rip off the concealing band aid to allow air, truth, and cooperation to heal the devastation from poor planning over the years? If we were not in a position to take these brave steps earlier, I believe technology has made it possible to provide the secure survival resources which will allow this evolutionary, mind expanding step to take place.

In order to avoid a mass panic when overpopulation concerns get aired publically and regularly with those already suffering the most lifestyle setbacks, arranging for all to have access to survival resources and a sense of welcome and belongingness will need to be present. Then, the discussions about overpopulation will not lead those who feel pushed to the fringes like they may be asked to depart completely and as quickly as possible.

Even if actual numerical over population is disputed as an issue, still the presence of technology reducing jobs and the opening of the job market place by technology to include all locations on the planet expands the available work force well beyond the jobs available to efficiently and reliably provide needed resources. The problems created by surplus people for jobs range from administration complexities, idle hands, and loss of mental health self-esteem and security when a person feels unnecessary.

In any event, my private little dream for happiness, equality and a safety net of resources aside, before more consideration for my dream and point of view will be deemed practical, a thorough examination of acceptable meritorious productive behavior as extracted from religion motivators and economic motivators needs to be analyzed. Others may be performing this task; nonetheless, I will throw in my helpful thoughts on the matter, using my full range of emotional responses to events to develop an unscientific version of motivators for Acceptable Meritorious Productive Behavior, just like everybody else, including the scientists currently in emotional denial.

With few exceptions, most religions have encompassed within their myth an afterlife of some kind. Usually the quality of the afterlife surpasses the current earthly experience enormously and in many cases the quality and certainty of the anticipated afterlife can be secured by actions taken in the current earthly body. Future promises in religious myth are designed to obtain AMPB (Acceptable Meritorious Productive Behavior).

Up until the present moment where science has undermined quite a bit of religious doctrine of all types and creeds, the myths worked to maintain a level of emotional motivation which allowed the scarcer, concrete material resources to spread across an expanding population, even if unevenly in almost all cases. The lack of outright material equality was endurable due to the uneven distribution of emotional rewards derived from religious devotion, and AMPB was generally achieved. From what I can tell during the beginning of this period, economic theory had not developed as a serious scientific discipline beyond the individual or small group. In more modern times economics has taken on a scientific flavor.

One of the earthly problems of an anticipated afterlife is that it allows for the miseries of overpopulation. By providing imaginary vistas of pleasure for the future which not only distract productive labor from being in the moment while performing work, the blissful afterlife also provides little to no incentive to curb population numbers that will be arriving in heavenly paradise shortly. Workers engaging in prayer or other imaginative reliefs to in the moment misery are no doubt responsible for much of the corrupt data in economic experimental information gathering, for which, as the gentle reader will recall, there is no mathematical magic to remedy.

Other than the imaginative flights of fancy throwing unanticipated shocks into economic data collection, devout religious observance can complicate behaviors beyond strictly predictable competitive responses. A person patiently present in the moment to do a good job may not be responsible for the erratic wild card conduct which permits a person to throw their life savings into the lottery or simply tune out of their job periodically throughout the day allowing all manner of gun permits, for example, to be issued to uncertain characters. However, persistent patience does permit nimble competitive problem solving, which believe it or not, does create snags.

Economically speaking, pure perfect competition is the foundation of quite a bit of economic theory, especially in the capitalist model of free private enterprise. In theory one supposes that patience allowing for nimble competitive problem solving would be a good thing, but in practice, what happens to the losers in real life terms, not on paper as faceless numbers, causes varying interpretations of survival behavior. Realistically speaking, the losers do not always, or ever, cleanly lose by admitting defeat, closing up their losing concern, and looking for some other business to develop as quickly and as discreetly as possible, if possible.

For various reasons, a losing concern may not behave according to described perfect competitive behavior which acts as the foundation for economic theory. These reasons can range from not knowing precisely what the rules for perfect competitive behavior are, stubbornly refusing to give into defeat, giving up too easily, or taking pure perfect competition to a ruthless plane unimagined by economic theorists. Also, nimble competitive solutions do not always behave within the confines of projected economic outcomes. Perhaps if a little more dangerous survival emotional electricity had been in the air rather than supportive patience, much of the current technological workforce now putting many employees out to pasture would still be in the ground as raw materials awaiting a future moment of invention still.

Do not mistake me, I am not arguing for or against the progress which has made life easier and less hampered by dire survival concerns for many people, some of who might not be here if population had not boomed in the wake of readily available manufactured goods. I am just saying it is not surprising upon reflection that economics requires such long time frames to allow for erratic competitive behavior and world shaping inventions. However, I guess I will also say it may be a thinking mistake to suggest that the lengthy timeframes allow for the mistakes to correct themselves rather than creating a compounding error exponentially. I cite the current financial misfortunes, along with the ongoing overhaul to economic structuring which occurs fairly regularly.

The emotional atmosphere improvement of moral tolerance and patience can also create some amount of social environment stagnation, undermining nip and tuck competition. Personally, I am not alarmed by the specter of slow or no change to social environment conditions caused by tolerance and patience, but many people who have lost the ability to invest in love are addicted to the challenges and accomplishment possibilities which come in the wake of constant vertical structure changes due to improved technology.

41

I am thinking that if the social environment were allowed to rest, as it were, it might be able to recognize and heal some of the ongoing social injustices and make a social consciousness leap forward to a horizontal social structure, rather than making vertical structural adjustments for new innovations all the time which simply move the social injustices around without identifying the problem which needs a solution. After all, AMPB is not only about technological progress.

If technology has hogged center stage so long it is because large growing numbers of population needed provisions. Additionally, it may be the ongoing technologic innovators are settling for an ongoing shuffling of injustices as an imperfect social remedy which is better than nothing. Imaginatively, the edgy technologic innovators may be hoping the constant swapping of social injustices will lead to a social consciousness leap forward, but I fear everyone will be too busy with survival concerns to question or think about injustices, as witnessed in any struggling third world nation or in detention camps of any sort.

Since direct confrontation of the injustices inherent in the hierarchy structure to civilization is personally scary and to a degree self-destructive when no improvement is on the horizon, it takes a stubborn, brave, crazed or desperate person to start egging the civilization hierarchy structure. I refer the gentle reader back to my earlier books to gain a complete picture of my cocktail of motivations.

If AMPB is not achieved using the religious motivators of an overseeing Omnipotent presence and a promised afterlife, what then? Throughout human history man made laws and systems have always existed right alongside of manmade religions which are understood to be the result of inspiration from a god or gods. Removing the input from religions is hypothesized to simplify the job of economic scientists, leaving just manmade laws and systems.

Since the emotional rewards of religious devotion, anticipated rewards, invigorating hope, and simple love attachments are invisible and immeasurable by scientific devices, gaging where individuals and the aggregates of populations created by individuals employing these types of motivators are, in terms of potential productivity, is undesirably unpredictable. Without the obfuscating clouds of motivations stirred up by religion, science reasons, men will engage in predictably rational behavior to secure survival resources and to avoid punishment, simple as that.

It is easy to see where the logical error is here and why it occurs over and over again in one form or another. Because the scientific person is utterly unable to credit some types of emotional experience due to lack of personal experience or the ability to visibly witness first hand emotional rewards, the scientist assumes that the emotional experiences are being artificially stirred up by faith and hope in unreal entities. Remove the unreal entities and the emotions built from their presence will evaporate into thin air as well. In a way, the Bible emphasis on "the Word" as representing god completely supports this outlook, and this emphasis is the result of the inspired writers. Language is a product of human invention and the collective decisions to call a particular animal a cat, rather than a tac, are pulled out of thin air and random.

It may be, to ease the task of economic planning, that humans will be returned to ongoing instinctive responses, which can be routinely counted on when life is lived on a day to day survival basis. If a person manages to get their hands on some food, they eat it right there and then before some other animal comes along and takes it away. A less instinctively motivated person might take the food home, put it in the refrigerator, consult a recipe book, go out and buy other complementary ingredients, prepare a guest list and throw a dinner party.

Obviously I am utilizing extremes here to make a clear point, but I personally do not feel civilization will benefit by this kind of aid to improved economic forecasting, especially when the larger group of people occupies the easily forecast edge while in the apparent interests of promoting clear thinking, the forecasters are permitted the less instinctive territory and better emotional lives. Without some kind of religion structuring the expression of faith and hope, for instance, will faith and hope disappear?

Survival resource providers may do their level best to remove any security and routine from resource dispersal to prevent these calming, complacency creating emotions from slowing economic activity and responses. Will that be enough to make these emotional experiences extinct?

Besides faith and hope slowing economic activity, there are also deep personal attachments like love. On the occasions when faith disappears, hope is crushed, and love turns into grief from separation and loss, economic activity forecasting suffers predictability failures. In the instinctive economic ideal, setbacks take place, but people still soldier on pretty much at the same pace as previously when faced with day to day survival challenges.

Mourning a lost spouse occurs, briefly, but the search for a replacement spouse starts almost right away, or even before the spouse completely departs in many cases, not because the people involved are heartless, but because they are occupying the edge of survival resource territory with anxiety as a fierce motivator. Under more secure circumstances these same casual swappers might not look for another partner until they had fully made a psychological departure from the earlier relationship.

It may be the anticipated case that the depth of connections to others, even those we share a bed or home with will diminish in strength due to intensification of the survival struggle with no religious salve available. Thoughts of fellow human beings as equally deserving members in the community will be replaced by a necessarily self-centered concentration on personal survival and advantage.

The experience of sharing time together will be replaced by a wary vigilance for openings to gain advantages or valuable intelligence gathering for use at a later date. Instead of length of duration of shared companionship acting as an intensifying bond of camaraderie, the result will be improved ability to push a companion's buttons as needed, creating the desire for the relationship to end by the more abused party, or for the more abused person to want to spend more time on his own.

As for the button pusher, this person may be trying to extend their influence abilities with little regard to comprehending the actual individuals who are being manipulated. The specific personal details about any one person do not matter as long as buttons can be effectively pushed. Developing this skill across a wide range of people is the type of advantageous survival behavior which does not encourage people to cherish and enjoy their companions. Instead, it encourages them to appreciate the survival edge environment of scarce resources which makes people more predictable and easy prey.

Overpopulation considerations also complicate economic planning. In fact it may be the unabated forward movement of population growth which has driven the scientific community so hard in the removal of less material factors impacting the economic environment. Making too many widgets or some other product can create a false sense of security, or even a realistic limited sense of security which in terms of overpopulation and nimble AMPB is unwelcome.

Personally, although I would not describe myself as a drama queen, I would rather keep the hopeful, loving, faith inspired emotional life content in life experience, and I do not feel a reliance on some culturally inspired fairytale is necessary to accomplish this objective. Admittedly the presence of these emotions accompanies the ready provisions afforded by technological advances, which in my opinion allows the technologically focused people to enjoy a level of security as well.

If people are not reliably motivated by the loss of food, shelter, comfortable associates and leisure entertainment, what will cause a person to behave in a manner supportive to society? I believe a previous faith in god can in some cases be easily extended to god's creatures or in other cases simply placed in fellow inhabitants on the planet. Using my own inner compass, I feel what I label a natural desire to do my part to create a beneficial and wonderful environment as motivation supporting society.

The scientists may feel they have a valid point when declaring the emotions of greed, superiority, hate, anxiety and destructive rage are equally human emotional fare which will not simply disappear because a horizontal equality environment has encompassed the planet. If faith, hope, and love can be extinguished through the removal of tradition, routine and relaxation, then I suggest those other emotions will naturally diminish with healing time and good fellowship. If some emotional content is necessarily lost due to the close quarters of civilization, I prefer to lose the destructive survival edge emotions. Am I the only one?

Harking back to the laboratory conditions which will allow leadership and planners the necessary confidence and comfort to make decisions for the population which depends on their planning for the community, it is clear we have a choice about how we are going to gain predictable behavior, AMPB, which keeps leadership from going into a helpless panic trance. The choice is between a majority of people occupying the survival edge with the accompanying limited emotional fare adding few rewards into a lifestyle, or utilizing loving cooperation to maintain a desirable environment, providing genuine control and security to the individual with the accompanying rich loving emotional fare and some additional rewards of the individual's choice.

I admit that my conclusions are all based on personal observation and experience, none of which was accomplished in a scientific experimental setting. I have not organized a likeminded group of people to validate my findings through experiment or recounting of their personal experience. Nonetheless, I am certain confirmation is out there due to scattershot story gathering at various times.

I ask you gentle reader; does some of your personal experience outside of a hard competitive environment support my personal findings? Although my observations and experiences have not been carefully logged, recorded, and statistically analyzed to determine overall population demographics which fall into my stated results to provide reliable scientific support for my views, I feel my basic membership in the human race lends an element of shared species experience. After all, I am not a reptile or an insect.

Up until the point I was negatively labeled I received much of the positive experience I am using to draw conclusions, so I feel all others who travel through life unhampered by negative labeling also enjoy the same human membership advantages, even while dealing with all manner of other difficulties like sickness, personal losses, and personal realizations of mortality. I suppose it is my attitude and other's attitudes shared with equal confidence without the supporting documentation and carefully crafted investigations which cause the scientific community to shake their fist in despair and shout "Vague, contradictory, ambiguous, undetectable NONSENSE!!!!!!!" Maybe they just quietly whisper these oaths under their breath while searching about for more ways to undermine further such defiant, meritless, counterproductive opinions, a more practical approach.

Historically, scientists helped man rise out of the mire of destructive ignorance and spared the human race some amount of senseless suffering. While enhancing agricultural technology, reducing the ravages of epidemic diseases and reducing heavenly support for human sacrifices in wars and on alters, the scientist has kept a keen wary eye out for all manner of foolishness parading as truth. Very early on the scientist was no doubt the constant victim of societal resource deprivation due to physical limitations. When resources ran short, depriving the skinny shrimp male or female of their furtively hoarded resources for future uncertainty was a source of easy money, in a manner of speaking.

Later on, scientific acumen was realized as a source of resource production to provide social stability and the scientist began to enjoy a level of general respect. However, even with the growing respect of those tasked with mental accomplishment to support society, there was always a group in opposition to scientific endeavor. People, who in spite of known facts and scientific inquiry, sank their heels in refusing to budge due to their sureness in perceptions of reality.

Were these people stupid? Selfishly Defiant? Poverty stricken? Social Predators? I think it is safe to say some portion of the poverty stricken may have utilized any means available to get their hands on resources and did not desist from successful resource acquisition once their financial needs were seemingly covered, changing their label from poverty stricken desperado into sociopathic swindler. If only the desperados remained poor, the scientific survival alarm may not be sounding so insistently due to the economic interference sociopathic swindlers' activities create.

Desperados and swindlers actually do not make up the largest part of scientific opposition, although their presence helps to support arguments to enlisting the means necessary to unearth them, like the destruction of security, tradition and routine. In fact, successful swindlers may be adept students of manipulating reality and appreciate scientific endeavor for unearthing helpful truths, although the swindlers may engage in considerable efforts to prevent the spread of these useful and helpful aids to others causing defeat for their swindling efforts.

The largest part of scientific opposition is the scientifically labeled defiant and stupid, made up of people of extremely limited experience, but not necessarily stupid or defiant. It may be in fact that the reckless pace of scientific advance is responsible for the limitations on experience, creating the aforementioned stupidity and selfish defiance. The scientific opposition is almost an unconscious survival mechanism kicking in to protect folks chained to small territories of experience or locked into limiting closets of exposure to reality.

Calling up the personal experience of my youth, like many young people who are the legal responsibility of their parents, I spent quite a bit of time in a limiting mental closet to ease the burden of my parent's concern for having to deal with any youthful errors I might stumble into while they were spending a considerable amount of time outside the home earning a living, or securing networked resources.

Youthful mental closets contain the Easter Bunny, Santa Claus, the Tooth Fairy, some version of popular religion, and the assurances that society operates fairly, so please, please, please, do as you are told to maintain the beauty that is humanity notwithstanding the crazy witch/dirtbag of a parent/boss/association President/other experience limiting personality who is responsible for the omissions in your particular youthful lifestyle, but will be absent once you grow up and get to inhabit the more sane larger world.

As youth ages, first, perhaps, the Tooth Fairy disappears, then the Easter Bunny, and finally Santa Claus. All of these useful tools for maintaining harmony in the home where shared time was scarce get revealed as fun fairytales to create gift giving occasions. At some point the youth is assured they are too old to receive gifts of chocolate eggs and peeps from the Easter Bunny, but they can still buy them for themselves using an allowance granted for completed chores. In some cases the fairy tale may be revealed while still maintaining the annual tradition of Easter Baskets. Either way, the enjoyable uniting tradition is maintained.

For some religion never gets fully discredited or even questioned to help reduce the mental sheltering closet impact of a literal interpretation. Often this situation is the result of reduced circumstances resulting from a hierarchy of deserved and granted material rewards. The greater the situation of deprivation, the more the nonmaterial imaginary rewards of religion will be necessary.

Revealing a religious story as a product of inspired imagination will not improve material resources, but will set back psychological coping

47

resources when the explained symbolism of religious language does not intellectually stimulate the same hope, faith and smug righteous satisfaction. On the other hand, being the recipient of bountiful earthly rewards would make a person uncomfortable with their receipt of favoritism without the confirming tenets and mystery of religion.

For example, heaven refers to the heaven here on earth for those who are permitted a place in the good guy corral, receiving secure survival resources. Hell refers to life here on earth for those unfortunates who are placed in the bad guy corral and do not fully understand the artificial nature of their unfortunate predicament. Limbo represents the waiting spot for serial killers of others outright or serial killers of others reputations until the killers most likely wind up in Hell as a useful bad guy due to diminished serial killing usefulness. Serial killing is permitted to control populations since many people take the "multiply and be fruitful" thing way too literally, or otherwise engage in reproduction recklessly.

The story of Christ suffering on the cross signifies the suffering of the smaller group of negatively labeled people who must pay for everyone's sins by presenting the visibly public consequences to undesirable behavior. By keeping the general populace motivated by fear, or by feeling superior to others erroneously, leadership or god is pleased and forgiving of all sins in general and does not obsessively engage in pursuit of all criminals/sinners.

The sin forgiveness is caused by basic resource production and distribution taking place allowing leadership to heave a huge sigh of relief and bask in actual rare praise, or bask in praise to some Ultimate Being making conditions here on earth rich enough to cause some group to sing halleluiah. Leadership internally enjoys the conclusion that the praise is partially due to their earthly guidance.

Given the starkness of reality within the vertical hierarchy, the regular public unmasking of religion is not popular. One way this unmasking in useful in my opinion is when you are negatively labeled and confused as to why and how this situation took place, thus hating yourself and actively abusive to yourself and others. Naturally the unmasking of religion would be useful in creating tolerance and understanding of others.

I can see the merit with revealing the antecedents of all religions when the planetary population gets on board with equality in resource distribution, happiness, and respect for others, allowing material and emotional rewards to replace those provided by the unmasked religion. Perhaps easing up on the absolutes of hierarchy and competition in the social environment would allow for more useful tolerance and understanding to make a showing without removing all religious psychological relief.

Otherwise a hasty revelation of religious symbolism is a little on the cruel side when gross inequalities still exist in a hierarchy environment and the unmasking usually leads the unmasked into the bad guy corral where some of the previous emotional rewards of the good guy corral are not present. When this happens, a previous good guy corral person will have to either find some rewards not previously utilized or understood present in the bad guy corral by engaging in battle of some type, accept meekly the bad guy label and look for alternative rewards, or look for alternative rewards while refusing to acknowledge any change from good guy to bad guy status.

For those blinded humanely by religion in the current hierarchy of just deserts, science is being a little harsh in labeling the religion supporters as stupid, selfishly defiant, or demented. The last sheltering mental closet of youth which is usually not thrown open to the harsh light of day unless absolutely necessary is "the world operates fairly and sanely except for one cleverly contrived person who will no longer have responsibility over a given youth's life into adulthood". As long as a person does not find themselves useful fodder for the motivating bad guy heap this closet need never be fully thrown open.

While growing up the youth may create discomfort by wanting to pursue an inconvenient activity outside the closet, like skate boarding or cheerleading. Mentioning outside the closet interests as suggested activities will be met with a charge of selfishness or other reasons for not granting parental consent. Perhaps the mental closet will be maintained by parents carefully dressing children in clothes which will make the youth stand out and apart from some anticipated informative group.

Whatever the complex mechanism for securing the boundaries for the closet as long as possible, the limitations on experience are real and will cause the fiercely independent and observant scientist to label the hoodwinked as stupid and defiant, not realizing that real defiance of parental authority would land some of these dependents in line for more severe and limiting blinkers from the overwrought parents trying to prevent catastrophe in their minds. Also, closets vary. Parents who are members of the extremely vertically organized military will provide a different concealing closet environment than those parents who are production workers, secretaries, accountants or doctors.

No doubt the use of these sheltering closets to protect busy parents provides plenty of job security to psychologists. Unfortunately, from what I can tell, the psychologists only change the sheltering closet to

49

conform to the current or anticipated employment environment rather than attempting any social consciousness improvements by exposing the nature of the artificial hierarchy and exploring the usefulness of cooperation, equality and love, but as I said earlier, egging the hierarchy environment is self-destructive for many and only for the stubborn, brave, crazed, and desperate.

Governments in authoritarian nations or other authoritarian concerns like commercial enterprises of all sizes are also responsible for an amount of persistent closet blinkering. To be fair, almost any government or commercial concern engages in some small amount of misinformation by leadership to create harmony at some moments, and competitive motivation at others. The modern corporate mindset of reducing reality back to a cosmic jungle to dispense with the bad mental health created by living life under artificial, manmade constructs present in many religions and philosophies is equally missing the target of reality in my opinion.

Various species populate the planet and at any given moment a particular animal species may enjoy a less stressful environment due to plentiful food resources and a lack of predators, take for example the lemurs of Madagascar before human discovery of their island. Of course this supporting banquet can come to an end at any time when the earth is struck by a meteor, for example, but only a very foolish lemur would contrive to live as though the world would end tomorrow when the possibilities for today are so rich.

Will redundant conservation of lemur food and shelter resources be useful after a meteor disaster? After humans have rapaciously and indiscriminately cleared the island of vegetation? Can a lemur answer or even pose this type of question? Are not similar types of questions for humans equally, shall we say, fruitless?

Of course planning and conservation should be done for material survival resources within human control as far as the human mind is able to practically envision survival outcomes. In the absence of Santa Claus, the Easter Bunny, the Great Pumpkin, Jesus, Apollo, Zeus, Thor, Yahweh and Allah, the reality that remains is the human choice of emotional journey. Will an emotional journey be fueled by dreams completely contained in the imagination by contemplators of god, dreams in the imagination supported by media entertainment on computers or DVD players, dreams in the imagination supported by material props, animals and people, dreams in the imagination supported by real life accomplishments and won competitions, or simply real life accomplishments, won competitions, and control over people and survival resources?

Using the word "dreams" I am running the risk of having an accusing finger point out the populating of reality with make believe. As is often the case a person must first wish or dream about or for something before practical action leads to fulfilled reality with the accompanying cocktail of emotions. While economics covers the division, production and distribution of material resources, the material resources or the lack of material resources will be responsible for motivating dreams of action, or in the rare cases of one dimensional contemplators of god, inaction spotted by performance of god's perceived will.

Should economics be allowed to distribute material survival resources, leaving each individual responsible for the content of their emotional lives? Is it desirable to plan for survival outcomes after human initiated catastrophes such as wars where outcomes might be as tragic as a meteor strike or a super volcano eruption?

In my opinion allowing everyone unconditional access to the survival resources of shelter, food, and companions of choice is necessary, period, and may prevent catastrophic human destruction. An acknowledged set of people slipping through cracks, or getting turned away at the end of the line because the system works that way, is not acceptable.

However, in order to provide for all as an unquestioned matter of operation, people will also need to consciously control the growth of population so that resources will not be required to stretch further than they can realistically go. Otherwise, there is no way of assuring that conserved material will still be available in the aftermath of devastation, much like the resources of the less prophetic lemurs.

The more even the distribution of resources creating happiness and acceptable dreamed reality realms, without necessarily being the exact same items of interest for everyone, the better for emotional fulfillment and harmony. I am projecting that AMPB will be reliably and predictably present due to everyone having a meaningful investment in society and not having to worry that some naturally upsetting occurrence to a person located in a powerful position higher in the hierarchy will result in aimless punitive action by an empowered person consumed by negative emotions.

Equally people will not have to worry about the battles and mischief which take place while jockeying for a better position or to maintain a position. All kinds of lost productive energy and debilitating illness due to battle fatigue in the close quarters of society will be severely reduced to a level healed by a good night's sleep, health maintaining exercise, or other relaxing activity. Before we can get to this new economic model, the old economic models need some examination.

Autonomous Economic Order, Capitalism, Communism, & Socialism

With the exception of Autonomous Economic Order which in modern times is hardly used, nations employing one of the other economic systems spend time exclaiming the evils and shortcomings of the competing economic systems, much as political candidates in an election sling mud on competing opposition. Unlike politicians, economic systems are not elected, they are the result of ongoing military history, natural climate and weather, agricultural production of land, types of national problems, and the amount of leisure time available permitting innovation.

Capitalism, Communism, and Socialism all employ calculations, techniques, and guidelines for producing and distributing material goods. Mechanisms for achieving the ends of providing survival resources to the community vary, but at the end of the day, leadership is expected to perform this supportive task to the community which has placed their trust and faith in governing officials. In my opinion the three economic systems have much more in common than is usually reported.

Socialism and Communism are often stated as being very similar, the only meaningful difference being in the amount of government control over the production and distribution of survival resources. Personally, I would extend this similarity to include Capitalism as well. Government is present and responsible for the overall economic health of the American nation even if they are not visibly active making plans for resource production and dispersal. The government steps in to correct unhealthy economic activity in Capitalism, but up until some part of the economy, or in more dire cases the entire economy, gets out of hand, independent businessmen are allowed to proceed with endeavors within the previous legislated law enacted as health restoratives and preventatives.

The prudent businessman, like any citizen in the community who does not want to run afoul of the law, makes an effort to comply with legislation. Since any size producer and distributor of resources can have a heavy impact on population when they do not behave in a health producing fashion, the government feels in their position as overseer ensuring a beneficial environment that they should be legitimately informed about the ongoing practices in any business organization, large or small.

Ideally within Capitalism the government acts almost as an omnipotent god looking out equally for the interests of all citizens. If the government is not the entity actively performing the planning for resources, they are making the guiding rules to prevent disaster, providing the mechanisms to encourage compliance with the health creating guidelines, and generally keeping an eye on things to ward off new threats.

In theory or ideally is one thing, and the actual practical implementation is another. The idealism theory behind Socialism and Communism is equally far removed from the actual practical implementation. It is the disparity between the mental closets created by the various ideal economic doctrines and the actual application of economic doctrine which allows for all types of mudslinging to take place and in the worst cases of survival fears and threats actual armed conflicts. Capitalist champions point to the human rights deficiencies in Communist nations. Communist nations point to predatory Capitalist monopolies run amok beyond weak government control. There is truth in both comments.

Although technically Fascism is not an economic system, it is a form of government and exercises economic control over the populace which adopts or is subjected to this governing principle. Time for another helpful definition: Fascism: A system of government that exercises a dictatorship of the extreme right, typically through a merging of state and business leadership, together with belligerent nationalism (The American Heritage Dictionary). Fascism, like Communism and Socialism, receives an amount of bashing from the Capitalist champions because of the centralization and strength of the government impeding individual initiatives and freedoms.

On a personal note, I admit it is difficult to see past the horrors of World War II's German detention camps visiting slavery and death on millions of chosen governed subjects and not feel that all attacks on Fascism are well deserved and never enough. However, in its ideal theory Fascism differs from the other economic systems by the amount of government control used to achieve survival resource supply. Because Fascism assumes so much power over every aspect of societal set up, it has the strength of speedily achieving advances without counter balancing checks and raised objections. In economically depressed Germany this speedy climb out of previous World War I debt and economic depression was seen as a needed healthful tonic by those who felt the pinch of unnatural shame in limited resources.

Other German citizens may have gone along for the ride with varying degrees of willingness, after all not everyone could flee the country. Raised complaint or objection landed a person in a detention camp, so serious objectors went underground to form a resistance of some kind. What characterized people who supported the Fascist ideal, even after the ideal was warped by picking all manner of scapegoats to become slaves in detention camps?

All people kept busy, useful and securely supported with an amount of personal freedom would have supported Fascism, as they would support any economic system which arranged such a lifestyle. Being kept busy, a person would not have the free time to spend duplicating the government's job of keeping an eye on things. Spare time would be spent in cementing personal relationships and networks by sharing warm loving interactions, as in other economic systems. Feeling meaningful and useful a person would not be casting about for other sources of activity to improve self-esteem. Additionally secure support would also prevent a wanderlust from developing which makes people start scrutinizing the environment for possible sources of income and stumbling across human rights atrocities. More likely, having to regularly face anxiety triggering stimulus, a person would finally manage to create a psychological survival band aid to permit acceptance of appalling outrages, as occurs in any economic system.

One of the main problems with Fascism is the speed achieved in implementation of government plans of a questionable nature or more troubling, a ghastly nature. No one would probably complain if the Fascist regime was providing lovely living quarters, banquets of food and entertainment, meaningful occupations, and the ability to enjoy companionship at a rate permitting everyone to enjoy the ideal in the foreseeable future. In my opinion, the other main problem with Fascism is the premise of extreme, rigid hierarchy which as in all the other economic systems accounts for the complete departure from the ideal environment back into a masked jungle. As for belligerent nationalism, this national characteristic is present also in any economic system where the nation's leadership and government are feeling insecure and decide some kind of expansion or a war will make things better.

Historically, the very first economic systems were Autonomous Economic Orders where a lone wanderer or group of wanderers provided all their own material, mental, and emotional needs. At this early time economic science as a growing knowledge base to establish practical principles was unknown. The lone individual would have been the sole dictator of his life activity. When stumbling across other lone humans an assessment of personal survival resources and belligerency of the arriving human would have to be speedily completed. The choice would be enjoying the companionship of another fellow or destroying the angry rival consumer for scarce resources.

In the case of groups of wanderers or families, I suppose the most physically able person at acquiring survival resources would also distribute them or have final say in division if necessary, perhaps a dictatorship with a group of assistants. However, in the earliest of groups, most likely any assistant who was seriously disgruntled by the distribution of resources could always just leave and start hunting smaller game and harvesting other available plant matter on their own, unless the Fascist dictatorship took the most extreme belligerent position of hunting down and killing any departing grouch.

The Fascist Dictatorship model developed more fully with European Monarchies and Asian Emperors. With time, technical innovation and population growth, newer economic models made an appearance, capitalism, communism, and socialism. From what I can tell, the move away from the dictatorship model resulted from taking the path away from the hunting/gathering lifestyle of nomadic dictators.

As a minor aside, dictator is a word often considered to be the same as an oppressive or cruel tyrant, a menace to mental health and flexibility. Although the dictatorship model may have outlived its heyday in government, on a more private personal note, many people still wish to have some amount of dictatorial control over some portion of their day's activities to establish mental health and flexibility. Ultimately dictatorship's usefulness depends on context and the surrounding social environment, just as with any economic model.

With the growth in population due to agricultural technology, came craftsmanship to forge tools and aids in agriculture. The next societal innovation resulting from agricultural bounty was the use of money and mercantilism to sell crafts and other products developed from agricultural produce or the need to create agricultural produce, rather than using the previous barter system. Populations grew and people were working harder mentally and physically than ever before due to improved health and security gifted from technological advance and in many minds, a supportive God.

Adventurers and explorers began to travel and discovered other places across land and sea which in a belligerent nationalist fascistic economy were conquered and claimed for the royalty sponsoring the expedition. Does this model differ much from large capitalist corporations claiming the discoveries of scientific and medical researchers who exploit the monopoly advantage afforded by patent law? In the one case explorers brought a better standard of living and survival resource security to conquered peoples, while the researchers bring a better standard of living, survival resource security and possible improved health with the pace of lifestyle seriously increased due to the use of technology.

My point to the gentle reader is that although things appear to change substantially, or that two systems seem to be very different, in this case the Fascist economic model of land discovery vs. the Capitalistic model of research discovery, just as often there is common ground. The recognition of these parallels aids in creating tolerance and harmony or at least allows for clearly understanding the surrounding environment without the concealing fog of empty emotional prejudices.

Population growth in addition to necessitating the exploration of new lands also provided plenty of working hands to make work light and afforded leisure time for relaxation which in turn led to innovation, invention and more types of technological advance. Where previously the most physically able and charismatic held dictatorial/leadership positions, the spread of technological progress allowed knowledge gatherers and creators (less physically able and charismatic in many cases) to assume the reins of totalitarian control, either in actual person (rarely) or by stand-in using the physically appealing charismatic leaders who did not relish replacement. Who would?

Capitalism thrives where raw material resources are available and plentiful, perhaps explaining the popularity of the economic system in the vast continental nation of the United States. Even when mistakes do take place, the material abundance allows for redundancy planning when building in large safeguarding buffers of prepared excess resources. When the excess resources do not get consumed in this country, they are often used to create solid good will interdependency with leadership in other nations. That is not to say that before material excess is shipped elsewhere that everyone is absolutely taken care of and accounted for in this country via a resource safety net of some type, but that the important core of production staff needed to assure provisions is accounted for, while still leaving the motivating shorthanded under class of apparent bad guys.

Communism established popularity in lands of poverty, infertile soils, and overpopulation requiring the educated, informed, unemotional hand of government to step up and remove control from anxiety ridden peasantry making masses of poor judgment calls due to inability to gather and process knowledge calmly and carefully. Economic control was also removed from emperors and their dynasties deemed selfish and corrupt. Poor planning in nations with poor agricultural technology meant many people starved creating enough unhappiness to destabilize organizing efforts by weak government, strong government or anyone else, escalating further the poverty/starvation problem. When poverty is this destructive, people opt for the solution which moves quickest to bring relief.

Rather than having Fascism morph into Capitalism with population growth, Fascism morphed into Communism. I have noticed the highlighting of the historical predecessor to Communism as Fascism here in the

Capitalist United States. I wonder if Communist countries engage in the same use of highlighting to create bias in the teaching of elementary history classes to the young? Socialism, since it is an economic system which arrived on the scene in the wake of monarchies and dynasties is also historically linked to Fascism.

In both Communism and Socialism the government is a strong centralized entity which plans for the economic health of the nation. Communist nations have the government distributing resources equally to support the populace, whereas in Socialist nations, the will of the people is in some manner determined and the agreed upon preferences of the majority are implemented via government planning. The Communist economic model uses the best minds to determine the proper path of production and distribution of resources to everyone equally, while the Socialist economic model polls the populace to determine goals then uses the best minds to accomplish the jointly embraced plans of the majority.

What is to stop a majority population high on legalized marijuana from choosing slavery for all people who will not smoke marijuana? Maybe all of the employed will choose to no longer provide any kind of resources to those displaced by globalization and technology thus unemployed. In my opinion Socialism's use of polling the people sounds much more in line with Capitalism's polling the people via the movements in the market place in supply and demand. On the authority of giving people what they want the United States Media Industry produces violent entertainment content.

The reduction of government oversight used to restore national health is no longer counterbalancing the unhealthy effect of this violence supporting all kinds of personal justice actions like lying, cheating, ruthless competitiveness, murder and so on. Thus a violent competitive environment is pushing the lifestyle pace into the stressful spectrum, just as if we were subjected to Fascist government insisting we had to slap our neighbors or be shot. In this case the supporting logic to the slapping mischief is "Slap to prove your willingness to keep society from becoming soft." Instead of declaring the overpopulation problem outright, the loss of sympathy and compassion for others is anticipated to reduce life span.

I suppose Socialism does have some built in ideology stating the government steps in when majority opinion takes an extremely unhealthy turn, preventing the elevation of all blonde, blue-eyed people to a special class of super person granted extra votes due to their genetic superiority. Besides linking Germany to Fascism in World War II, it is also linked with Socialism. However, in light of the previous fact and general tendencies, I also suspect that Socialism is just as prone to idealism lapses just like all the other economic systems. Quite frankly, when everyone is subjected to the imperatives of moment to moment survival, it is almost impossible to tell these economic systems apart in practical application.

The question becomes which system is better at making the decision for creating scapegoats and apparent bad guys, the informed government or popular majority vote? Obviously spreading out the responsibility makes it easier to face legitimate devastation being visited on a group of chosen sacrifices, or accountability can be removed from the table completely by executing any challengers to authority endorsed actions in the case of strong government. Frankly, I personally do not care for having anybody making this decision, not the majority vote, not the informed government, not the strong centralized government and not the perceived will of god interpreted by inspired writers (although some inspired writers come closer than others when embracing everybody). Everyone is equally deserving of life and quality of life.

The Big Bad Brother Regime of Communism as depicted in general American media is actually looking like a pure white rose of reason right about now when providing resources equally to everyone. Why are so many people frothing at the mouth in dread and revulsion from this economic model? In the case of Communism, the practical application of the ideal has taken the same unpleasant turns all the other systems have taken when departing from the ideal in everyday life experience.

In particular, Communism bans religious observances to win favor with a powerful Omnipotent God and replaces this human tendency with reverence for the government leading to additional bribes and other persuaders to corruption. Also, although material resources are being evenly divided, the people have no mechanism in place for making suggestions or to point out where a miscalculation may be taking place.

Verbal dissent, as in any economic system with hierarchy and empowered leadership, brings punishment. Where the government is visibly strong, punishment is sure and swift. Although other apparently weaker government systems deliver punishment as well for dissent, dissent is a legal activity. The presence of protective legality is not an assurance that no consequences will be delivered to dissenters, just that the consequences will not come from the government, but rather strong government supporters who feel threatened by opposition and can legally visit consequences. The government may not be able to get a rebellious person fired from their job, but fellow employees in competition with the defiant may register the remarks, deciding to make the most competitive advantage out of openly expressed bad moods.

Also, the opposition located half way around the world is an acceptable target for complaint and rage people might more accurately use to improve their local situation if they were not in fear of reprisals. The reprisals may not be death and prison, but a loss of survival resource security can lead to a loss of standard of living and acquaintanceship one has become accustomed to, a loss which is just as frightening and which acts as a stepping stone on the way to prison and death in economies where the pace moves more slowly.

All this knowledge, innovation, invention and theories of understanding and still the population continues to grow. If minor rustlings about the extent of population growth are hitting the airwaves, little actual containment and reduction of population numbers is openly taking place, except for communist China where couples are limited to one child. Equally absent from discussion of problem initiators is the civilization structured by a vertical hierarchy.

Again Communism appears to be taking the lead by treating everyone essentially equally in material deserts. If you consult popular prophecy outside of religion, China is assumed to be the winner of World War III, taking over the entire world. After that conflict, very little prophecy is available from future forecasters of some reputation, although less acknowledged psychics may try their hand at forecasting after Oriental domination. Will the Orient take over? If they take over will the Biblical Revelations story still be in the offing, or will the unified world of equally distributed resources be the symbolic equivalent to the city of heaven descending to earth?

These are interesting questions, but right now, I would rather skip the contemplation of World War III and the aftermath. I would rather suppose that the human race can by pass another major conflict and globalize more peacefully. I will just add competing internationally with other nations with differing views on resource production and distribution also helps create stress and temptation to Communist leadership, in turn causing more loss of idealistic implementation in Communist regimes, just as competition takes a toll on the idealism of any economic system.

Besides the answer of limiting population and the vertical hierarchy to dampen competition which I have been harping on for two and more books, what other mental acknowledgements will help remedy the problems present in all the economic systems practical operation? Various cultural religions are shaped and modified to address this problem, but as an individual trying to find a path of happiness while supporting the community flow, what other mental perceptions of truth will be an aid to creating a humane laboratory environment helpful to leadership?

Defiant, Meritless, Counterproductive Behavior

----I am the captain of my own damn ship!!!!!!----Captain Meekness

Strictly speaking, if everyone could agree on the definition of harmful behavior, or agree on the definition of helpful behavior, lots of time and energy spent writing books could be saved and used more productively and helpfully. Stealing the theme from a popular peace song written by John Lennon, imagine if everyone engaged in helpful productive behavior, and then imagine no one doing so.

Before you can engage in this imaginary effort, you personally must pick a course of productive behavior to place mental focus on. Perhaps everyone is employed using their talents either growing food, making apparel, making electronics or other commodity to supply the general store or working in the general store as a clerk of some kind. Others may be fittingly retired.

Best case scenario, everyone is satisfied and able to perform their job or is voluntarily retired with income. Will being able to perform a job and having easy access to resources at the general store be enough to create a peaceful environment? In my imagination everyone will only be working 20 hours a week, maybe less, given technological advances. After contributing 20 hours of work a person would be mostly free, within the law, to do as he pleased. A person could be captain of their own damned ship and still be meekly supporting the lab.

It is a nice dream, fairly simple in outline. Who would object to this outline by engaging in defiant, meritless, counterproductive behavior in the remainder of their free time, or more dangerously, at work? I am going to answer the above question for a vertical hierarchy civilization environment and then for a horizontally organized civilization environment.

A Look at the Vertical Hierarchy Environment

In a vertical hierarchy people are awarded varying levels of freedom and material resources. As a result, right away, visible material differences support dissatisfaction and reduced self-esteem leading by design to competition. The greater the differences in freedom and material resources, the greater the ruthlessness factor in the competition. The competition to remain alive will engage everyone and is going to be much rougher than the competition to win a quart of sand which may get no one involved.

Thus when designing competition the prizes must be compelling such as sizable compensation to acquire better food, shelter, clothing, transportation and other accessories to personal wealth such as general public status and prestige companions. Ruthlessness inducing panic and anxiety in competition cannot be stimulated by the loss or the gain of bonus movie passes, amusement park passes, or designer clothing, unless the possession of such items is linked to survival within the networked groups providing protective support to an individual.

In order for designed competition to be meaningful it must have winners and losers. Even if everyone could be a winner in some category of competition, the ranking of worthiness in competitions and the fact that everyone wants to win competitions labeling a person worthy planetary material, places some in unworthiness situations unsatisfactorily. When some large group does not win competitions self-esteem loss follows only marginally healed by the presence of god in many religions.

If loss in competitions leads to uncovering the networked appearance game in won competitions, some people may make the ability to win competitions be reliant on more than talent and merit. Ruthless antics will also be necessary. Often these ruthless practices can be individually justified by the forgiveness of sins in the Christian religion, rendering defiant, meritless, counterproductive behavior cleansed of bad karma due to the sacrifice of the human incarnation of God's son. See what can happen with the mixing of religious/philosophical hierarchical doctrines?

So what if everyone does not win a competition some say. Not everyone is going to be or should be President of the United States, Police Chief, an Office Manager, or Production Team Captain. People can still maintain healthy self-esteem through personal connections and the liberal use of religion and philosophy. In theory, that outline of ideal implementation is true, but in practice, the lives liberally or fully supported by religion lack quality of experience and most people know it and avoid it. Take for example the change in many churches from priests who remained celibate to priests allowed to marry and have families so that gifted supporters and sharers of religious lifestyle would not opt for other more attractive religions, causing the religions with a larger emphasis on religious rewards to die out naturally.

Whether or not the Ultimate Creator of the Universe loves you, for the sake of the argument and in my opinion because it makes the most sense, let us assume He does. Good will from the creator if he is there, again in my opinion, is the limit of what common sense supports. Therefore, a person in civilization needs physical survival support, emotional survival support, mental survival support and spiritual survival support provided by his civilization when he cannot realistically strike out on his own anymore.

At the least, if civilization does not step up and deliver physical, emotional, mental, and spiritual support, it should not prevent citizens from providing for themselves. Humans do have brains with a variety of needs over and above getting enough food and oxygen. I would venture a guess that many more animals are capable of developing these needs as well.

Many state that while technology provides the physical resources, it has removed the emotional, mental and spiritual rewards. Personally, I would caution against dismissing technology as harmful, mostly because it allows general humanity to move beyond the need to dwell in the possibility blinkering, survival concentration lands of stark necessity. However, recognizing that the presence of technology has reduced available jobs is desirable by removing the cause for job loss from individual responsibility. When a person feels he lost his job for some reason related to his performance, he loses faith in his right to enjoy his personal gift of life, beginning the descent into all types of destructive behavior to himself and others.

The fact is no human being can compete with the performance computers or manufacturing equipment deliver for the jobs which the machines are programmed to do. When a machine is utilized instead of the human work force, some amount of human workforce must be dismissed. To maintain the motivation and emotional attachment of the remaining workforce, the dismissal must appear as if the departing individual actually deserves the upheaval visited into his life. General acknowledgement that this person is leaving because his work is going to be done by a machine leaves everyone waiting and wondering when their turn is next.

To some degree everyone is beginning to deal with this realization and thus possible eventual job loss. Overall lack of ability to generate commitment to workplaces is causing ripples in accomplished goals for production and distribution of resources. Now more than ever a core group of people with untainted motivation to stabilize the works at any organization is needed. This core must not be in fear of eventual job loss and must feel like the organization is reasonable and fair in requests, otherwise disillusion sets in. In this way the same group of people keep stable long term employment and another group becomes labeled dispensable and flawed, being dismissed regularly as needed to accommodate technological change.

All and all this arrangement might be okay as long as physical, emotional, mental, and spiritual survival needs did not become totally destroyed in the nomadic journey from company to company.

Unfortunately due to the environment supporting the belief in good guys and bad guys of various types due to religions, philosophies, and entertainment media, people do suffer losses in character and standard of lifestyle. Although the presence of a logical, sane world would prohibit these events from really being able to take place, the presence also of insecurities due to competition in a hierarchy, globalization, overpopulation and technological advance, make the regular occurrence of these events very real.

Briefly, let's back up and summarize some of the emotional, mental, and spiritual needs to feel socially secure, since material needs are basically food, water, shelter and maybe companionship. As a member of civilization a person needs to be needed by society, ideally. Barring being needed, a person will have to be feared or protected to ensure a feeling of security and comfort. For some being needed is enough when they have supportive family and friends who they do not have to compete with while sharing time. Families where everyone has roughly the same social position would represent this situation.

If one family member is born exceptionally good looking, exceptionally charismatic, exceptionally intelligent, exceptionally athletically gifted, or some other outstanding gift, the presence of this gifted individual in the family creates tensions. With the presence of a civilization hierarchy structure, these gifts may well translate into elevation of social position, making the fortunate gift recipient feel not only needed, but also wanted and popular. Depending on the rarity of the gift, the recipient person may enjoy admiration and even imitation if elevated sufficiently by leadership to perform this exercise in molding the populace.

In terms of creating a nimble, receptive to change workforce, having people feeling satisfied and needed in a supportive family unit is not entirely desirable or desirable at all. What is useful to create this nimble open to change population is the tension from feeling unneeded. If everyone is employed and feeling needed, then perhaps the tension can be created by being unwanted and unpopular in jobs of slightly less stature which anyone could fill or as a workplace nomad. If everyone goes to some trouble to receive training to insure credentials and desirability, then the tension can be created by being not admired or not imitated.

At any given time a group of stabilizers allowed long-term ongoing, uninterrupted employment is needed by leadership, along with nomadic employees who fill in the emerging gaps and shifts due to innovation and technology. The desirable size of each group varies according to the amount of innovation and change. In times of little technological advance stabilizers were more numerous, but their presence created loss of self-esteem and survival resources spurring on criminal innovation and invention. Criminal innovation and invention may have led to some technological advances, but other catalysts to advance were increasing populations of people in a stabilizing position who felt they needed some kind of competitive edge in the sexual market.

Barring being able to start a legitimate family, a person may have redirected all energy into embracing all humanity as family or as delightful providers of admiration, discovering useful models for describing reality. Using these models as a base allowed others to originate technological inventions. Others who did not marry and start families may have become fiction or nonfiction writers in their time over and above stable employment.

Leadership, like everyone else, has a need to feel secure in their leadership positions, or barring security, feeling feared or protected by military forces. Leadership personnel may be another way of saying the most active and interested pursuers of the diverse advantages and opportunities bequeathed by the gift of life. Early on they perceive the rewards to be reaped internally by observing the environment and thinking about it or soaking up the beauty of earthly surroundings. If a person shares these feelings and thoughts or renders these thoughts useful in practical application regarding others he may enjoy popularity, being wanted, admired, and imitated.

Leadership does not eat a bag of cookies and take a nap. Leadership eats a bag of cookies and looks for a boat to sail, or if that has already been done and fully appreciated for the richness of beauty and experience, looks for a car to take apart and put back together, a place to build a house with garden, a business niche where an empire can be started, or some other novel experience not yet fully milked for enjoyment and learning. So while leadership needs to be needed by the surrounding civilization to his gift of life, he and his predecessors are largely responsible for the vast, sprawling civilization which has encased the planet in a layer of interconnected human life.

The above description is of modern day leadership, constantly on the move to acquire knowledge and be bigger and better in some fashion. Was this restless quest for excellence always present, or was there a period of history before villages and small human gatherings began rubbing up against one another where the pace was more relaxed? As it happens, there was a period of technological stand still very early on in human development. It occurred right after man invented the handy axe. For a million years, a period unheard of for absence of technological advance, no new tools arrived on the scene.

Instead of thinking up something new, people made the axe over and over again with slight variations in artistic expression. Apparently, people sat around making axes for some portion of the day, and then used an axe once to perform a kill. No need to have one exceptionally long wearing killing device due to the economic demands of having more than one. Any given person could make hundreds and did.

Drawing on my personal experience of knitting, I find knitting the same simple scarf or fingerless gloves to be rewarding in a ribbing knit/purl pattern. I found this activity most rewarding as a relaxing ritual in times of overwhelming anxiety over job situations, previous to my realization that I actually had no personal control over my job situation.

Oddly enough not feeling absolutely personally responsible raised a large burden of anxiety from my shoulders. Needless to say other anxieties took the place of personal responsibility and power to effect change in my life, but this realization changed the quality of anxiety into something I felt more capable of coping with.

Therefore, I suppose the ongoing making of axes to be an attempt to achieve personal control in early human life by being always at the ready for when a good meal prospect wandered down the path. While making an axe an early human could be dreaming of his next meal when he may not have enjoyed one recently. If an early human was not dreaming of dinner, perhaps he was dreaming of providing dinner to a friendly and comforting companion.

The leadership role may have developed as simply as this, one person providing dinner to another. Initially, maybe the companions traded meal provisions, or one companion hunted while the other foraged for edible plants. The actual actions of leadership may have been swapped back and forth between people. At one moment a person with a better vantage point to a well-travelled deer path might instruct his partner when to charge, while at other times the positions might be reversed. If a group of early humans was nomadic, following prey animals for food, the group might have a meeting to determine the best time to move camp in which all participated, but the oldest most experienced follower of the prey herds provided the most respected input influencing other's votes.

Apparently the axe was a fairly huge advance and permitted early man to have a crucial advantage over all the animals used to provide food, clothing, and other sheltering items. Maybe it took a full million years for the species as a whole to be able to relax enough to innovate and invent. If only one person innovated and invented without the rest of humanity being able to appreciate the effort, technological advance would have been quite slow, and probably was at the outset. With more people being able to feel calm and thoughtful due to ready resources, others could understand new ideas, or come up with them as well.

Who would be the lucky folk able to achieve calm and thoughtful demeanors, thus becoming leaders? My guess is the men would be the most physically able hunters and gatherers of food and materials, thus able to utilize the thinking, planning, and learning advantages. The more survival resource access is improved, the more people who can, in theory, contribute to leadership and progress. Take for example the presence of a group of male elders in tribes of people, and the presence of a group of nobles in European nations, both topped by a chief or king.

I am not sure the second class role of women and others was so much a result of human evil and sin, as a reflection of the secure availability of survival resources. As access of survival resources spread to women and others, the new found security permitted lower hierarchy members to calmly reflect and think. Once populations had reached a size to start dividing up labor to create efficiency in resource collecting, men practiced thought and reflection in the roles of leaders, while women and others used thought and reflection to aid in their established roles dictated by the need for efficiency, not entirely as a result of men exercising dominating leadership decision making.

Even with the very beginning of population growth from small egalitarian groups to villages and tribes, the increase in numbers of participating people in culture allowed for extra hands over and above the needed number to secure resources for the group. These extra hands took over thinking, planning and learning, and thus took over the reins of leadership control. In my first book I suggest that even in the earliest days of labor division things remained classless and only with some serious disaster creating the first ongoing resource shortages did the idea arise that to maintain the health of the most important, needed members of the tribe and in turn the tribe itself, some group would have to sacrifice an amount of health, or life altogether.

Other tribes and villages may not have chosen to make this decision to embrace a vertical organization. If the thin even distribution of severely depleted resources did not compromise the health of all members of the tribe into extinction, then the tribe would have carried on. I can easily see an egalitarian tribe of this type managing by allowing the most physically vulnerable to naturally suffer during the resource shortage until the resource equilibrium was restored due to population depletion. As long as all the women or all the men did not succumb to some strange disease, at some point equilibrium would be restored with no loss to social cohesion maintained with one class of social equals, if not absolute equals in receiving of nature's gifts in hardiness.

Unfortunately, in the history books there is no shortage of stories where some peace loving egalitarian people run up against the other type of decision making tribes. Vertical organization leads quickly to competition, strife, and violence. It does not take long for adventurers and explorers to arrive at the idea of providing a relief valve for competition through the expansion of territory and conquered peoples who will provide still one more vertical rung in the class ladder. Essentially, once a group of people has assumed the role of leadership, either because they are at the moment the most able, or the persons chosen to front for the most able, the return to an egalitarian way of life is unthinkable.

The above egalitarian outline sounds rather harsh, letting nature take its course in times of extreme hardship, but the vertical outline, as you can see, is no better. In the vertical outline the men structuring civilization make the choice of removals, not Mother Nature's mystical mechanism of granting physical hardiness. Some might choose to substitute in God for Mother Nature achieving an absolute, omnipotent upper hand for their side of the argument. The other side would argue that at least utilizing the most intelligent men of the age insures a kinder response than that provided by indifferent Mother Nature, pointing to all the bounty provided by technological knowhow.

If all that bounty were made unconditionally accessible to the current planetary population without recourse to apportionment via the carefully crafted vertical hierarchies, I might almost be on board with the No God, No How people. As it is, quite a large portion of people are well taken care of in the societal plan, the majority even, but since I personally occupy the left out minority, I must disagree.

What if the physically hardiest were in charge? Would we be living in an egalitarian dreamland then? No, the hierarchy set up would be different, not equal. The physically fittest thoughtlessly began the overpopulation dilemma, leading to the decision by force to use competition to thin the crowd. Once the competitive remedy to overpopulation took control of the environment establishing degrees of rewarded usefulness, the stage was set for the thoughtlessness to continue via craftily enforced mental perception blinkers, exhaustion, and panic, establishing an unquestioned vertical hierarchy.

Besides feeling emotionally secure or some variation of secure (wanted, admired, imitated, feared, protected) there are mental needs of stimulation and its variations, and spiritual needs of feeling unique and its variations. Mental stimulation may result from survival imperatives.

67

Naturally the anxiety and panic from survival imperatives can act as a deterrent to successfully meeting these mental challenges. Otherwise mental stimulation can arise from chosen areas of desirable personal challenges, for example, designing a sail boat with the world's tallest mast and sailing it.

Those who live smoothly on the edge of personal disaster do so because they do not care whether they spend time in jail or personally mind the conscience dilemma of blaming someone else. For them morality is flexible, and they bend it to suit their purposes of the moment. For everyone else being short on the survival resources of food, shelter, and friendly companionship is truly an unwelcome hardship.

Some people never have the desire to address spiritual needs. Either they are enormously endowed with survival resources and thus assured of their place in God's heart, assured of their own personal skills at avoiding the poor house, or utterly disillusioned at an early age. Alternatively they could be enormously short on survival resources and feel so overwhelmed with anxiety that they are willing to cast about everywhere for relief and consider the path of spiritual inquiry, and most importantly, the social networking found in spiritual institutions such as churches, temples and sanctuaries. Although to outside appearances a spiritual quest is underway, it is actually a practical undertaking to secure survival resources.

Genuine spiritual yearning does not mean a person neglects material or mental concerns, living under a tree with one bowl and spoon. On the contrary, spiritual seekers who arrive at an answer can be quite materially well off by founding a church or due to successful networking in a well-established church. This type of spiritual seeker within the competitive hierarchy almost always attends or establishes a church with a vertical hierarchy and achieves some level of status. Even in poor countries, a poor spiritual seeker who comes up with a philosophy which supports the hierarchy or does not present a well-argued logical challenge to the hierarchy will be supported by the rich who will arrange for supportive speaking engagements.

Whatever the precise tally of total physical, emotional, mental, and spiritual rewards, the societal mechanism of competition practically applied by the pickers and choosers punches holes in the idealism for excellence in accomplishment and the idealism for spiritual focused life, just as this mechanism takes its toll on the ideal economic dispersal of material resources. The diminishment of materials distributed to those invested in mental accomplishments and spiritual yearnings is achieved when the pickers and choosers calculate the equivalency of the mental and spiritual rewards with actual material rewards. In cases of lower hierarchy positioning, the calculations allow for the thinnest possible distribution of material survival resources to those who can utilize their imagination spiritually or mentally to create useful substitutions.

In order to create competition with this group of imagination utilizers, their ability to manage with meager survival resources must be undercut to the point where the competitive gnaw of anxiety and insecurity is felt in spite of all spiritual succor and mental solutions to extend resources as far as possible. Under these circumstances it is supposed the imagination utilizers will want to improve their lot instead of using their imagination to support society through traditional spiritual morality using popular religious behavior guidelines and making do with their thinner than average allotment of survival resources through thrifty crafts.

Thus are born creative writers who encourage readers with few personal sounding boards for advice to engage in all types of reckless behaviors, some heroic and some merely favor seeking, which will land the socially disadvantaged on the downward slope to negative labeling, increasing the creative story teller's usefulness and placing more hapless, neglected example people beneath his ascending heel. In some rare cases a thrifty person may invent, for example, a post it note out of junk mail, and by the vagaries of cosmic luck find themselves the possessors of vast fortunes not even imagined in their, the imagination kings and queens, wildest dreams.

Why can't the pickers and choosers leave these imagination utilizers alone as examples to the poor of how cheerful and easily tolerated a life of restricted survival resources can be? Wouldn't that be a kind thing to do? Wouldn't that encourage peace on earth? First of all, if the imaginative example is generally followed, the lower class would manage to evade the rigors of competitive battle which ultimately handily reduces life span for the lower class.

Additionally, the pickers and choosers find the creative productions very useful for setting up their tiger traps to land some group of unfortunates in the negatively labeled domain. The creative may or may not realize this use, but I would guess if they are popular and well supported on an ongoing basis, they must have some inkling.

For example, a busy, panic stricken, verging on the extinct tiger (a creative symbol for overworked lower class human) not utilizing careful detail oriented scrutiny of the characters in a police drama, witnesses a police detective using established police procedure when questioning a suspect. The procedures can involve pretended support, lying, and/or blackmail using some lesser usually unenforced transgression.

In the real world when a training co-worker lies about work procedure or tells this newly employed panic impaired tiger that everyone will understand if he takes long panic trance naps at work, the tiger foolishly believes the devious co-worker. Most likely the tiger is also being subjected to some amount of blackmail to take bad advice or be fired through combined gang deviousness.

When this hapless tiger gets fired, he does not blame the co-worker because he sees upstanding officers of the law engaging in the same types of behavior, so it must be okay. The tiger does not register the detail that the officer is dealing with a criminal who has an established recorded criminal spree, whereas the co-worker is taking complete advantage of their trusted position as trainer to mislead an undesired rival in the competitive work place.

Eventually the tired tiger may wise up, learning to sift the good advice from the bad advice, or the tired tiger may opt for performing work poorly becoming the lazy stupid bad guy. In both cases the poor panicked tiger may still be fired for some other trumped up reason. A person may be allowed to stay as the blame taker at an organization performing work incorrectly, but he will not be allowed the personal dignity of a job well done, and of course, appreciation from others is out of the question.

To be fair, the training co-worker may be equally panic stricken and not utilizing careful detail oriented scrutiny when deciding it is okay to engage in this behavior. Sadly, if the newly employed deceived tiger reports the misleading training to a manager whose responsibility is to sift these matters of competition gone awry out, the tiger may be fired more swiftly.

Ideally, the manager should question these dubious practices by the trainer and if the trainer is trying to spot criminal behavior by inducing criminal behavior, the trainer should at the very least be corrected. However at times, the manager subjected to the same panic producing environment as everyone else decides if the police are doing it, it must be okay. The police are after all supported by leadership and network TV.

Police dramas abound on TV. Actual police procedure varies depending on which show you are watching. Sadly, all too often the officers who abide by the rules wind up dead or removed from the force via injury, disillusionment, or gang deviousness. If they do not suffer removal, they remain as uncool characters who do not manage very much successful law enforcement activity.

Of course rules must be broken on occasion, I am just not certain rule breaking should be taking place all the time. Perhaps breaking the rules is a spiritual activity, where a person feels he is special as the unique exception to the rule. I suppose it is natural that the police officers as enforcers of the law might begin feeling special and unique in their understanding of the spirit of the law. Again, this would be another instance of not sifting details when the general population assumes this unique spiritual understanding of the will of society when throwing the general code of decent behavior and the actual procedural code of an employer out the window.

Still, what about peace on earth, the right to happiness and equality? Wouldn't honesty, starting with the overpopulation issue be a huge help to keeping up morale and efficient production? It may be the case that overpopulation actually supports the implementation of technology, which is why the subject does not receive the media attention which it should, in my opinion. Well, that just sounds crazy doesn't it? First everyone is worried over the complications and resource losses due to overpopulation, and then overpopulation supports the deployment of technology. Which one is it?!? Both.

No one wants to be responsible for the outcome of an announcement that population numbers need to be contained. Such an announcement will have a frightening impact on members of population who imagine they are tagged for dismissal. By allowing everyone to feel secure and emphasizing that population reduction will only take place in the birth rate, this fear can be minimized. On the other hand, once this security is generally felt, people who performed picking and choosing services to publically place labels as well as those highly placed within the vertical hierarchy may have some discomfort to deal with, as outlined in my second book, but at least they will still be here on equal footing with everyone else.

As far as overpopulation being deemed useful, naturally those who do the picking and choosing amongst population will no longer have that source of power, so they do not want any reductions taking place. Besides providing usefulness merit points to the pickers and choosers, the population consumes manufactured goods. If everyone buys the least amount of goods to be socially presentable, demand for goods is created, but not as much as when people consume competitively to achieve protective network membership and rank, conspicuously to maintain network rank, obsessively as a way to obtain stress reducing pleasure which can become an addiction, or as a means of providing personal meaning when networking feels empty.

With the growth in demand for food and other consumer goods comes the need for improved technology and the puzzles which keep the mentally agile happily busy and secure. When the mentally agile run out of such puzzles and sources of status and self-esteem, feeling the possible presence of a pink slip of dismissal on the way, they begin thinking up mischief and ways of demonstrating the weaknesses in the system which will hopefully continue their employment into the indefinite future.

It may be that these job saving glitches are programmed into the system to appear periodically as a redundancy plan. Otherwise, the more honorable puzzle solvers will start looking to the social and economic system with their acute mental ability and point to the weaknesses in these larger systems not providing adequately for them in particular and others as well.

Unemployment and low wages keep people from spending money, jeopardizing the stability of the hierarchy. The addition of more people to the consumption market, while creating the problem of overpopulation, insures some amount of predictable social stability within the rankings. Without a degree of stability to hard fought social positions, the loss of positions would lead to hefty amounts of disillusionment, eating into the core of needed stabilizing pillars of stone.

Thus, competition requires growth in order to be socially stable, specifically growth in consumption of manufactured goods, population, and levels in the hierarchy. When growth is not present, upheaval and overthrow of the ranking order creates destabilization, making the current economic and political system, whatever it is, look ineffective.

When uncertainty does influence the environment violence such as blackmail is needed as a motivator. In terms of keeping people off balance and willing to sacrifice health and relationships, a person must be driven to the cliff edge via competition, which is best achieved when there are plenty of replacements for the disillusioned in poorly executed social engineering strategies. Otherwise, not feeling easily replaced, a person might engage in ethical judgment calls regarding his own work situation. A worker does not stop working because he feels empowered and equal; however, he does stop working in a health destroying manner demanded by a blackmailing network.

The disillusioned in poorly executed social engineering strategies must be permanently labeled as flawed in some manner via the appearance game (see earlier books) and be restricted to minimal or no survival resources, if possible. By making serious health sacrifice a precondition to employment, the employed will develop a cruelty edge and feel those not employed, for whatever reason, can be removed from the planet.

After a few generations of such general mental states, people will live for the day and accept, albeit somewhat unhappily, when their turn comes for early dismissal and eventual resource depletion with all the horrors that will entail. This socially engineered design gives the advantage to anyone who stirs up competitive lust over those who seeing through the whole mirage, don't feel like taking down anyone for a few extra days of questionable quality existence once resources become extremely limited.

With luck the destruction in health will result in people dying shortly after 50, certainly no later than 65 when most people retire. After 50 most people take a hormone reduction hit, seriously curtailing their inborn sex drive which fuels quite a bit of competitive consumption to be socially appealing and fuels general social anxiety period. If a person does not feel a strong pull to find a partner, to be considered socially acceptable (i.e. sexually stimulating to add interest into the surrounding environment) or to continue to impress the competitive judgmental partner he is currently involved with, he will spend less money on accessories and apparel, making do with what he has already and daily showers.

One of ambition's rewards or a reward for keeping meekly in neutral territory where allowed, will be attaining a level within the hierarchy which will prevent dismissal or making the journey of diminishment long enough to allow a demise by natural aging. Population will continue to grow by those creating network members, those reaping rewards in the day as quickly as possible, and by those who suppose that having dependent mouths in tow will allow some amount of necessary social position and prevent their early removal. Not to mention the population growth due to the fortunate who go about the business of life with rose colored glasses and those who suppose that their genetic superiority requires them to make as many replacements as possible, and all because no one wants to own the overpopulation problem.

A Look at the Horizontally Organized Environment

So now, let us look at an egalitarian horizontal arrangement. Ideally, as outlined in the constitution of the United States for example, everyone recognizes that all are born equal and thus deserving of equal quality of life. A fusion of the liberty and freedoms available in the Capitalist economic system with the democratic election of government officials providing oversight is the practical application of this constitutionally stated idealism. In practice, the popular majority casts votes for candidates running on promises and platforms of planned action.

A candidate could baldly state that they wanted to reduce the poor to beggary and death by poverty, but instead they speak about cutting government spending and waste nonspecifically, speaking of cutting taxes in short 30 second publicity spots. Candidates can support decentralizing the government to aid in problem solving which is the exact opposite of economic theory encompassing the entire nation. Perhaps more regional economic theory, science and goals will be a new development to keep planning personnel from feeling utterly adrift from the solid ground of realistically forecasted and achieved targets. Lastly candidates can speak about international policy and relations with the currently identified foreign creator of all the national evils taking place. When the majority speaks by casting a vote, they are picking a candidate and his choice of advisors to fulfill these vague assurances.

The time may come in the future when such wanton admission of inhumane goals is no longer likely to damage popular appeal, but I don't think we are there quite yet. Personally, I do not believe that the leadership who goes out on the campaign trail addressing the public understands the effects some implementations of ideals have on the chosen negatively labeled group. In order to present a believable face of wanting to solve problems fairly, a person must really believe he can solve problems fairly.

Otherwise our political candidates would have to be sociopaths who can lie convincingly at will. If they are sociopaths lying to the public due to lack of empathy and compassion, what prevents them from lying to each other in further sociopathic disconnection from human feeling and understanding? They have to be honest with someone or how would they get anything done, problem solving or problem intensifying?

Basically, I feel it is fair to say the huge gaps in the levels of the hierarchy create an experience disconnection between leadership and the middle to lower classes. Also, leadership is overwhelmed by the sheer enormity and complexness of their undertaking and sadly do not look to the one simplifying solution which would make everything much easier, flattening out the vertical hierarchy. Why won't leadership go there?

The overall civilization structure will not have to radically change that much. A lot can stay the same. Leadership, laws, and law enforcement will still be needed; the compensation will just be on the same level of material and social rewards as everyone else. Once survival insecurity has been erased as an ongoing concern for the general population, the leadership jobs will be that much easier, not requiring huge incentives to get interested parties to step up, take responsibility and plan action.

Some detractors from the ideal of peaceful existence feel people will generally become lazy without some dire incentive spurring them forward. I understand the perception error taking place. Those overworked with a heavily developed cruelty edge understand fully how much they have unwillingly sacrificed of their physical and mental health to win the cooperative meekness competition. When the equality ethic governs the social atmosphere, their losses will still be present and making the overworked feel the very insecurity they were willing to compromise health to avoid.

The overworked sacrifices will not be needed, the sacrifices will definitely not be wanted since they will be considered a bad example, and obviously, the overworked sacrifices will not be admired or a subject for imitation. The replacement ideal will be those who still want to work hard can do so because they want to, not because they are anticipating being able to exercise power and control over others they put out of a job achieving personal security.

At present the overworked are deriving security from their willingness to senselessly destroy their health, motivating others to the same bar of destruction which helps to compromise clear thinking, creates early mortality, and stunts emotional growth. Others derive security from their exceptional good looks, athletic skill, intelligence, charisma, being well networked and so on. What the currently secure in the vertical hierarchy fear is the source of emotional, mental and spiritual quality of life once the playing field has been evened materially.

Health sacrifice can only be delivered a few times before work performance starts failing. Good looks, intelligence, athletic skill, and the like are all gifts with fleeting value within the vertical hierarchy unconcerned with overpopulation, or in some cases even desiring the circumstance. Competitive stress takes an early toll on all these gifts.

So when an ability to offer an outstanding performance gets sacrificed by too many outstanding performances, when good looks, intelligence and athletic skill fade with the stresses of competition, do these people used to their place at the top step aside and let the next group of unmarred achievers go for the gold? No, if they could they might be on the way to embracing equality.

Instead, they utilize pickers and choosers to winnow the up and coming field into work place nomads where possible, allowing a clear easy path to job security only for those willing to assume positions below already occupied territory to remain. In many cases due to sheer upcoming numbers, not even those will get to stay. In fairness, not all of the previously well positioned, for various reasons, remain in their secure positions. See my earlier books for further insights.

The boon which competition for social position brings to the table for the individual is the ability to act freely in any manner deemed fit as long as a person is personally able to cope with the consequences. An individual can choose to destroy his health to achieve security and thereafter, when health impedes actual work performance, perform networked favors for others to help maintain the group position, play favorites amongst willing pickers and choosers, and engage in any other self-promoting activities absolutely freely as long as the activity is within legislated law.

Some people may not even feel the conscientious urgings to wait until they are damaged and impaired in some manner to begin these networked activities. Based on sound parental advice and experience, the informed will start these networking activities in private schools, on sports teams, in churches and in college activities. The person who waits till they begin work or until their skills are compromised will be late comers to the game. Society, like the Cosmic Universe, may not much care about the details as long as resources get produced and distributed. Intelligent law breaking is even tolerated to a point.

Essentially liberty and freedom in situations where survival resources are not readily available by design, as a matter of social policy and generally accepted belief, as in a vertical hierarchy, boils down to the freedom to acquire security within the bounds of the law, not decency. Starting with a mild equality distribution of survival resources would mean everyone has access to food, shelter, some small amount of disposable income, and companions without the loopholes created by leaving some groups out via the law. Even those who have broken the law and been caught are covered as they occupy prisons and rehabilitation centers.

Basic physical needs are securely covered in a horizontal civilization structure. Freedom over and above the freedom to network and connive is still subjected to law, just as it was in a vertical civilization structure. It seems to me the incompatibility of freedom and equality coexisting, as voiced by many who oppose a horizontal civilization, refers to the loss of freedom to break the law without consequence due to high vertical placement in the hierarchy and carefully limited amounts of law enforcement. The freedom loss could also refer to the ability to use excess survival resources to spend competitively, conspicuously, as a way to obtain stress reducing pleasure and to create life meaning where necessary.

Of the four, competitively, conspicuously, as a way to obtain stress reducing pleasure and to create life meaning, the only motivation which strikes me as immediately socially destructive is competitively. If a person creates life meaning by trying to surpass another person in a contest known only to and organized by him, I imagine he is still free to do so. However, the competitive person is no longer free to subject others to his pace of achievement which he wants to establish by making others have to suffer a loss or become meaning centered in competition as well. By making everyone compete in a vertical hierarchy, the civilization structure is robbing every one of their freedom to perform comfortably and healthily with dignity.

Obviously some people are going to be able to perform better on the job than others, standing out and becoming conspicuous in this event. In fact with the social predation present in a competitive work environment causing people to avoid sticking out in a crowd absent, people will feel safe to compete with themselves, indulging in work they find rewarding to their personal limit. Perhaps a person here and there may irreversibly damage their body in some manner "going for it". If a nimble group of people is needed to move about into various new jobs as innovation and technology progress, these people may be happy to oblige, or they may be so happy with their line of work that even with less ability to express work performance excellence, they still want to do that job, or something just like it.

When people use consumption as a social activity or to obtain the pleasure in ownership of something perceived as fine, valuable, and life enhancing, stress relief occurs from these experienced pleasures. However, sometimes this type of consumption can become an obsessive addiction which creates more overall stress in the individual's life rather than a balance tipping into a total of pleasurable stress relief. This experience can take place in the achievement of collections and support gear to a leisure activity.

I think the real issue of freedom is what activities will receive the most support from society creating the most availability of freedom in those favored areas. Religion could just as easily be banned in a Capitalist environment as in a Communist one. If our democracy can pass a law forcing everyone to get health insurance or pay a fine in spite of large portions, even the majority portion of the population not wanting anyone who does not want the insurance to not be required to buy it, then freedom of worship, and even freedom of speech can just as easily be the next casualties.

The vehicle which must be in place allowing the freedom to practice religion is the freedom of speech and dissent without consequence. I am not suggesting law breaking without consequences. However, I am stressing the ability to point out errors in planning and express discontent with departures from the idealism in the Constitution regarding a separation of church and state, or passage of a law dictating the manner a person disposes of consumption resources.

As it happens one of the clear economic differences between Communism and Capitalism is in the first case government can tell citizens how to spend their money, whereas in the second, the freedom to choose purchases is up to the individual. Confusing the matter of evil apportionment to economic systems, Communism provides healthcare at the expense of the state without recourse to any personal individual investments. Of course, since the Communist government controls all the wealth, one supposes health insurance expenses are removed before wages ever reach an individual consumer's hand, much the same as in the Capitalist system where companies adjust received wages for benefits.

Usually the company in a Capitalist system asks the individual whether or not he wants insurance and few turn this benefit down. On one occasion, I did turn the health insurance benefit down because I tend to lead a safe, healthy life and because the price of insurance, even from an employing company, was to my mind, ridiculous. Shortly thereafter I was laid off. If a right to choose does not actually exist in practical application of a democracy, then perhaps calling it boastfully a democracy is not quite the right identifier after all with the economic system creating a dishonest application of ideals.

Ideally a democratic government may not visit consequences on individuals by law for speaking about personally experienced injustices. Removing the ability of the whole surrounding larger population to visit consequences on those less fortunately placed in the vertical hierarchy will allow democracy and equality to be a part of the real experienced world. Competitors using the content of a person's free speech as a tattle tale mechanism to improve advantages in the hierarchy will not impair a person already adequately provisioned and unconcerned about material resources, allowing the democratic ideal to exist in applied practice more completely, if not absolutely perfectly.

Believe it or not, I have on occasion made the odd dissent filled remark or two. I was not rude, crude, or loud, I was simply disagreeing. Although I was aware dissent could cause career damage, at some point, after I realized I was clearly going to be the nomad scapegoat due to my single status with no children, or other attached family, I was in a devil may care land of recklessness, speaking freely about things taking place in the environment. Additionally, even a very modest dissent filled remark can prevent a person from the descent into self-loathing occasioned by speaking in contradiction to one's own strongly held opinions.

I may not have always agreed with the spontaneous procedures made up to promote favorites and said so to the manager who was throwing years of established method out the window when I came on the job and refused to perform poorly. Usually my remarks were a result of answering a question, like, "Don't you think this is now the best way to do things?" To which I replied, "No". I was still willing to work as directed, but I was not going to agree with a procedure which would prevent me specifically from performing well. On one occasion I wrote to corporate officers and alluded to the fact that stockholders would have an interest in the loss of efficiency so carelessly dispensed with to pick favorites, see my first book.

Dissent is dissent and if a person is obviously not going to be in complete agreement with his being negatively labeled in the work place, he can look for work somewhere else where he will only be permitted the exact same option due to managerial networking and no further changes to a poorly networked person's network resources. The presence of the competitive hierarchy environment creating levels is doubtless responsible for this situation.

Some group of onlookers who have no experience compass to understand the reality of the situation, tsk tsking away, are the vocal supporters of the need for hierarchy and competition to keep people active, motivated and behaving correctly. Little do these onlookers realize that if the blackmailing hierarchy insisted some employees take a nap, these sidelined workers would have little choice than to curl up and pretend to be sleeping or have to find another job that much sooner.

When all types of human needs - basic physical resources, energizing emotions, mental stimulation, and a spiritual specialness connection – are covered in a horizontal environment, what may happen is some group of people heavily burdened with responsible planning chores will find more people willing to help plan and be responsible, lightening the previous heavy burdensome load. If others are encouraged to share responsibility and allowed to do so in an equality environment, those exercising these new aspects of their mental tool box will not be additionally concerned about sounding rebellious, critical, or negative when providing input to those previously placed higher in the hierarchy.

There will be no one higher in the hierarchy visiting consequences for presenting a bright new better way of doing things, or simply fielding a new idea which elicits a helpful, informative discussion about why that idea cannot be utilized, improving future input from others all around. Obviously this model of equality requires freedom of speech for starters. Otherwise keeping the competitive hierarchy ensures that all offers to share responsibility and planning chores will sound like an offer to share the accumulated personal power and the survival security of the person currently doing the responsible planning job, thus, not a welcomed advance.

In situations where volunteers are in charge of organizations why is disagreeing comment so threatening? These people in charge should not be afraid, but they are, I guess. Where does the fear come from? Being afraid of losing sight of who is in charge?

On the rare occasions when I have been vocal in my disagreement with a board of directors whose meeting I was attending, I found the whole group of directors almost immediately seize up and halt all further discussion. I would ask a question trying to understand the heated situation about (a fictitious illustration) the continuation of banning all previously forbidden books in spite of complaint from the Free Love and Literature Brigade. I would query "Are the books unfair, prejudiced, misleading? Would it be accurate to say the books were X-rated?" To which the reply would be "Read them yourself, we've moved on."

I tried to warn the group that others were probably looking at the situation the same way the original complainers were and I was, to no avail. A short bit later, a person in the community charged with keeping a general eye of my wayward attitudes started a conversation about how a complaining person or group is actually in charge of a board of directors without producing any useful effort when seeking their attention and trying to guide their discussions in meetings. Couldn't I see how wasteful complaint is for the volunteers who run for these offices and selflessly perform public service for no acknowledgement or reward? Well, I guess if you put it that way, but what happens when an issue needs to be addressed? Do we all just cross our fingers and hope the board will stumble upon our concern sooner or later by blind luck?

Leadership must be open to hear comment, and if that means employing a few extra volunteer ears to help sift through all that comment, than time to add a few more seats onto the board. As for who is in charge, the public is because they paid the taxes which support the organization the board is overseeing, the laws of the land are, and a general consensus about what constitutes civil courteous behavior.

I suppose that all sounds vague and some people are more comfortable with Mr. Churchill is in charge, or Ms. Leadfoot. Fine, as long as Mr. Churchill or Ms Leadfoot has the capability of handling the abstraction that the public, the law, and common decency are really in charge, then they can assume some mantle of responsibility and leadership for being in charge. An invaluable aid to this abstract thinking and not taking oneself too seriously will be the reality of equal material rewards to all, rather than the leadership group being weighted down by their material success in the community which egotistically blinds them to valuable input from others less fortunate in reward receipt.

The paranoia resulting from regular brushes with those teetering on the survival edge will also be reduced, allowing the fear of predation from time wasting complainers to be characterized more accurately as the voicing of public concern by utilizers of a public service. If in fact some complaints are voiced to help a person establish some needed self-esteem or to help reduce a feeling of helplessness with an impoverishment situation, then these sources of complaint will disappear within an atmosphere of general worthiness and security for all.

In economic systems of equal distribution of material resources, why is comment so discouraged? I speak about equal distribution of material resources as if this circumstance were really present in reality and not the artful advertising and propaganda of the appearance game as played by Communism. It is my contention that if resources were more evenly distributed with a definite comfortable safety net of survival security then fear of comment would not make Communist leadership sick with worry, opting to speedily silence all detractors.

Personally when I think of equality I think of equal access to survival resources for all individuals, equal opportunity to relax and enjoy whatever is personally considered the finer things in life, equal access to the positive, healthful emotions of love for self and others, equal access to the mental assessment of being a worthy, productive helper to society in some manner, and overall the equal right to embrace the gift of life within the bounds of the law and decency if a person is in public. I suppose my definition of equality is running the risk of getting me labeled as a self-centered hedonist, a slave to material trappings and the need to be accepted by the artificial manmade civilization of the planet earth. I realized I was running these grave dangers when I came into a better understanding of how Communism defines equality. The full definition is quite an eye opener both in terms of revelation and stark hair raising horror.

In school I remember the lectures on the bloody collectivization of newly established Communist lands. I remember wondering why every time a Communist regime took hold of a new nation, blood shed had to be so prevalent and terror inspiring when the regime was delivering the very same ideal of equality so praised and lauded in my very own democratic America. I remember thinking that perhaps the free spiritedness of Capitalism was not present in these Communist lands, but was the running of farms and industry by the government really so terrible?

The teachers talked about how Communism was a doctrine of equality but I do not remember them informing of me of the equality taking the form of the individual becoming an indistinguishable entity from any other individual, that is absolutely equal in every possible way, including what would seem to me quite impossible ways. Also I don't remember there being quite such a huge emphasis on the individual not owning any private property so much as all the means of producing goods being at the disposal of government and hence the entire public rather than hoarded goods of Capitalist exploiters.

Perhaps by glossing over the impact to the individual the teachers were hoping to glean early lazy Communist leanings in the student body. Perhaps the teachers were aware of how closely this doctrine parallels many religious teachings and did not want to risk any appearance of critique to sacred doctrines. Maybe the teachers themselves were closet supporters of the Communist ideal.

Teachers walk a difficult tightrope between stirring the right amount of nationalist fervor, and reporting completely within limited time the wide fact base of knowledge in history. Not to mention the impact of current events. For example, during WWII when Russia became an ally, there would have been less stirred up communist animosity than later during the Cold War so teachers would have adjusted accordingly. Perhaps in communities heavily populated by scientific researchers at corporations like DuPont, the teachers lean toward an emphasis on the positive aspects in Communism reflecting general parental wishes to globalize into one peaceful non-religious community.

Also the U.S. has its fair share of atrocities like slavery and the treatment of Native Americans. If teachers did not strike a balance portraying Capitalism and Communism, the teachers might inadvertently breed a whole generation of ethically oriented political activists writing boat loads of letters to elected representatives, who although paid, would feel overwhelmed, out of control and definitely not in charge even as interpreters of the law and decency for the public with so much unsolicited input clogging the works. Who knows?

Besides creating absolute equality in material goods by making sure no one had any material goods, ideally, in Communism a person did not consider his body to be at his personal disposal, therefore destroying any natural inequalities which might turn up from being born tall, well-muscled, and good looking. Much like the prevailing code during times of war, the individual's hands, feet, eyes, ears, in fact any part up to and including all of his being was at community disposal as deemed appropriate by the hereditary leadership. Hereditary leadership? I did not hear about that in school either.

Apparently in order to maintain control of the populace shorn of all possessions up to and including the body he was born into, absolute totalitarian control had to be maintained by having the upper leadership class placed advantageously for life, passing the advantageous position onto children. Hereditary leadership of this type does not sound like equality or anything approaching equality as far as I am concerned. If I did not understand all the need for blood shed previously from my high school history classes, I came to understand it much more fully reading books on the subject recently.

Another key element of Communism is central planning. Since Communism has suffered defeat in the USSR and is heavily blemished by reports of human rights violations, central planning is assumed to be the culprit responsible for the economic failure and inhumane practices. Personally, I would point more specifically to the rigid, steep vertical hierarchy where the planners are elevated well above the general populace.

To keep the larger population in line with the Communist definition of equality, i.e. no private possessions, not even your own body, public services and facilities are planned to be time wasting and inefficient to keep some kind of discomfort edge present. If you think about it, the social engineering mechanism is not very different from the discomfort created by constant competition curtailing relaxed clear thought.

Returning to my version of the John Lennon peace song, imagine everyone having the reserve energy resources after work and the encouragement to take an interest in national planning, current events, and wanting to act locally. People wouldn't have to take an interest, but they could if they wanted to, or felt that at the moment circumstances required their input to protect their personal situation.

Some frown on the late to the party arrivals of those motivated by personal consequences, but very often these people provide a view of the practical plan's repercussions in an early warning system. If heeded, the warnings would help prevent much larger damages requiring more complicated solutions later on. These people act like the canary in the coal mine, but only if they are free to speak up.

Every so often I hear remarks in the wind about the Bill of Rights and free speech being the hall marks of an antiquated age and no longer applicable. These new era people are expressing their disenchantment with the responses to their priorities of wanting open sexual relationships, same sex relationships, or some other organizing lifestyle in a commune, for instance, which does not receive general support.

Attacking the Bill of Rights they are trying to emphasize the personal choice element in all life style decisions. Of course, if freedom of speech were removed, these folks would be just as heavily impacted as the rest of us, so you have to wonder if they are counting on people empathizing without really looking too deeply into their flawed logic analogy, a very common practice I have discovered.

Frankly it is not illegal to set up a commune, live with several partners, live with a same sex partner, or some other variation on the family unit. Because the one on one opposite sex arrangement produces children and feels more comfortable naturally when resources are available, it has been around, and sustained for a much longer period of time and hence has subsidizing legislature and general public opinion approval.

As far as that goes, the horizontal, equality organization to human cultures has been around much longer than the vertical hierarchy arrangement, which only arrived on the scene 150,000 years ago, roughly. The progressive drive forward has not slackened since. Just for the record, some type of man has been on earth for at least 2 million years.

For these detractors to the Bill of Rights (BOR) who have been living life legally but not in the warm and fuzzy main stream with material benefits, having to constantly be on competitive alert has made them too well aware of the networked appearance game which by passes all of the rules they are calling antiquated due to hard life experience. The BOR cynics feel these rules were used corruptly to support networked married bliss as an arbitrary lifestyle elevated above all other lifestyle choices. Bravery and honesty are important character traits which the life style innovator inhabits by living openly in a non-traditional manner, and announcing the futility of investment in the BOR can be justified as honest advertising to them.

In fact, the BOR cynics may have managed to achieve a level of networking skill themselves. Perhaps they are not ousting the life time married couple as the preeminent lifestyle, but they have achieved enough career success and advantage to be placed above the lower class all out fray and do not want to return to life coloring inside the BOR lines now that they have finally made it. Worn down by competition, they can see it will be much easier to maintain social stability personally if the defense of the rights of people in general is linked to belonging to a powerful protective network, not belonging to a strong nation which actively supports its ideals.

The BOR cynics sound so selfish, but they are no worse than the rest of us. In order to achieve that elevated position, probably on subconscious, instinctive automatic pilot to survive, they engaged in the competitive networked appearance game until they made it or perished trying. Although I am not applauding, the majority of people, also operating on blind instinct would and there is no shortage of entertainment media devoted to this achievement story.

Democracy is linked to Christianity historically by the early settlers' religion. Equality in being well loved children of God the Creator was the deeply held conviction supporting the stated equality in the Constitution, even with the separation of church and state. With the flight of religion's foundation caused by the revelations of science, the BOR cynics now have an example demonstrating how transient all human held convictions are, in the greater scheme of things involving the wide infinite Universe.

Oddly enough many consider Communism to have a lot in common with Christianity as well, although Communism bans religious practice and uses the oriental philosophy of Confucianism, the principled life as the way to guide a life path. Popular Christian religion is very useful in creating guilt ridden personalities, and it may be Confucianism has this effect as well, although according to the media, books, and other sources, fear and terror are the most relied on motivators.

Calculating persons can take advantage of weakened mental states and survive by manipulating others, achieving leadership status, when vertical civilization structure demands such cunning. Perhaps the ease with which the cunning can interfere with ordinary day to day activity is the practical explanation for the removal of a loving God in heaven. If anyone is going to interfere with day to day activity, it is going to be planned and directed by the hereditary government.

Christianity hopes to enhance love and cooperativeness by deemphasizing the pleasures of this world and if human nature cannot be sidetracked, then worldly pleasure is subordinated to the pleasures of brotherly love. Brotherly love, agape, the love for everyone, these find a parallel in the Communist loss of personality in one bonded organism moving harmoniously and not getting lost in distinctions of personal property, merit, accomplishment, beauty, or luck, all manmade illusions creating mental slavery. Naturally the Communist ideal does not want people getting lost in the slavery throes of addictive pleasures as well.

I do not care for the mental slavery of manmade illusions or for destructive physical and mental addictions. I am all about brotherly love; I think it is the natural state when survival resources have been acquired via cooperative efforts. People can recognize when their life has been improved and why the improvement has taken place when they are not being otherwise misdirected by emotional triggers. Unfortunately survival stress, jealousy and loss of life experience throw a real whammy into brotherly love when people get officially vertically ranked in artificial categories.

Both the Christian religion and Communism while in favor of equality, leave large loop holes for the vertical hierarchy to slither in. Both systems deal with the loss in quality emotional life visited by the hierarchy by pointing to distant future circumstances when things will be better, death or having taken over the entire world. To a degree both philosophies embrace expansion to include everyone via some form of conversion.

In the middle ages the crusades in the Middle East were a violent form of spreading Christianity. Some history books point to the more practical motivation of reducing the number of young men wanting to start a family and travel the peace time life path as the more likely motivation. Otherwise, these young men who were not well provided for in those difficult times prior to technology would become disturbances in the cities of their own homeland rather than more conveniently somewhere else.

Similarly, Communist regimes look to spread their form of government everywhere that has a group expressing an interest. Very often resources will be diverted from the sponsoring homeland of a Communist regime to the nation expressing a willingness to embrace Communism. The provision of resources to foreign lands allows for a handy excuse for limited resources in the established Communist nation creating desirable discomfort and reduced mental clarity.

Both philosophies have had moderate success in the spread of their doctrine. Interestingly, Communism has taken hold in many devout Catholic nations due, in my opinion, to the emphasis on one brotherhood of man where everyone is the same. I suppose in these cases exceptions to the banning of religion take place, especially when the religion helps support the government because of the rigid vertical hierarchy of priests, bishops, and the Pope present here on earth.

In religions without the vertical hierarchy of religious personnel here on earth, the emphasis on a God in heaven supported by a believer's faith and hope could lead to divided loyalties, again, introducing the ability for charismatic leaders or active imaginations to undermine government efforts. On the other hand, in Communism all the humans who are brothers in one unified organism are present here on the planet. Surrounding humans are able to be perceived by each other via sensory perception, so no act of faith is involved reducing the chances for imagination induced disturbances.

Faith and hope in Communist nations may perhaps be desirably crippled by the easily perceived lapses in the government's fair and equal distribution of resources. Keeping the populace unable to utilize these psychological mechanisms as a tonic to limits on other life experiences helps create the desired effects from shortages and other terrorizing methods, producing predictable useful instinctive responses.

I say all these things about Communism fueled by the scary specter present in the books I have recently been reading. In fairness, someone in a Communist nation might have just finished reading some books on Capitalist America and is reaching for a valium bottle equally disenchanted with the vastly different outline in the national philosophy. Most likely it is all in what you get used to and I suppose a book designed for American consumption would have a slightly different bias than a book written for consumption in some other nation.

That being said, I am used to expressing my individuality and personally enjoying my very own private personal gift of life. Knowing that the spread of technology has accomplished what the heavy handed spread of philosophy via blackmail and battle could not is reassuring. The more reliable arrival of agricultural crops and industrially produced necessities has permitted many Communist nations to start enjoying a relaxation from being tied into one large unit of alike material. I believe the Christian missionaries caught onto this trick of material bribery early on in their efforts too.

The enormous philosophical obstacles to be overcome between Capitalism and Communism is how to enjoy brotherly love without removing the brain via enforced human constructs about how brotherly love expresses itself between the enormous numbers of humans on the planet and also performing the exact same type of brain lobotomy by requiring everyone embrace some kind of artificial hierarchy. While Capitalism does not support in living practice equality, in its initial theoretical design, it too supposed that the atmosphere achieved by perfect competition would lead to a fairly even distribution of resources, if not absolute perfect equality in every possible respect.

It is funny how easily these theoreticians embraced the possibility of perfect competition while denouncing the possibility of absolute perfect equality in every respect. When trying to accomplish absolute perfect equality in every respect the arbitrary gifts from the Universe of stronger physique, better looks, solid mental focus, and other favors must be neutralized, as well as any feelings which ensue from the ability of the environment to strongly stirrup emotional energy and productive activity. For example, being in a position of insecure resources within a rigid vertical hierarchy might motivate some, while not changing the motivation of others, or demotivating still another group, depending largely on who anticipates winning, or being favored by hereditary leadership. The vertical hierarchy emotional effects may be the hardest element to equalize. Perhaps the isolation of hereditary leadership is also designed and justified as a help creating this type of emotional equality, although still being an imperfect solution.

How is equality supposed to be accomplished in a setting of perfect competition? It almost seems as if the idolizing of competition and the insistence on competition would create a violent tension in everyone trying to acquire survival resources so as to explode the civilization adopting this method. Fortunately, the very same accursed human nature reviled in the Christian religion which seeks to make life easier and looks for short cuts is the saving mechanism for the Capitalist economic system, and also it's undoing in terms of achieving overall equality.

Communism is flawed by supposing everyone will be able to access the "harmony as one being" center in the brain well before actually having solidly secured survival resources. Additionally, after the heyday of physical survival resources arrives, everyone being primarily motivated by "harmony as one being" is assumed over feeling the pull of enriching emotional rewards, mental challenge rewards or unique spiritual connectedness rewards. These rewards are omitted and ignored, although they are present mucking about with the applied theory of absolute equality.

Fortunately harmony aids in producing tolerance which allows individuals to go about business in these other regards relatively incident free. Harmony while soothing and calming does not erase the presence in the brain of these other human potentials creating visible differences in lifestyle actions, but not necessarily producing harmful inequalities if everyone is free to pursue his own path after delivering some amount of service to the community.

Capitalism supposes that everyone will be able to access the "calm rational thinking" center in the brain, and feel energetically motivated to act on concluded thoughts also well before actually having the same secure survival resources. Additionally, perfect competition assumes a certain amount of both consumer and producer omniscience to propel actions of price/wage adjustments. Ideally, in perfect competition, prices and wages adjust to be in equilibrium such that no one is making too much more money than anyone else.

Perhaps the simplest summary of the situation is the Capitalists have an unwarranted faith in market magic, an unwarranted faith in the presence of environmental circumstances knowledge, and an unwarranted faith in the desire for personal lifestyle changes required in quitting a job not paying the going market value. Capitalism also has an over reliance on the ability of human perception to anticipate and to act at the precise moment when, for example, the horse cart market is no longer sustainable, fold up shop, and accurately pick a new business endeavor, providing seamless support for both business owner and employees.

I suppose that the Christian religion's emphasis on not keeping things too simple, or to embrace hardship with the knowledge that eventually the Almighty will bring some type of relief helps to stabilize these moments of technological innovation completely overhauling the business environment and job market. Otherwise, ignoring the warnings from the prophets penning religious doctrines, many wage earners and corporate price setters alike resist the hard scrabble life of perfect competition and get together over a beer, or in more official meetings and undercut competition. At various times both worker's unionized strikes and corporate monopoly have been illegal. More recently, unions have fallen into serious disfavor, and many transportation and utility companies are permitted to function as monopolies with government regulation and oversight.

Personally, I would like to point out that the avoidance of the hard life of competition which impairs the ability of Capitalism to function effectively is an indicator of human nature being more peace loving and cooperative, given the freedom to pursue natural inclinations. I am not ready to label these inclinations as evil and lazy, as many philosophies do, but while reducing competition within a class of workers or class of owners of a certain type of business, both of these bonded class networks remove the mechanisms ensuring equitable material dispersal present in perfect competition, via the time honored practices in networks of blackmail, coercion, and other bullying techniques utilized with some degree of ease against faceless consumers.

Ideally, perfect competition involves each individual consulting his own rational assessment of what job will suit him best, how much he should get paid and how much daily output he can achieve in a healthy manner to be a dependable daily attendee in the workforce. Inhabiting the lofty clouds of objective accurate appraisal the musing worker will determine that although he would most like to be a male ballerina amidst a herd of gazelle like female dancers, his body type is too boxy to perform this job as well as others, and so he wisely settles for being a welder of heavy metals building ships surrounded by other men all day long. At least he gets to talk about women and fling the occasional light hearted remark with resonating wolf whistle at passing ladies.

The devilish pulls of getting some type of sales or advertising job where more women are present, or at least the opportunity to interact with women is present do not cross his mind's noble exercise of lucid thinking. The perfect competitor shuns marketing activity as a career because sales and advertising are parasitical occupations producing nothing of added material value other than psychological cotton wadding clouding straight thinking in consumers. By spreading more disabling fictions to others for selfish profit and the opportunity to chat up pretty women the perfect competitor would be undercutting perfect competition further by engaging in the sins of vanity, lust, and doubtless at some point, greed.

Believe it or not perfect competition does not promote vanity, lust and greed as all of these human frailties lead to ignorant consumer behavior, supporting industry which is frivolous and unneeded. It sounds a wee bit Communist to me but it is the underlying foundation of ideal Capitalist perfect competition. Continuing with the musings of our virtuous welder, without recourse to any discussions with work buddies comparing the green pasture of one work place over another, one type of welding work as compared to another, or even within one company how much work seems like a fair trade with the company owner, the aspiring welder to perfection does not allow his chums to influence his logical path of community serving self-interest.

How likely is all that? Well, I did it to the degree that I delivered the best work performance possible on a regular basis. At the time, however, I felt like the only one, and as a temporary employee, I was heavily discouraged. Trying to dictate wages from my personal experience is not possible.

This perfect competition scenario, especially amongst temporary employees, is about as likely as people being satisfied living life alike in every possible manner. Truly, I can appreciate the philosophical premise behind all the blending on the one hand, and competition on the other, but to me, both miss the whole point of being given a healthy feeling body in the midst of natural bounty, with survival enhancing brain power, the ability to enjoy good supportive companionship and the beauty and diversity which is this gorgeous planet earth.

On a more realistic note, let us suppose our decent but flawed welder does engage in dialogue with pals, and they all agree to weld 10 seams a day. Regardless of whether some or all can weld 15, more comfortably even, the flawed welder and chums spend a certain amount of time looking busy, engaging in time wasting sharing of confidences and feelings they may later regret, and planning pleasurable events outside of work which causes them to fail to produce with expert craftsmanship the originally determined 10 units.

Whether or not they are all getting along better than they would have performing to ability within a few units of each other, or even with large differences in output, they choose to make themselves all alike in the land of democracy and freedom to choose, while cursing Communists in good safe fun. One supposes that eventually the psychological wear and tear of peer pressure and coercion convince fellow welders to support the performance limiting group plan, or, if they are still trying to inhabit the principled mental lands of perfect competition, leave for another company where they will doubtless be appreciated by observant ownership and enjoy the work day more fully amongst likeminded associates as well. Chums and pals are for after work.

On the other hand, the owner, inhabiting the rational land of perfect competition and wanting a decent night's sleep decides to look for replacements in the case of the quota setters wherever he can find them from Indiana to India. In the case of individual performers, as long as the welders are all suited to the job and performing to meet deadlines comfortably, the owner might be quite content to let a good team remain intact to prevent upsetting the chemistry, or hiring a replacement who might sneakily initiate the poison of setting unofficial quotas. However, also in the spirit of perfect competition, the owner will always be looking to cut costs, starting with labor, and foolishly initiate the poisoning of his own well of employees by being too pushy and unappreciative of a genuine good day of work.

Ideally though, like the virtuous welder, the owner looks to his better, logical, rational self and picks a business he understands completely, or will understand completely with further diligent study. Aside from the costs of labor he examines carefully the market and prices for all the ingredient metals and other support material to his ships. He knows to the penny what is the fair price for everything in the ongoing business and when setting his own price for his ships, and mind you this part is very important, he adds in only a reasonable and fair margin of profit for himself, ideally.

Under perfect competition labor is responsible for keeping an eye on the profit margin of ownership to determine if the laborer is getting equitable pay for his participation in the enterprise. If labor asks for a raise pushing costs too high than the owner can refuse the raise, take a pay cut, or pass the cost onto the consumer.

Ideally, the owner is not supposed to get carried away with delusions of grandeur regarding his superior planning prowess and risk taking. After all, he is usually not doing a lick of any other type of labor. Once the planning gets done initially, changes come up, but not every day, month, or year even.

As for risk, unless the owner goes out of his way to destroy his failing plant, equipment, and inventory, he will not suffer the huge loss imagined by many of losing absolutely everything. Unless he has been engaging in sharp practices of not paying bills, not paying taxes, or racking up other debt in a poor business manner which disguises his failure for longer, causing more damages, the business owner is protected by supporting banks, the government, insurance policies and business law. Additionally, all employees of a corporation are also engaged in some amount of risk when hitching their cart to a particular corporation with physical and mental shaping activities.

The consumer's responsibility under perfect competition is to shop around for the best price and the least greedy labor and owner in the ship building business. Everyone is responsible for keeping an eye on his brother, being his brother's keeper perhaps, in the ideal effort of achieving perfect competition.

No wonder some look to undercut this overly prying, senselessly invasive, theoretical construct. Are you sure you cannot stay 4 more hours and weld 15 units a day for the same pay daily? Are you really sure you can't pay us more, you skin flint?!? This price is outrageous!! Surely it doesn't cost this much to make this ship!! Give me a break!!!! Give me a break!!!! Give me a break!!!!

Imagine this going on all day, every day. Labor asks for more money, management turns around and wants more output. Consumers want the ship for less; labor fails to make a boat that floats. Everyone is competitive and dominant and nothing constructive is happening. Boo Hoo!!! I want to eat!!!

I suspect all this mental calculating to reach equilibrium prices which determine the action of consumer, labor, and ownership, creates insult from ongoing accusations of shirking in one capacity or another, threatening the stability of perfect competition in actual application. Competing companies worn out, frayed, on the mental edge, seeking some stability and security, unite to set prices, regardless of being reviled by the religious and regardless of how the price setting will impact the ideal of perfect competition and overall equality for everyone.

On the sly, labor does so as well, or publically forms a union. Unless absolutely all employees in every type of employment engage in unionized blackmail, inequalities set in between those who are unionized and those who are not. When unionized employees get raises, the employing company raises their prices. The unionized employees can afford higher prices due to their raises, anyone not receiving raises due to union involvement falls behind economically and inequalities start arising.

Ideally, prices should not be raised to give ownership or labor more spending money just to have more spending money, but in practice, largely due to the idea of vertical hierarchy and the need to advance, ownership sets profits higher giving himself a raise, and unionized staff wants a cut of that action as well. If they did not resort to this relief valve to create some security and stability, the pressures of competition would lead to violence and mayhem amongst ownership and labor, or perhaps some strong governing body as in Communism might have to take over.

In situations where the surrounding environment has been fairly stable and friendly, extra money can translate into savings. When leadership is ignoring the overpopulation issue, some amount of extra money being spent translates into economic growth, as does money being saved in a bank. Money saved in a bank allows the bank to use that money as loans to companies trying to grow as a startup or trying to grow from a more established position. Population growth makes the extra goods provided by new companies or longer established companies necessary, while providing some amount of new jobs.

Perfect competition assumes that population growth will balance out into the correct amount of extra spending, savings, new jobs, and new companies, which is where quite a bit of the government oversight, ideally, comes in. If there are too many large corporations stifling smaller new corporations, the government is supposed to even the balance with an array of supportive policies and incentives. If jobs are being hoarded and condensed into fewer personnel, then government again intervenes with laws or incentives promoting new jobs rather than overtime.

Ideally, government ignores the cajoleries of lobbyists and special interests trying to forge a path away from idealism and equality. We are all witness to how well the government composed of harassed overworked humans, suffering numerous cutbacks themselves, has been managing at that task. Heeding objections that centralization in government is unhealthy, decentralization and deregulation has been a new popular trend.

Personally, I prefer centralization. I am pretty sure decentralizing the government has not meant less overall government staff. In all likelihood, decentralization has probably afforded a lot of job duties duplications, good for employment, bad for efficiency. In addition to allowing each state to determine which industries they are going to regulate, if they are going to regulate, it also allows corruption to explode exponentially by a factor of fifty.

If media are the watchdogs of leadership, informing the public about what is taking place in legislative sessions, then media needs to expand to cover all the new bases. Unfortunately media news has not been expanding; it has been condensing into larger conglomerates. Apparently news companies in keeping with the popular trend of compacting all companies with like end products under one purchasing umbrella, have merged numerous publications into media conglomerates. While these conglomerates achieve purchasing efficiency for themselves, they undercut perfect competition in the market for all the companies which must sell raw materials to them at the requested/dictated price.

Additionally, many have voiced the concern that media news has been hopelessly weakened by individual technology in cell phones and other portable computers. To a degree anyone can report news if they happen to be well placed as an eye witness at a particular moment. Some forecasting fire spotters go so far as to say that traditional media is almost dead since the economic model of supporting the business through advertising dollars in no longer viable. Those anticipating the end of traditional media say that the public and organizations like Wikileaks which receives information from whistle blowers are doing the job without being hampered by traditional newspaper elitism and fears of government retribution for compromising national security.

I suppose that if an eyewitness were reliably capable of writing a fair unbiased story every time news worthy events were witnessed and also could be counted on as a certainty to write such a story, traditional media may truly be in serious trouble. But even with the financial woes plaguing media these days, they still have the deep pockets and networked sources to be at the right place at the right time to act as an eye witness to new events. Also, if the government can make its heft felt among newspapers, the impact on individuals taking a feisty stance would be just as imposing, perhaps more so.

Wealthy newsmakers and the like do not want your average citizen to start assuming the role of unbiased observer cherry picking relevant facts for the limited time and space most hardworking and otherwise worried Americans have to devote to the larger picture of events beyond their local area. For these reasons, traditional news media as the hand chosen interpreters of leadership activity have nothing to worry about, other than a shakeup of how the news will be reported and how many people will be required to present the necessary appearance of free speech democracy. Technology has been shaking up everybody's job; it was only a matter of time before the news industry felt the pressure.

If traditional media were to go on strike for an extended period there would not be a complete void of available news information, but the stories which would seep in to fill the empty void would be delivered without professional news people utilizing professional news contacts to confirm details or hedge their position with no comment. Barring official confirmation or even with it, speculation would fill in empty holes and add flashy amateur conclusions, some crazy, some coincidentally right on the money, and some chillingly accurate from careful sifting and research of the surrounding environment.

Without the sobering restrictions created by losing via loose lips validating journalism news credentials which cost thousands to obtain, the average man on the streets unaware of possible risks might and could say just about anything. Until the disillusioning cold hand of blackmailing larger parties accurately found his soft spot on which to apply pressure for as long as necessary, the amateur investigative reporter could ply his new found craft offering a new and refreshing perspective on current events.

Leadership would no doubt be very dismayed and uncooperative with amateur journalists pursuing news in relatively the same manner as professionals by confirming facts through the same sources and the same public relations people officially designated as an organization's mouth piece. The amateurs would produce varying results and lots of open speculation. Predictability of the masses consumed interpretation of events would be missing, however, leading to lost control through manipulative ability of the population which is counted on to maintain the appearance game of the hierarchy as an absolute natural phenomenon. As bad, some amateur journalists would become disillusioned by the necessary steps taken to direct their reports, causing an unanticipated and undesirable tear in the appearance veil, forcing a group of people to begin populating the ranks of the negatively labeled rather than being solid supporting pillars of stone.

On the one hand government has been vilified for being centralized and overly controlling, while on the other, many industries are centralizing into large units approaching in many cases a monopoly, utterly defeating the operation of perfect competition. If the timing can be arranged properly, I suppose the ability of government to act as an invisible hand correcting economic activity will be severely depleted by being under state and local jurisdiction. Companies could simply move their headquarters around at will from state to state to find favorable laws where the lobbyist's efforts were most effective, or where newly elected political candidates seemed likely to want to implement favorable changes.

Adding in additional destruction to the foundation of perfect competition in Capitalism is technological innovation. The introduction of fast change into industries creates large amounts of unemployment, removing any power the employee, who is also a consumer, has as a balancing check to ownership of corporations. As a double whammy, the company which has ownership of competitive cutting edge technology can get an advantageous lead or temporary monopoly over other companies not aided by this technology, being able to cut prices and thus attract a larger group of thrifty, penny pinching shoppers, always a plus.

I still think equality is a good idea. Just because both Communism and Capitalism have embraced flawed mechanisms and systems to implement equality does not mean it cannot work. The Communist expectation that everyone will be satisfied as a faceless, interchangeable cog in the wheel of life neglects all the humanizing bonuses present in the granted gift of life which are impossible and undesirable to completely stifle. In Capitalism the expectation that the individual will be able to exercise the scope of responsibility necessary to keep in check the vast seas of inequalities created when circumventing competition to favor the more natural relaxing cooperation, undermines the ideals of equality via perfect competition.

Some kind of new economics which permits humanizing individuality in conjunction with cooperation seems like the more natural, practical road in my opinion. Competition is not particularly natural at some point of secure resource availability or maybe even before the arrival of secure resources since so many people can be blackmailed into the absolute nature of a vertical hierarchy, opting for cooperation, albeit coerced, over freedom to compete and behave morally.

Most people, in a natural setting of sharing adequate resources would not probably spend a lot of time trying to determine the life time impact on rewarded desserts from holding beauty pageants, sporting events, or chess tournaments. The civilization might still have these events as entertainment, but not taken so seriously that winners got special treatment over and above the achievement of winning in the moment.

There are the nay sayers to equality, worried about the presence of freeloaders and their impact on others. With new implementations of helpful technology, extra hands cannot be avoided, but the distribution of available work and free time can be rotated, more evenly distributed generally, or recognized as a possible individual difference of lifestyle. Some might prefer the activity element in work while others prefer the reflective element available in thoughtful contemplation at work or away from work, while still others prefer the activity element which is under complete individual direction when not at work. More personal choice in these matters will be comfortably possible.

The careful accounting of all types of rewards encouraged by both the Communist and the Capitalist economic systems to keep inequalities from destabilizing the works will no longer be necessary. What might be termed inequalities in terms of personal choice for life focus and activity will be present, but couldn't we just call it personal choice differences rather than inequalities? Anyone can change their mind for their free time activity whenever they wish.

Yes, some people will be naturally better looking, more able to maintain physical activity, more able to maintain mental focus, or more able to maintain ongoing interpersonal interactions. None of these natural talents is so meritorious as to demand special status. If some group is experiencing a shortage and overworked, then the other groups can be polled for those desiring a happily coincidental job change, or simply having a willingness to try something new. If a particular job is so undesirable as to have no voluntary takers, the job needs to be changed, or discarded altogether. Crass manipulation of others into uncomfortable situations to motivate good behavior will no longer be required.

The Price is Right

Having established the depth of similarity between the popular economic models, it may now be helpful to consider factors which drive economic activity, regardless of the economic system surrounding the considered factor, specifically price, supply and demand. Price can refer to the price of consumer goods like food, or to the price of labor, like the salary of the President of the United States. In the strictest economic terms a person is remunerated with money which can be spent on material resources. Economic scientists focus largely on countable money and material resources since both can be seen and measured.

Other incidentals which may or may not accompany any particular consumer good are emotional rewards from ownership, types of status rewards from ownership, and types of perceived spiritual rewards from ownership. Starting with President of the United States, Supreme Leader of a Communist nation, Supreme Leader of a Socialist nation, African dictatorship, and South American Communist Democracy Supreme Leader, we can look at some of the rewards above the material rewards which are assumed ample for survival in all cases in the ownership of these situations.

When the President of the United States, for example, is elected after a grueling election campaign, he can bask in the emotional glory of winning and being wanted. As elected leader of the nation he can mentally acknowledge his accomplished position and be well equipped with mental and emotional energy to meet decision making challenges. In many cases the President may enjoy some feeling of having the Ultimate Creator's aid and ear in meeting all of his tasks. What an enormously intoxicating cocktail of supportive emotions, mental thoughts and spiritual affirmations, all of which are needed to confidently choose a course of action and implement the plan in the face of many who will feel their interests slighted within a vertical hierarchy.

I suppose that most national leaders have the same variety of resources available, with slight differences. The leader of an African dictatorship may enjoy less perceived future stability, but then as compensation, until he is fully ousted, he does not have to deal with much embarrassing public dissent. Obviously, the leaders of nations with more access to natural survival resources and the ability to turn those resources into useful commodities will have more inequalities and challenges obstructing smooth sailing when structured around a vertical hierarchy civilization structure, but the emotional, mental, and spiritual rewards will be a supportive aid when confronting those ongoing trials. Poorer nations utilizing some degree of vertical hierarchy may have less perceived inequalities simply because there is less material available to create these visible spectacles of conspicuous consumption.

The more homogeneous the population and the conditions of the population, even with less material support, the easier the job of leadership to implement the governing function of taking care of the needs of the community. Where each family unit grows their own food and makes their own simple tools, very little government interference will be necessary to correct errors in the market where planning is done on such a small scale for short time frames. Not too many of these nations labeled as impoverished in comparison to higher standard of living nations exist now a days due to massive imperialism and exploration in earlier times.

There may be a few here and there in Africa and the Amish and Mennonite communities in Pennsylvania and other scattered communities in various localities in the U.S. The Amish/Mennonite communities are examples of religious leadership directing a community under a larger national umbrella while still maintaining lifestyle independence essentially for those choosing that religion centered lifestyle. The lifestyles are extremely simple materially, with a large emphasis on the imaginary rewards created by the tenets of adopted religions. The very simplest leader would have a lot in common with the head of a small company in more diverse complicated hierarchical nations.

The famous economists whom I have read about recently agree that conspicuous consumption is a result of man living in communities and expresses a desire in a person to win competitions, or to publically demonstrate winning ability and status. These economists have a lot in common with the psychology genius Freud who reduced the substance of life to the sex and death drives. As stated more fully and clearly in my second book, I believe that life blossoms in substance after survival resources have been secured to encompass all kinds of desires over and above sex for many people. The death drive is a result of being a constant loser in the sex and survival resources market competition, or in some cases so prominent in winning as to attract abundant predation.

For example, due to some earlier volunteer work at a thrift store to support a non-profit organization, I made a variety of hats to promote the non-profit. I wore the hats during my volunteer hours spent stocking the store. To be able to sport a variety of hat apparel I also acquired decorative accessories to rotate, mix and match. Admittedly I went out of my way to make sure I did not look ugly or unattractive wearing those hats. I tried to emphasize my femininity secondarily to supporting the organization.

If appearing sexually appealing had been my first and only priority, I would not have been wearing hats at all to allow for the free flow of pheromones from the top of my head to any nearby appealing male possibilities. I would not have made myself somewhat ridiculous by making enormous balancing acts depicting some element of the nonprofit organization as a reminder of its needs for funding and a reminder to generously spend dollars at the store.

In fact, if sex was my only motivation, I would not be performing any kind of free volunteer work. I would be competing ruthlessly for the best job available, or being the utter loser which I am by refusing to network, I would have picked an addiction of choice to fully realize and articulate my self-loathing until I successfully slaughtered myself. There is no shortage of this type of behavior in the environment and the only reason I have been spared the ultimate degradations of being an ordinary loser is my ability to intellectually sift the surrounding environment and see the appearance game for the sham it actually is. In other words, my ability to access mental focus and rewards has sidelined the absence of emotional rewards from beneficial interactions with other human beings. Luckily I also have my cats who are not blinded victims of the appearance game either.

In the previously outlined religious communities or small nations with limited resources, spiritual rewards add enhancement to the emotional rewards, reducing or eliminating the pull of conspicuous consumption to express sex appeal. Other off beat communities may offer other emotional rewards stirred by dreams above the need for survival resources. The dreams being unrelated to competitive consumption would create another type of simple material lifestyle reliant on brain wave manufactured substance of quality of life. There may be some small need for material supports to dreams where each individual writes his own story of attainments, but the need for a corresponding competitor pushing forward the attainment efforts will be absent as will the obsessive accumulation of material goods.

Instances where the dreams achieve a close approximation to stated national idealism, as in ideal Socialism which allows for some individuality, everyone enjoying the dream of shared appreciation of life which is not crashed into reality via visible leadership corruption, can also circumvent the stop into conspicuous material consumption due to the nature of the idealism. In the case of visibly corrupted ideals destroying the foundation of perfect competition or harmonious oneness, decay into bitter disenchantment with the sacrifices demanded under false pretenses also circumvents the stop into conspicuous material consumption while creating instead widespread mental depression.

Considering all these possibilities, what would be the price of one of my homemade, artistic, comfortable hats or any hat for that matter? To complicate things further, one could suppose that red and purple were the colors of leadership jacking up the price on all apparel of these colors including especially cleverly torn and sewn jeans and t-shirts. To answer this question, let's consult the lists below.

Very Comfortable Handmade Designer Red and Purple Sequined Hat:

In a *Horizontal Equality Civilization Structure* the price is irrelevant. Personal taste is the deciding factor since everyone has roughly the same amount of money to spend according to individual priority.

In a Vertical Hierarchy Civilization Structure the price is $10,000.00, nice if you can afford one.

In an Amish Civilization Structure price is irrelevant; the hat will not sell here no matter the price.

In an Intellectual Civilization Structure price is irrelevant; the hat will not sell here no matter the price.

For those In an Emotional Dream Civilization Structure the original price is irrelevant. The hat will only be purchased by a dreamer in a second hand store for under $5.00.

In an Emotional & Physical Relaxation from Competition Civilization Substructure to a surrounding vertical hierarchy, the original price is irrelevant. The hat will only be purchased at a garage sale and repurposed as a casserole warmer.

White Engineer's Cap:
In a Horizontal Equality Civilization Structure the price would have to almost be payment to wear as very few people look good in white and still fewer brides marry in engineer's caps, white or otherwise. Given a choice, handymen would probably not want a too easily permanently stained white cap, so the answer is... Price is irrelevant; the hat will not sell here no matter the price.

In a Vertical Hierarchy Civilization Structure the price is free to anyone fool enough to want to wear such a garment advertising their loser status while simultaneously looking as hideous as possible. If you are good looking enough to sport one of these caps chances are you are a winner, so let me be the first to congratulate you, and beg your forgiveness.

In an Amish Civilization Structure the price is the cost of materials as the Amish will sew their own, roughly $1.00.

In an Intellectual Civilization Structure the price is related to the cost in passing certain exams and certifications bestowing membership in the elite political class of hereditary leadership or some variant thereof. Cost is essentially being in the right place at the right time, or priceless.

For those in an Emotional Dream Civilization Structure the original price is irrelevant. The hat smacks of all kinds of serious anti-emotional dream killing symbolism so... the hat will not sell here.

In an Emotional & Physical Relaxation from Competition Civilization Substructure to a surrounding vertical hierarchy, the original price is irrelevant. The hat will only be purchased at a garage sale and repurposed as a dust cloth.

Religious Cap:
In a Horizontal Equality Civilization Structure the price is irrelevant; personal taste in conveying religious devotion is the deciding factor when everyone has roughly the same amount of money to spend according to individual priority.

In a Vertical Hierarchy Civilization Structure the price varies depending slightly on material and more importantly on place of manufacture. Although Capitalist perfect competition should make the prices all roughly the same, in practice, distinctions of brand name will allow for easy visible identification of wealth.

In an Amish Civilization Structure price is the cost of materials as the Amish will sew their own, roughly $1.00.

In an Intellectual Civilization Structure price is irrelevant; the hat will not sell here.

For those in an Emotional Dream Civilization Structure the original price is irrelevant. A dreamer will enjoy the relaxing process of making their own hat out of either suitable materials or a close approximation of suitable materials creating a close approximation of the religious cap in question the price and cost of which is free to $1.00.

In an Emotional & Physical Relaxation from Competition Civilization Substructure to a surrounding vertical hierarchy, the price is irrelevant. The hat will not sell here no matter the price. It may be grudgingly accepted as a gift, in a peacemaking gesture.

Black Bowler Hat:
In a Horizontal Equality Civilization Structure this popular hat has doubtful amounts of inherent personal appearance taste appeal. Someone

may want one, but as can be seen in many other cases, the price is irrelevant.

In a Vertical Hierarchy Civilization Structure the price is $80.00 or more, a hat which bestows some amount of status and prestige.

In an Amish Civilization Structure the original price is irrelevant. The hat will only be purchased by an Amish man in a second hand store for under $5.00 when a shortage of the more traditional wide flat brimmed hat is not readily available.

In an Intellectual Civilization Structure some intellectuals inhabiting the lofty financial realms may take a shine to this style, boosting the price in pseudo-perfect competition to the outrageous range of $80.00 or more for an essentially attractiveness destroying hat.

For those in an Emotional Dream Civilization Structure the original price is irrelevant. The hat will only be purchased by an emotional dreamer in a second hand store for under $5.00 and then madly embellished to improve lacking visual appeal.

In an Emotional & Physical Relaxation from Competition Civilization Substructure to a surrounding vertical hierarchy, the original price is irrelevant. The hat will only be purchased at a garage sale and repurposed as a ferret bed.

Double Beer Can Holstering Cap with Straws:
In a Horizontal Equality Civilization Structure everybody wants one of these, but limited disposable income may encourage more practical choices. As before, price is irrelevant.

In a Vertical Hierarchy Civilization Structure everybody secretly wants one of these, but the vertical hierarchy is a hard task master so many will forgo this relaxation luxury, making the price irrelevant.

In an Amish Civilization Structure, unless a youth has opted for Rumspringa, price is irrelevant since the hat will not sell here in most circumstances.

In an Intellectual Civilization Structure price is irrelevant for most who are too terrified to possess such a selfish, self-serving item. Fine imported alcoholic products may be relished, but for the upper class which can partake of such excellences, price is irrelevant due to good fortune.

For those in an Emotional Dream Civilization Structure the original price is irrelevant. The hat will only be purchased by a dreamer in a second hand store for under $5.00, and chances are the dreamer will use the beer cozies for stuffed polar bears and the like. The straws will be rendered into vertical antennae with shiny stars on top.

In an Emotional & Physical Relaxation from Competition Civilization Substructure to a surrounding vertical hierarchy, everybody wants one of these and has several, just in case. Price is irrelevant as like many other necessary items, this hat will be purchased if possible at a garage sale.

I tried to cover a variety of hats within various civilization structures. The point I am demonstrating is that in all cases price is irrelevant because the most important factor influencing decision making is the type of civilization structure and the person's fortunate or unfortunate placement within that civilization structure.

If I wanted to waste my money, I could buy a black bowler hat expecting it to confer some amount of respect and status on me for owning such a head cover. Without the supporting social network and career within the vertical hierarchy, however, the hat will look meaningless and silly perched on my unemployable head. It would not be long before I realized the best course of action would be to decorate it, repurpose it, or try to recoup some money by selling it for a fraction of the original price.

In economic circles there is a lot of discussion about supply and demand pushing and pulling price up and down in amount. A lot of people want to be rich and occupy winning status in a vertical hierarchy civilization, but not everyone gets to do so, in fact hardly anyone enjoys this elevated condition. Therefore, in theoretical terms, the prestigious, status bestowing black bowler hat which only works effectively as a respect magnet with the proper accompanying career, etc., should not be in heavy demand at all, and therefore not too many producers would consider supplying this small market making the price as small to nonexistent as the demand for the product itself.

Producers do however choose to supply this market because of the ability to jack the price up on the hat higher than is usual for ordinary serviceable, or even stylish serviceable head covers. By making acquisition of a black bowler hat an investment of money, the ability of the hat to act as a mark of distinction is practical and reliable. Similarly for women, the Very Comfortable Handmade Designer Red and Purple Sequined Hat acts in the same manner as a status symbol whose actual demand is extremely limited, making the supplier of these crafts able to set a price well beyond cost in materials and labor. The higher the cost on unique consumption goods, the more responsible the demand filler providing supply will have to be making sure his product has distinguishing characteristics not easily copied and sold in underground markets.

Visible marks of class distinction, while they sound vain, serve to help those placed highly in the hierarchy to avoid easy predation destabilizing their lifestyle. For the extremely wealthy the safest company is also extremely wealthy, rendering all parties unconcerned with each other's bank balance. In following with this practical protection, the old saying that if you have to ask the price you cannot afford it, also protects the fabulously wealthy who must always be on the lookout for predators when sifting possible companions having genuine interests and common ground for sharing experiences from more opportunistic parties.

Very often the presence of wealth is associated with scandal and dishonorable practices to fleece the less fortunate rather than resulting from hard work and effort. The sharp practices associated with enormous wealth cause many to discount the self-defense element in pricing and go for the absolute label of vain, competitive, conspicuous consumption.

In some cases the presence of extreme competition in a family of husband, wife, and children destabilizes supportive, healthy, loving relationships between the various members. Certainly I have been exposed to my fair share of tabloid headlines about all types of unfortunate relationships among the rich and famous. Some fare better than others, and for those who manage to leave competition out of the inner family circle of relationships, there are a range of developed noncompetitive personalities who will need the protection provided by visible signs of class membership, or run the risk of losing valuable status and community support.

Some, particularly economists, would call these accessory folk parasites enjoying the ride on the back of the competitive capitalist, whether he is hard working or simply adept at fleecing others. However, call the black hearted capitalist what you will, his accessory folk provide meaning and supportive companionship where the relationships turn out to be good, so like any type of support personnel, they earn their keep. In terms of producing material goods, many people occupy support or parasite type positions due to the demands of recordkeeping, logistical planning, and marketing.

Lying on the couch, my kitty cat propped on my stomach, (don't you dare call me a parasite; I am producing a book) I read about the foundation of quite a bit of economic theory being ruthless competition among fierce capitalists who care nothing for each other or for others, ideally (Oh my). The motivations attributed to these single minded competitors are at times appalling, and I know that I personally have very little in common with this mind set.

I suspect however that the attribution of motives is similar to the slanderous fictions resulting from my negative label. In general others are in regard to me, regularly quite unpleasant, rude, and at times outright deceitful. In contrast, the general behavior amongst the average population when they do not have access to a person they can safely stomp all over, is probably very cordial and friendly.

How can the theoretical economists come up with their abstract logic driven theories based on the types of motives attributed to indistinct humans in Communism on the one extreme or rapacious capitalists in Capitalism on the other? Generally the theorizing economist expands all motivations into the general range of life experience for everyone. In the ideal of Communism where the plan is to treat everyone essentially the same the reasoning is easier to understand.

However, within Communism practical application of the ideal fails almost right away due to scarce provision of survival resources to all, natural differences, and harmless expressions of uniqueness, creating tensions. The situation is rescued by a supplied undercurrent of terror stifling the full expression of these human differences which threaten to destabilize an environment without tolerance inducing secure survival resources.

Using mathematical formulas which assume that any minor ripples in behavior will be diluted in a vast sea of uniform behavior, economic statisticians formulate their action plans. If necessary, government command to the populace can be counted on to right any severely flawed mathematical computation. Upon this economic reasoning, supporting the good of the entire population, rests applied theory which reduces all behavior to one set of predictable motivations within Communism.

As for Capitalism, how is everyone heaped into one set of predictable motivations here? The free spiritedness and individual choice would almost seem to lead to unfettered chaos, and in fact, economic theory in opposition to the Capitalist model, Communism, insists that this shifting, unstable foundation along with other factors will be the undoing of the Capitalist system. Undaunted, Capitalism has marched forward from century to century, surviving in spite of no apparent stabilizing support structure in many cases, while suffering the predicted failure in others.

Is the success magic? Is it the gift of the gods, God, the Universe, Mother Nature, or the Easter Bunny? In my opinion Capitalism succeeds, for the moment, due to the historical imperialist foundation which got the nation off to a planned start by the English monarchy. Also success was achieved, until recently, by careful government oversight to correct problems. Other factors are enormous amounts of raw material resources, clever marketing which uses sex among other things to talk people into buying things they do not need or even want masking poor planning, the necessity to create visible artificial differences in consumed products to protect support personnel from rampant predation, the vast amount of consumer goods supported by addictions, and an array of meaning generating holidays supported by material goods sporting the appropriate symbolism, for example, the Easter Bunny and Santa Claus.

Communism is founded on conquering the world by establishing the same type of government form in all nations. The system depends on the constant state of anticipation for desired results and expansion accompanied by a general thin spread of resources to the assimilated conquered peoples. Hence, the price does not matter. Once the results are achieved, the pressures and stresses from competition with other economic systems will be gone, allowing for blissful harmonious blending of all in one unified supportive entity, whatever that means exactly, and price will still be immaterial.

Capitalism creates growth by using stress in the vertical hierarchy to create addictive consumption, to create the need to avoid predation by having vast price differences and amounts of consumer goods within classes, to create poor buying decisions prompted by stifled and distorted sex drives, to create comforting traditions in regularly observed holidays, and to create meaning through gift exchange or shared purchased experiences. Prices matter in terms of purchasing to correctly express an individual situation, to cunningly create a false impression of an individual situation, to innocently express a complete lack of understanding of the limitations of an individual situation, to audaciously express a complete lack of concern with the realities of limitations on an individual situation, or to desperately acquire a material fix of the addictive substance in an individual situation.

To maintain the stability of positions at the top and throughout the artificial hierarchy all of these types of consumption, and others, must be present and growing. Therefore, except in cases of planned weeding of specific individuals or the necessary amount of visible suffering to create general stress motivation, the consumption needs must all be met successfully, making actual price basically irrelevant.

When I speak of irrelevance, I am not speaking about the individual consumer carefully counting his pennies to determine whether he will continue with his newspaper subscription, buy some soil for the garden, or spend some money on gas to perform volunteer work. Obviously individual decisions can be more harrowing, like whether to buy breakfast or lunch, but in the majority of situations food is available through various charitable outlets. The group which slips through government programs and other resources are the planned group of motivating bad examples the premise of the hierarchy cannot do without.

Naturally, to me having to make the above types of decisions are personally quite relevant, but to economists advising leadership on overall plans of operation to provide for the general welfare, the fact that some will go without food or have to make other restricting lifestyle choices is a part of enjoying the capitalist economic system. It is all part of the plan. Can't have an omelet without cracking a few eggs, right?

Economic theory, much like the musings of a sociopathic mind, bypasses value and ethical judgments and focuses entirely on the usefulness a person provides to the sociopath, or in the case of the economist, the community in which the economist/sociopath is well placed. If the economist embraces any ethical construct at all it is "Everyone must be useful". Suffering addicts, prisoners in jail, the homeless to name a few would fall into the grave sin of being useless parasites if they did not visibly provide avoidance motivation to others who do not want to find themselves walking a mile or ten feet in negatively labeled shoes.

Economists suffer very little frustration in their lives as they are well placed above the fray and are extremely useful to leadership as the visible coordinators of the failing plan of financial organization. When everything is going well, leadership steps right in there and takes credit for good judgment calls, but for the occasions when things really go crazy, the economic profession can take quite a few pies in the face.

The stock market collapses, unemployment skyrockets, inflation is growing, and Communist nations are having a banner year. It all sounds bad, and all the fingers are pointing at the theorizing economist, who due to his sociopathic thick skin is calmly musing away on his next theoretical concept which will rescue the whole mess, or provide a period of relief from ongoing accusation. With any luck, things will magically correct themselves with some new innovation in technology, expansion into new territory, worldwide epidemic and catastrophe, or war.

The sooner the better as far as the economist is concerned for rescuing mayhem, but if he has to, he will think and think and think until he can convince others that it is not really his fault, the theory was applied incorrectly. Probably the theory was applied incorrectly, but the premise of the theory was also probably irredeemably flawed, and impossible to apply correctly without transferring everyone's brain into an ongoing permanent trance state via drugs, survival panic, or ongoing brain reducing stress.

I say all this on the heels of the most recent set of economist labeled scapegoats, the savers, of which I happened to be one until I became fully unemployable. The presence of personal savings in banks is not the problem, as stated earlier; this money can then be lent to someone else, a person or a company.

Nonetheless, apparently the savers are to blame for the current world financial crisis. As a saver I always thought I was behaving responsibly, doing as I was advised in planning for a rainy day or my retirement future. I guess a lot of people just like me followed the instructions putting some money aside, did not overcommit financially and did not become habitual gamblers.

Adopting the responsible mindset in regard to personal finance however often carries over into adopting the responsible mindset in regard to discharging work duties and responsibly running a business with a comfortable margin of profit rather than building up debt, which leads to bankruptcy. Also, a person who concentrates on saving is not going to be taking out a loan. Only people who do not save their own money will need the use of other people's money.

Previous to the enormous bounty provided by technology, people were urged to frugality so that everyone could eat, have shelter, and other elements of quality of life. Quite some time ago technological leaps appeared on the scene providing excess resources which disappeared due to equal leaps in population growth. Networked competition is still encouraging population growth, but now other discoveries are calling into question the ongoing march forward with population numbers.

The environment is suffering. The human race is killing off all the other life experience enhancing animal species on the planet that can never be replaced. We are also killing off plants, and we are polluting our own air, water and soil. Perhaps we should stop killing everything including ourselves, but how?

Well, for starters, the economic theories which depend on growth and expansion will have to be replaced. I know, I know, we were all planning on expanding into space and time by putting people in 50 story buildings and having work shifts around the clock for 24 hours. Also, over and above filling secure survival resources, we were going to add the fulfillment of secure emotional resources, secure intellectual resources and secure spiritual resources helping to hold the Capitalist, and perhaps even an enhanced version of the Communist system together for the foreseeable future.

How exactly can emotional, intellectual, and spiritual resources be expanded and turned into material fueling the economic machine? First, when thinking of economic material or items of trade, these items do not necessarily have to have a solid form. Belongingness can be turned into an economic commodity by spending outrageous fees to attend the concerts of popular artists. If a person does not choose to attend, they lose out on shared experience and belongingness. When belongingness is treated as a competitive opportunity within the demanding vertical hierarchy, a person loses status each time they choose not to participate in a networked event requiring a large outlay of cash.

More traditionally, some have managed to turn love into a box of candy, flowers, diamond rings, vacations to exotic locals, dinners in restaurants, and nights on the town dancing. Through advertising and marketing, it is possible to educate the community on just what gifts and shared experiences constitute a solid, meaningful relationship for the type of people occupying the highest rewarded group. Down to the least rewarded recipients, rented movies, fast food, and trips to amusement parks are available to demonstrate a willingness to participate as directed. Only the extremely wealthy can make their own rules because they pay the advertising company, or the extremely poor that have to improvise much of their emotional meaning.

What exactly are secure mental/intellectual resources? The need for mental resources arose when men gathered together into supportive groups. Humans on their own or in very small groups had no need to corner the market on opportunity to solve survival resource production dilemmas; they necessarily performed all duties themselves as a lone wanderer or the most experienced human in a small group.

When groups were small enough for everyone to be aware of all goings on, who actually got to solve problems was not as important as solving the problems and keeping the whole happy band intact and available to perform their bit. During the very earliest of times there may have been some expressed admiration for the practical smarts of finding an oasis of food near water, but I find it doubtful that anyone other than the problem solver came up with the idea of allocating more survival resources to the predictor locating future natural deposits of food. No doubt in the earliest of times when almost anyone could take over the problem solving reins this privileged dispersal did not take place.

As time went on and the band grew supported by the fortunate arrival of oases, additional smarts may have been utilized to mislabel the observable indicator of food to preserve a source of community usefulness and power. Perhaps a person said they utilized their inner guide to communicate with an omnipotent being to locate the oasis, knowing everyone else would not be so bold as to dispute this claim when suffering from anxiety and panic hallucinations themselves.

Maybe a person crossing the brink from strict survival focus in finding food employed a bit of anxiety relieving imagination to suppose that future sources of food would be so easy to find as first identifying areas containing water. After all finding water does not appear to be that much easier than finding consumable food when the burden of everyone's dependence weighs upon responsibly concerned minds. In any event water covers 75% of the globe, an enormously useful statistic not readily available at the time, but nonetheless a truth offering unappreciated emotional support or more solid observable support to anyone carefully monitoring and measuring the environment.

Very often emotional support comes from being attractive and popular in some manner. Having a degree of thoughtful concentration and intelligence can also provide emotional support, albeit of a calm confident nature to meet survival necessities rather than the exuberant rush of being sought after and desired due to physical attributes and the ability to make people feel happy or relaxed, perhaps also providing survival necessities.

In the strictest sense of simply enjoying solving puzzles for the exercise of the intellect, very few isolated activities exist, because the intellectual exerciser, much the same as the athletic physical exerciser, is anticipating the need to keep sharpened skills available for unanticipated contingencies. If thinking skills become rusty from disuse, they can get out of shape just like the physical body. Some minor amount of maintenance thinking exercise must take place to keep a flexible, open, keen problem solving mind able to perform mental gymnastics, and maybe even able to learn new needed methods of addressing problems which do not yield to traditional problem solving.

In itself, physical activity is rewarding since it reduces anxiety, works the muscles, and helps circulate the blood to all parts of the body, including the head and brain where mental problem solving takes place. Generally, those who enjoy exercising their physical faculties enjoy some amount of social companionship where the stresses of competitiveness are absent. While these people are not looking to create problems for themselves or others which would impair the experience of communal enjoyment, they also find serious, stern attention to tasks to be somewhat tiresome and an effort to be avoided if possible.

Naturally, if necessary, the physically focused will develop the mental faculties to perform more strenuous mental endeavors, but, they will feel a wee bit put upon and expect at the least, recognition for this pleasure sacrifice. After all, if left up entirely to them, most technology would not have been developed, and life span would still be short and full of tragic derailments. From the strictest physical focus point of view, a long life full of changes, aging, the ongoing loss of abilities and the loss of personal power is not all that appealing, even if the mental abilities step up to improve pleasure possibilities or the imagination can be employed to enhance emotional pleasures and hence, physical pleasures.

Thinking on the other hand can take place in a body at rest or a body moving around performing routine tasks that do not require absolute clear mental sensory perception. Either way problems get solved, although more complicated problems will require a more focused, sedentary approach. Due to the growing complexity of problems, more sedentary life styles are required to address problems, and physical wellbeing is suffering somewhat. Taking the place of physical sacrifices to a degree is the emotional rush of solving a problem or receiving an inspiration and knowing this information will be helpful at least personally, and perhaps, in a larger social context.

Engaging in prolonged periods of mental concentration on problems stirs up a variety of emotions which are not to be found amongst those who spend prolonged periods of time cultivating the fields or some other more routine task allowing for more free ranging of the mind to socialize with others, enjoy the sunny day, or contemplate what to make for dinner. Naturally when the mind is loosed a bit to enjoy these harmless diversions, oversights take place, but due to the nature of the task, usually the errors do not cause serious alarm.

However, because many of the problem solvers are not enjoying their physical body and are making other pleasure sacrifices due to sedentary necessity, they feel the injustice of their sacrifice of bodily pleasure all the more deeply when observing others sporting about with little care or concern for responsible outcomes and achieving an element of sexual desirability and popularity simply by performing their community service.

It just does not seem quite fair in their minds. Clearly for some portion of the mental performers the emotional reward of accomplishment, like bagging an elk for the community dinner for the hunting group, does not offset the sex appeal loss, diminishing access to the most alluring members of the opposite sex. Unlike the large game hunter's accomplishment demonstrating bravery and clear physical strength, support and protection, mental problem solving puts provisions on the table after the problem solver or their significant other goes to the grocery store and picks out the provisions, clouding the source of support and diminishing sex appeal. Other than taking the bus, walking through bad neighborhoods, driving a car on crowded roads, and wrestling bargains from other shoppers, the danger aspect of shopping is negligible comparatively speaking.

Hunting produced protection and support are very primitive aphrodisiacs for many women, which does not cross over as sex appeal when a woman is doing the hunting/shopping, or the mental problem solving which provides less visually glamorous access to survival resources. Although women are drawn to mental problem solving occupations, their sex appeal to all but the most sophisticated and enlightened of men is limited. However, as bountiful sources of survival resources, these women can still count on attracting more than their fair share of social predators.

The damaged sex appeal problem is doubtless compounded by the lack of emotional and physical development in mental problem solvers, making them the object of overall ridicule as well as slighting in the sexual market. Many religions would call this sexual lust evil, but there is no denying the force sexual yearnings have over human behavior, almost as much as the need for food, shelter, and basic companionship.

The sense of injustice is felt all the more so in observations of warriors whose goal focus of destruction leaves responsible care completely out of all mental calculations. When civic engineers and planners perform their efforts a definite cast of cooperativeness must overlay their exertions, while the warriors due to the ever present possibility of loss of life, must emphasize their self-centered competitive edge or perish.

On the other hand, since the warriors could depart at any moment, investing in the rich emotional rewards of ongoing long term relationships while possible to indulge in for the granted term of life span, may not allow for enjoying many of the facets of life available when a more devil may care approach to relationships is the standard. Hence a warrior may choose to enjoy both, utilizing some people for long term relationships and others for indulgent quick fixes when the appointed hour of departure could arrive at any time.

While warriors of old played early sports to keep a physical edge for battle, community problem solvers were constantly employed to create, for example, running water and other conveniences employed to better the creature comforts of the environment, and then went home and played mind exercising board and card games. The life and death nature of battle on the one hand, and the enormous numbers of people served by public utilities on the other created an urgency to performance perfection not experienced by musicians, cooks, crafts people, actors, and others.

The ability to assume a more relaxed attitude toward the environment surrounding life experience permitted those in less pivotal fields to desire the development of more sensitivity to others, more emotional connections, and more empathetic understanding. On the other hand the stress of trying to achieve perfection under competitive circumstances created the desire to develop strategy, tactics, and battle sequences. The cooperative environment creators tried to achieve perfection by motivating support personnel to install pipe carefully and correctly, for example, and any other task required for establishing an efficient comfortable public environment. It may be these strategies and motivators employed against brother nationals created the felt urgency for increased sensitivity to others and empathetic understanding by the less perfection oriented individuals.

Clearly the daily makeup of workday experience was in some part responsible for the early gaps in division of material resources. Even the most novice tactician would be aware of the importance of limiting resources to others, even friendly others of one's own nation who the engineers were eager to motivate usefully. It may be this type of knowledge which the wise writers of biblical history were condemning in their tale of the knowledge apple of sin.

Knowledge is a vast landscape containing many reservoirs of facts and observations to examine and put into useful action. Besides the strong arm tactics of blackmail with survival resources to motivate behavior, there are the soft persuading methods of explanation and honest sharing of knowledge, planning and directing of community goals. People who are consulted as to their input on particular problems are far more likely to participate cooperatively in solution implementation.

Even if some people choose to go out and play rather than attend a planning meeting, they will have had the chance to mold society into a more comfortable shoe. After all, planning is not for everyone and if a person feels essentially taken care of, he may decide to leave the planning to those who have devoted their work hours to gathering information which they can be reliably counted on to share should they be asked to do so.

Additionally, the more fun filled pleasurable diversions out there removing various personality types from the grueling ongoing planning of resource production and distribution, the easier for the planners who do participate to focus on a solid plan. Another little tidbit of knowledgeable strategy which may not appear awfully menacing until one discovers just what the plans turn out to be. One may depart for a game of golf to return and find a tax on all golfers.

As for spiritual rewards and resources, secure and otherwise, these are comprised of things like hope, a clear conscience in regard to life code and action, charity to others less fortunate, trust in and from others, the ability to enjoy serene observation of the environment, a feeling of love for and from others, and the pinnacle of spiritual experience, communion with the great forces of creation outside of oneself.

As with all other types of survival rewards, emotional, mental, and spiritual rewards are impossible to list in their entirety. Similarly, as with these other types of rewards, the ongoing presence of these rewards in a lifestyle will come to feel like necessary accessories to the life experience once fully appreciated, even if a person only experiences an adoration visitation from the Almighty once in their lifetime.

Also, as with the other types of rewards, material goods do play a part in spiritual rewards, as do the accompanying emotional and mental experiences for spiritual activity. As recounted in my first two books, and to some degree in this third book, I have lived a stress filled life in my opinion caused by my choices to live a conscientious, hope filled, love containing, and spiritually centered life style. I personally can attest to the ongoing relaxation, health, and life experience sacrifices I have endured by pursuing these choices.

However, I can also attest to the fact that although the sacrifices are indisputably present, the sense of loss from these sacrifices is less than the sense of loss and grief I would have without the spiritual accessories I have chosen instead. I suspect this is the criteria by which everyone makes their ongoing lifestyle decisions when accurately informed as to the real possibilities. Obviously people choose a variety of rewards the overall balance of which depends on upbringing, chosen associates, the surrounding local environment, and in these days of technological modernization, the plans and actual outcome of the plans for the global environment.

For leadership a huge global concern is providing adequate nutritious food for all at a minimum, and palatable and satisfying food on a more elevated emotional level. To this end of secure food provision, the modern day controversy over genetically modified organisms has received attention in documentary films, news stories, and as a source of legislation presented for popular vote. Some years ago I developed a wide ranging food intolerance and read any book and website I could find on the problem.

To cope with the discomforts created by food consumption I settled on a diet of no soy, dairy (except yogurt), wheat, yeast, corn, sugar, grapes and cooked oils. Basically I ate yogurt, few fruits, vegetables, beans, rice and other grains. Let me tell you, this is not a diet rich in the emotional comforting rewards to be found in rich creamy ice creams, melted cheese dishes in tomato sauces, and cooked nut products, a large part of my previous fare along with salads and cereal.

Well, I suffered on this restricted diet for a couple years or more, and then, I just had to have some chocolate so I bought a quality dark chocolate candy bar with a black panther cat on the cover advertising the fact that some of the proceeds went to endangered species. The candy bar had the fewest extra ingredients possible, basically sugar, chocolate beans, cocoa butter, and perhaps one or two other ingredients. Miracle of miracles, I did not have a reaction, so I decided that at any rate that particular brand of chocolate was okay, and occasionally tried other quality chocolate bars with good results.

Although my food life experience was limited, having the door to chocolate thrown open again was a huge boon. One day I was browsing in the library through the DVD collection and discovered two DVDs on genetically modified food. Since the DVDs were on the food topic still near and dear to my heart, I picked them up. The rest of this personal tale is best summed up in a letter I sent to Monsanto which follows.

Dear Monsanto,
I recently checked out of the Public Library two videos on GMOs. From the moment I checked those videos out my life started to be impacted by GMOs. First, I live in a small town which maintains records of a person's borrowing materials, so I was not overly surprised when I was waylaid in the library by a person who was heavily anti-GMO. It took me a while to get to watch those videos, but when I did I observed a definite bias against the GMO industry.

Back in September 2011 I came down with an intolerance to many foods and over the years since then, by limiting my diet to fruits, vegetables, grains, non-fat yogurt, rotating foods, and completely avoiding most corn, soy, yeast, honey, grapes and a few other foods I managed to slowly get better. In the beginning I was able to get a handle on possible problem foods by reading books in the library regarding food intolerance, which by the way, make no reference to the GMO industry. After watching the videos, I gave eating strictly organic foods a try with good results and now I am feeling much better.

The person at the library continued, I felt, trying to brow beat me into developing a fighting aggression against the GMO industry, although I told the person I believed I reacted to GMOs because of the long term stresses of my life style. Out of curiosity I wrote the manufacturer of my pet cat's food and asked if they used GMOs in their production, and they informed me that they did.

My cats are on a prescription diet because one of my cats was having seizures which were diagnosed as kidney disease. Unlike me, eating the GMO food reduced his seizures until finally, he has not had a seizure in years. I attribute the difference in reaction to the fact that I provide my cats with a fairly stress free environment.

I informed the person I kept running into at the library about the disparity of my experience with my cats experience and my guess that most people tolerate GMO products without mishap. I suppose this person expected me to agree unreservedly with them and when I did not and additionally mentioned the undermining personal pet experience and the unsupportive general population experience facts, he told me he would be prepared for me in the future. It felt like a serious response to my saying goodbye with the words "See you" and getting the response in a lightly menacing tone "Not if I see you first". Usually that little exchange has a more joking quality, albeit the kind of rough joking I do not usually participate in.

Since this unusual exchange, it was quite some time until I ran into the fellow again. I did not see him in fact until I left a draft of this letter to you in my house. Also, since that conversation both of my cats have been attacked. One of them is still not eating for himself and now refuses the food I offer to feed him by hand, although he permitted this feeding arrangement for some time. I suppose most people would say I have let my imagination get the best of me and that the whole sequence of events is one large coincidence, but I cannot help but feel differently.

My cats do spend time out doors on my patio garden area. I am always at home when they are out. When I go out, they come in. Although I have heard the occasional rumblings of the beginnings of a cat fight, I am always out there in a flash to break any quarrels up, so I am not sure how these cat on cat attacks are taking place so quietly that I cannot get out there to interrupt them, as I always have in the past. Additionally, whenever the kitties get scared they high tail it straight for the patio and apartment. Neither one of them is a "fighter" unless cornered.

Previous to the GMO video watching, I have responded to people trying to conscript me into some kind of battle against some target by explaining the possible motivations of others in a positive light, which has of course caused me no end of trouble.

As a result I have written two eBooks which I self-published on the Internet as a means of trying to make money since I am now unemployable due to my reluctance to engage in dishonest networking and battles, but also due to improved technology producing numerous job cuts, globalization sending jobs overseas, and the fact that I do not have dependents impacted by my continuous job losses. I am planning on writing a third book in which one topic will address my GMO experience. What I would like to do is to present the GMO industry point of view. To that end, if you have time will you please answer the following:

*Why and do you sue small farmers for seed science theft when the wind carries seeds between farms?

*Is your company concerned with maintaining a supply of unchanged DNA seeds?

*Is your operating conclusion that the small amount of people who suffer health setbacks due to GMO products is easily offset by the improved health in the certainty that crops will not be devastated by disease or bugs?

*Do large corporations engage in summits to discuss pressing issues of the day, like large nations do?

*If large corporations do have the previously mentioned summits, do you discuss the problems of overpopulation and possible solutions? If so, what are those solutions?

Personally I would suggest the overpopulation solution of an enormous, priority funded campaign by large stakeholders in the world, like yourself, endorsing voluntary population control and increased approval for lifestyles that do not create population (same sex unions, any heterosexual couples who focus on hobbies or other interests outside of work rather than children, people who choose the single lifestyle with no children for whatever reason – disinterest in children, not finding the right love partner, etc. – and so forth), rather than unquestioningly supporting with jobs those who have families and putting everyone else trying to behave responsibly by not recklessly creating dependent commitments regularly out of work.

Although you will probably not agree with everything I have to say in my eBooks, my website is CWPPRESS.com and if you are interested, I would be happy to send you both books free of charge (one of the books is in audio version as well) on DVD if it will help to make the environment on the planet better and less stressful. Just say the word.

Well, those are my questions and a suggestion. Please answer them if possible. I do think you should be aware of how difficult it is for people to maintain a peaceful demeanor and lifestyle in the current environment of heavy job loss from technological advances and globalization. For me, although I try to avoid having political conversations, the only way to avoid these deadly exchanges is by not interacting with other people at all. Agreeing to disagree is apparently not an option anymore.

Sincerely, D.A. Hewlett

Well, that is the basically the letter I sent. I sent it in June of 2015 and to date I have had no response. Obviously Monsanto is a large, busy corporation and must get thousands, maybe even millions of letters. Also, I would not be surprised if they felt uncomfortable addressing the issues I raised due to the amount of ongoing negative publicity. In large part the substance of the publicity may be true, but presented with a bias that colors perceptions darker than the complete detailed truth might do if time and media space permitted those subjected to media scrutiny the ability to fully disclose their side of the story.

For example, in the two DVDs I watched, both mention various incidents which took place in India and South Africa where cattle who ate GMO food died in a few weeks, and some humans also suffered death and impairments. Additionally, some 250,000 farmers in India committed suicide after losing hope when the extremely expensive GMO cottonseed technology turned out to be causing rashes on farm laborers and killing off some of the animals grazing on the picked cotton fields.

Although I am a fortunately placed American in the land of plenty of material resources and still able to access resources due to savings, because of my ongoing unemployment and the expressed attitudes of coworkers while previously employed, I have essentially lost all hope of being able to participate in the job market without becoming some kind of punching bag to motivate other members of staff with feelings of superiority to be maintained or feelings of terror to be avoided.

While I am uncompetitive, still I must stand side by side with all others allowed to maintain constant employment through their own questionable activities or as the solid pillars of stone permitted untainted motivation due to other's questionable activities. Public judgment and contemplation of possible future choices, unless I can become a successful writer or some other type of business success, leaves me feeling a little down if I allow too long a focus on these subjects to go on.

In India, the caste system does not permit hope for the current lifetime to exist. One is born into a social position and remains there until death, no matter what they do. After death, a person may go through a transformation due to good karma to be reborn into a higher social caste. However, many interpretations of Buddhism do not grant even this small amount of future hope, stating that fate determines a person's ongoing incarnations in each life, a closer reflection of practical abilities to impact the current life experience in the present incarnation regardless of what may happen after death. Also this interpretation subtly supports the appearance game by discouraging lowly untouchables from inspiration to heroic acts causing unpleasant nagging doubts for witnesses.

Hence some amount of population in India suffers from the loss of being able to access practical applications of hope, similar to my loss of hope of being able to get a job in a company and stay with my conscience intact. Also, this same lowly group and I have in common the general treatment of lower level personnel in the vertical hierarchy. Personally, in moments when I am not feeling too embittered to access my try and see the glass half full capacity, I like to think the poorly executed implementation of cottonseed technology explains the huge amount of customer service jobs which found their way into India.

Stress comes in many shapes, sizes, intensities, and durations. Some types of stress are actually healthy, spurring a person on to greater challenges. These are the stresses a person has some control over and can meet the challenges and problem solving readily without outside interference blocking success.

Being assured there is no relief from social position stress is not healthful. Neither is being assured that given the need for bad guys to support the vertical hierarchy, most negatively labeled people have no ethical alternative to advancing their status or recovering their lost status. These designs may be deemed the kindest treatment of individuals within various types of vertical hierarchies, but personally, I dispute the unquestioned need for the vertical hierarchy. Hence I believe the particular stress occasioned by permanent loss of hope has been a factor in my personal susceptibility to genetically modified food crops. Other factors may be the loss of positive emotional vibes which trigger healthy body chemicals from having a family, husband, long term associates, and a sense of meaningful purpose.

I do not believe that wholesale conviction of modified food crops is helpful. Most likely Monsanto developed these products in response to the impact of pesticides on the environment killing off birds and weakening eggshells and bird offspring, further devastating the bird life cycle. The current group of GMOs (genetically modified organisms) depicted in the DVDs are engineered to require less pesticide application, protecting food crops from insect infestation and the diseases which inflict weakened plants after insects have ravaged their leaves and structural supports somewhat.

It is an unfortunate truth that most technology is dispersed into general application before being fully tested. Thus the need to correct for phosphates in washing detergents, the pesticides destroying birds and helpful insects like bees, and now the GMOs creating food intolerances in people for various reasons, perhaps being low on hope and receiving ongoing negative vibes.

The DVDs also have spokes people declaring that plenty of food could be grown organically to cover planetary needs. They are insisting that the absolute necessity of GMO crops is grossly overstated, and in any event, organic production of food should not be undermined and withdrawn altogether since untainted seeds are the only hope for returning to food which will not hurt humans. I suppose these spokes people are anticipating a future date when everyone will be low on hope and receiving contemptuous deceptive vibes as general social fare or other emotionally destructive circumstances. Given my personal situation, I have to say I agree with keeping some amount of organic food production.

It seems most people are managing somehow, though. How are they doing it? If most people are allowed to occupy the neutral territory of solid pillar support, while some small portion are actually winners, the only people left out of the general hope spring fountain of youth are those who being negatively labeled, do not have access to the hope and good vibes of harmonious participation in society anymore. Some large group of this negatively labeled subset of the population instead of losing hope and not effectively replacing it with small hopes in becoming a writer or business success due to limited resources, turns to the hope generated by illegal acts and initiating battles where ever possible.

Of course, if I am wrong, and it is only a matter of time before everyone succumbs to food intolerance, then I have done what I can to inform Monsanto, and I am here by warning all the rest of you to keep an eye out for this eventuality in your life and speak up loud and long so all the rest of us can know when the condition becomes more wide spread. No one is going to worry about a problem which impacts a small fraction of a percentage point of people, but, if it turns out the food intolerance is actually more common, the problem will merit concern then. Remember, the experiment is to go completely organic and see if physical symptoms clear up. It is up to each and every one of us to air their concerns as they arise. I know I have.

I believe that organic food alternatives should definitely still be made available. Besides the benefits of physical comfort to me personally, organic food containing the seeds with DNA from natural processes which have served mankind well for many years do not seem like a gift from the Universe we want to recklessly throw away with such limited trials of our own technology, especially when some portion of those trials in real world applications is uncovering problems. It does strike me as a basic common sense conclusion that food which is designed with its own insecticide which disrupts insect digestion and reproduction would in long term doses create problems in the human body as well.

Given my personal experience, the presence of outcry in various media venues, and the mental consideration of how the genetic modification works, I would definitely caution against too widespread an implementation of food crops which will be difficult to reverse and may leave many impaired, while also leaving some without a source of healthy food. Although I am running the risk of sounding somewhat schizophrenic while simultaneously being a self-serving sycophant to leadership, I would posit that the reason the crops were implemented in such a widespread, all-encompassing manner, 90% of all soy and corn roughly, was to spread the possible damages as evenly as possible if something went amiss or maybe to conduct an enormous experiment which encompasses again everyone when really, experimentation on unsuspecting humans is very shaky ground.

On second thought, I am not altogether certain leadership would be happy with my characterization of their thought processes regardless of the amount of truth present in the speculation. Still it sounds like a softening of motives compared to many others who condemn leadership as trying to kill off or poison the lower classes. If indeed such dastardly purposes do underlay action I would say it is as much a self-defense action as anything else when the lower classes in their turn would send leadership gleefully to hell, or inflict outright earthly mayhem and revenge where and if possible.

Returning to the discussion of types of survival resources, in all cases the nature of work after division of labor created the emotional, mental, and spiritual barriers which isolated people from complete understanding of each other causing them to feel they were making sacrifices when witnessing others enjoying unavailable pleasures. This sense of loss has been the source of much accusation and at the least needs to be healed with recognition. In many cases recognition is simply not enough.

In addition to healing recognition of other's possible sacrifices to keep the works afloat, an ongoing overall tolerance aided by material resource equality would help in repairing serious senses of loss and give people the resources they need to set up a settled supportive lifestyle which would enable them to meet cheerfully the ongoing technological changes of the present age. What I am discussing here is an economic problem just like the economic problems of all the years past. The problem is and always has been how to produce and distribute survival resources and allow for ongoing quality of life so people will participate reliably.

An Examination of the Equality Economic Plan

For starters, I believe identifying the social engineering elements in previous economic theory which did not work, or at least thinking about what the specific shortcomings are, will be helpful. We don't have to throw out the Communist or Capitalist baby with the cold dirty bath water; we can keep the baby and make sure we use health promoting soap instead of punishing cold water for creating a clean economic plan.

Most importantly, I feel it is essential we remember and keep an ongoing emphasis on equality for all. Equality does not mean everyone has to be exactly the same, or that being alike in any manner is desirable other than everyone having equal access to survival resources. After a person performs their community service, whatever it may be, this person can take their allotment and go fishing, or go dancing, or go to the theater, or go to the race track. A couple can start a business, or they can start a family, or they can build their own house, grow their own food, make their own furniture and clothes and perform similar services for friends in their free time or as their actual community contribution if their appetite for such activity allows.

So what did not work effectively previously in the Capitalist and Communist economic systems? Like Communism, Capitalism has relied on expansion to fuel economic growth. Capitalism had access to tremendous amounts of natural resources present in the North American continent, hence the populace spread over the territory staking property claims where possible. Technological advance permitted industry to grow by leaps and bounds, creating population growth and trade with other nations, although international trade involves a lot of importing of goods as well as exporting of goods. The predominant national religion of earlier times, Christianity, was an enormous philosophical support for these endeavors.

Communism expanded into countries where poverty made the communist form of government more appealing than the alternative of starving to death in terrifying circumstances or where the prevalent cultural atmosphere was one of unified brotherhood with a spiritual vertical hierarchy as was present in many poor Catholic nations. In both systems growth is seen as essential to create a stable atmosphere which spells economic success. Fascism also has an element of belligerent expansion, while Socialism, depending on popular opinion and coercive influences, may or may not promote expansion.

It almost seems as if it should go without saying that the foundation for Hitler's Nazi regime, Fascism, and the belligerent governments of World War II's Japan and Italy, Socialism, need no further consideration and should be plopped into the dustbin without further ado. The Socialism expressed in Russia was rife with violent expansion, but perhaps no worse than the violence of slavery and pseudo slavery in Capitalism and the similar violence expressed in Communism to keep hereditary leadership strong and intact.

At the risk of the last vestige of my fading popularity, I would suggest that all these economic models, Communism, Capitalism, Socialism, and Fascism all basically rest on the same flawed foundation of a hierarchy of privilege whether the initial intention was equality or survival of the fittest in the first place. Once practical implementation is underway, social networking between those people who spend the most time together creates, naturally, stronger supportive feelings between warm, friendly bonded people, and less comforting attachment between strangers and those who spend almost no time together, again, naturally.

In the present world theater, many religions already have strong networks, large corporations have strong networks, some professions such as scientists and doctors have strong international networks, as do computer technology people, and the many who choose to do some amount of social networking online via Facebook, LinkedIn, and other sites developed to get people with something in common, in touch with each other.

With the possible exception of large corporations, none of the previously mentioned is the beginnings of a new worldwide foundation for economic unity, but to some degree the presence of all these various connected peoples in strong networks requires the other networks throughout the world to step up connections beyond the constraints of state geographical borders to keep pace, or lose out on the information available via networking and the possible social maneuvers executable through strong social contacts. Governments are of course the official largest networkers internationally, but to a degree, they are getting a run for their money from some of these other groups.

Economic theories abound but the one thing they have in common, other than practical application failure, is the reliance on treating human behavior as predictable in the same manner machines are predictable. When achieving practical results, in order to ensure predictability, availability of survival resources is kept within carefully confined ranges to ensure most people will behave impulsively yet predictably to secure restricted resources. The justification for keeping the workers who help all the imaginative others to accomplish their artistic work, productive work, administrative work, and so forth on a reduced income is the assumption that the worker's contribution is less mentally strenuous, less risky, less inspired, less responsible and therefore less worthy of equal remuneration.

A much smaller group is isolated from those teetering on the survival resource line by having abundant supplies and the generous, cheerful, cooperative demeanor that comes with calm security and control over the content and pace of one's life. This smaller group is usually charged with creating much of the upper level logistical, financial, administrative and other professional supports for a nation and this group is generally more loyal and sympathetic with the classes above than with those below, as one would expect to serve survival interests in a vertical hierarchy.

There is also the group of musicians, artists, creative story tellers, new age spiritualists and others, of whom the portion which become enormous successes are loyal and supportive with their creative efforts to the classes above them and craftily deceitful with those below, again, as one would expect to serve survival interests in a vertical hierarchy. To some degree, if their deceitful propaganda serves to help boost some group into the helpful realms of being visibly negatively labeled, these artists will enjoy a surprising success that many of the more rigid line towers find difficult to understand.

Many of the artistic/intellectual types find themselves relegated to the lower classes of survival support also limited to mechanized responses. To a degree within any profession – athletes, entertainers, scientists, writers, politicians, etc. – some people hit the jackpot lottery and enjoy luxury lifestyles and others do not. I believe the Bible hits it right on the nose when saying, roughly, the race is not to the swift, the smartest, or the most able, the race as often as not goes to the best networked, which given the number and diversity of networks and membership, can be a difficult outcome to predict for your average relegated machine part. Admittedly the Bible says all this in a much more beautiful and touching manner than I

125

just did, but perhaps my explanation from personal experience has a more direct practical usefulness.

In this manner theory can make a successful run for limited amounts of time until the imbalances created require government interference from Capitalism, Communism, Fascism, or Socialism. I would think given the errors this practice has produced in economic logic that theory manufacturers would know better. Invariably the predictability of motivation breaks down due to alternative meaning structures which exist under the larger national umbrella of an economic design, even when religion is officially banned as in the Communist system.

Is there perhaps some other method for predicting behavior other than keeping people in stressful competition on the survival edge? Additionally, and maybe even more importantly, is it absolutely necessary to predict behavior in the first place, economically speaking?

Although Capitalism has waged a huge informative campaign stressing the emphasis of this system on free enterprise which allows for the freedom in action and will to do what seems relevant and supportive, individually and communally, the fact is that Capitalism had a solid foundation installed by the planning monarchy in England which helped set the stage for having a balanced distribution of crops and occupations before the Revolutionary War which gained independence for the United States.

Government planning is an acknowledged facet of all economic systems even when these systems are planning and counting on expansion. Creating a general understanding within the Capitalist economic system that things magically fall into place with no planning is false, misleading, and harmful. After the Revolutionary War many of the rich plantation owners continued to plant the crops they had planted under English rule and direction. Wealthy land owners in fact comprised a large portion of early politicians found in the National Congress, Senate, and the state legislatures.

It is hard to imagine that the food supply grown and raised in this country was not a hot topic of government consideration in those earlier times. At some point when agricultural technology created such an overabundance of food crops, the government made and implemented a plan which paid some farmers not to plant food so that the price levels could be maintained, facts I learned in elementary school. Clearly, some kind of planning has been the norm all along, although emphasizing this dull, boring, ordinary state of affairs has not proven as popular for creating a sense of national specialness or nationalism, as depicting the successful outcome as a result of the magical coming together of all interests when everyone is allowed to act freely and choose their own destiny.

No doubt the Communist, Fascist and Socialist economic systems all have similar magical tales of wizardry making the ordinary planning for production and distribution of resources take on a more glamorous, challenging aspect which is likely to intimidate some while leaving them awestruck with the incredible results, a very desirable state of affairs for those shouldering these responsibilities. As with religion, economics relies on a certain amount of mystery veiled by the unknown in the depictions consumed by the average man on the streets. Hence the average man on the streets will not entertain the thought that he could begin to understand and participate in the leadership processes, still yet another bit of strategic tactical knowledge for controlling the course of events.

Well, if you look closely at anyone describing their work day and contribution to society, and I have, you will discover in everyone's account an amount of aggrandizing, intimidating emphasis on the trials and tribulations of their ongoing efforts. More rarely, some people will forthrightly declare the unadorned good fortune to be able to perform the job they have landed. This later group usually resides in the highest wage earners for performing creative works of art, professional athletes, and others who are allowed to exercise to capacity inborn talents. For these people, the downside which does not get mentioned is the enormous amount of competition it took to get where they finally landed, and the long, life shortening hours of work and other performance enhancing sacrifices.

I have personally worked in a lot of the jobs which get bad press as mind-numbing and soul destroying which now reside in third world countries. In my opinion, the jobs themselves were not so bad if as a worker you were allowed to like fellow co-workers, do a good conscientious job, and also not be required to be on 24/7 call availability ruining any life outside of work a person might try to establish.

Usually due to the aforementioned practices, people in these relaxed and yet productive and necessary jobs wind up stressed out unnaturally and unnecessarily or at least the portion of the work force required to become workplace nomads suffers from this type of stress. Contrasted with the high ambition group who gets paid fabulous sums while enduring many of the same career enjoyment destroyers, it seems the main difference revolves around the money incentive.

Does it really boil down to getting paid more money to be happy no matter what kind of work situation a person finds themselves in? Are the high paid athletes and artists so single-minded in focus that work is all that matters? Planning leadership likewise pipes up singing the praises of their career choice, but they label the decision as a response to a calling for public service.

Whether one uses talents in public service or as a hockey player, if one touches the lives of many witnessing onlookers directly, or as the more widespread agent of creating the rules in the environment, both types of career choices strengthen the overall chosen emphasis for the civic environment by participating unreservedly in widely distributed media support material.

Even amongst the large pool of people who express interest in these elevated positions to act as a role model educating everyone about the important highlights of the mental toolset which labels a person some kind of winner, not all of these hopefuls take to the program of brain washing insuring a person delivers the desirable responses whether they are surrounded by a group of helpful advisors or not. The more certain a person is, having deeply felt and thoughtfully supported convictions, about desirable beliefs, the more ongoing usefulness this person will reliably have. Still, others can manage an equally supportive performance if they pick their entourage carefully to include some wise interference runners who will prevent any unguarded remarks propelling a high flyer into a nose dive early collision with negative labels.

In my opinion, it is this visible position as one of the chosen superior beings, which also ensures an almost unlimited amount of get out of jail free cards, regular recognition wherever a person goes, and eventually getting to enjoy some amount of career expression freedom which makes up for the losses of privacy, being solidly happy with the artistic content, legislative content, or other content of work performance in the early career days, and being on edge with all associates while not being assured of the day's activities from moment to moment. Having enough money to spend on anything a person might fancy is icing on the cake only if the cake is somewhat digestible in the first place.

Naturally the picking and designing of role models is planned, if not by government, than by entertainment corporations. Although the appearance game would have the general populace believe that anyone with enough talent can make it, more recently, and refreshingly more honestly if not more ethically, an admission that a person must also have "the right stuff", "that special X factor or special something", "a certain quality that pops with the public", however the characteristic is described, it is merely an arbitrary means of sorting people out of the contest for filthy rich role model.

Since government has undergone quite a bit of downsizing of personnel and actual duties regulating various industries, one would hope their safeguarding and planning function was being done by the corporations previously a subject to their efforts. Personally, I do believe the corporations have stepped up to implement their own agendas and plans, although these plans are much more private and do not receive popular voter scrutiny and approval. As mentioned in my earlier two books, I suspect there is a large group of influential people who would be more comfortable with a reduction in population to make a better atmosphere on the planet in a host of different ways such as making planning and administration easier, sparing other species extinction, saving valuable resources and natural visual feasts to name a few.

I agree with their goals and I prefer that whoever is acting as planning leadership enjoys enough bountiful security keeping them in touch with their tolerant loving sides. However, I would feel more supportive if the agenda were at least more honestly declared as goals. Ideally making sure the people who would choose not to vote for this agenda, due to shortage of survival resources and a natural disinclination to compete, should find themselves with the materials and lifestyle which would also insure the addition of their heartfelt agreement.

Watching the movies about GMO food, people declare that at present the world has enough food to feed everyone one and a half times. The problem is not the amount of grown food; the problem is that many people cannot afford to buy the food which is available, a question of poor economic planning in providing the ready resource of disposable income to some large amount of the population. Additionally, biodiversity has taken an enormous hit. As many as 93% of previous plant species are gone never to return due to agricultural technology.

I wonder if the same anticipated reduction in population numbers which would make planning and administration easier was also determined as desirable for all the plant species. Perhaps the overall planners were worried that a person in New England would compare their heirloom tomato with a person enjoying some other type of tomato in New Mexico and raise a fuss. Perhaps the economic statisticians were having trouble making the necessary equivalences for various types of asparagus or the more complex and impossible substitution of apples for Jamaican kiwi oranges. Well, who knows exactly? What I do know is that economic calculations have gotten mighty complicated, as if they were not before.

Yes, gentle reader, I have been reading lots of economics books. All shapes, sizes, and colors of economics books. I will not pretend that I understand everything I am reading, but I am doing quite a bit of question asking. As is my general way, I have gone ahead, thought about the questions, and answered them for myself, rightly or wrongly, for better or for worse, and as before I am going to share my conclusions with you now, with the advice to think these issues through for yourself or find a few handy economics books to read if you feel moved.

How did things get so complicated and messy? In the earliest of times people bartered and traded excess handy crafts for someone else's extra apples. Perhaps a person would trade part of a slain deer for some vegetables from someone else's garden. Certainly these were simpler times in terms of economics, but might not have been so simple in terms of survival seeing as in many cases the deer hunter might simply be able to take the apples from an orchard or a garden in the dark of the night and kill anyone brave enough to raise objections. To avoid accusations of bias, the orchard tender or gardener could just as easily steal a portion of extra deer while the hunter slept a deep healing sleep from his strenuous impulsive exertions.

For the duration of this thought experiment I am going to assume that survival resources are fairly available for any who have the pluck and spirit to gather them up, rendering the less wholesome actions detailed above unnecessary unless some other underhanded transaction is taking place in regard to wives and daughters, etc. As time went on and population expanded requiring an even greater division of labor, money was invented allowing a person selling the service of carpentry to be able to purchase food from others who did not need the carpentry services right at that particular moment.

At some point money received a negative cast as the root of all evil, and I suppose that ideally speaking, trying to make such an exact accounting of services and food stuffs seems out of step with the spirit of love for everyone. If a person needs some apples, vegetables, deer meat or other tasty comestible, than anyone who has some extra food which may spoil in any event, might just want to share the extra. In turn, carpenter Aspen would render services on request and not worry about payment but have the mental assurance that because of his cooperative willingness to thatch Farmer Wilson's barn, he will find a ready source of corn which he can take to Baker Paddington to bake into corn cakes since he helped put out the fire in the Baker's kitchen and helped repair the damaged walls.

If the community is concerned with efficiency, then Farmer Wilson takes his produce straight away to a community kitchen where Baker Paddington, Chef Smith, and Fryer Jones all ply their trades serving food for some portion of the day so everyone can stop by and have a bite. Efficiency in this manner serves to bring the community together, while individual artistic differences in preparation of stews and other victuals cause some to want to prepare their own tasty morsels. A departure from efficiency and community spirit can take place when there is more than enough food creating security and feelings of trust, rightly or wrongly, that food is not being wasted or senselessly hoarded and squandered.

To a degree the presence of everyone at a community meal or some portion of everyone ensures that people will not help themselves to enormous portions leaving little to no food for others. Unofficially, no doubt, the food preparers would take on the portioning task simply because they would find themselves left without food at some point in the day and also without having served all hungry stomachs. The presence of the cafeteria organization is only possible when people have banded together in the belief that life will be better and easier, not worse and infused with more suffering.

Having just made the cultural move from individual or small family self-sufficiency to town and village self-sufficiency, I suppose the outline of perfect competition with everyone keeping a close eye on one another to be sure food does not get wastefully hoarded or senselessly destroyed would find its closest parallel in applied reality during this period. Everyone would still be in roughly the same experience boat creating similar motivations in this period right on the dawn of division of labor.

As people got better and better at their tasks, as happens whenever you do something over and over again and you have the freedom to implement possible improvements without undue red tape tying hands, production of resources improved creating more available resources for distribution. Thus the community cafeteria would be well supplied while allowing for some to make the occasional meal at home if they desired.

Of course it is possible at some point a cafeteria service person might get annoyed at a field hand who stole his sweetheart and decide to pretend there is no food available when the field hand comes into eat, but this deception would require that no better informed cafeteria person be a witness to events, or that the early network of cafeteria service persons was strong enough to permit this trickery when just as easily one of the other cafeteria people might be related or on friendly terms with the field hand, his new sweetheart, or live in minor discomfort with the eager cafeteria schemer in the first place.

Naturally a cafeteria person could poison someone he found despicable, but I have to believe in the earliest of times justice for this kind of thing would have been quite ugly, and hence a deterrent to all but the most black of jilted hearts. Additionally, before religion had a strong presence dictating all types of moral behavior, it may have just been a question of time before the cafeteria person was permitted access again to a lost love that got jilted when her field hand sweetheart had moved on.

Looking at the above emotional reasoning during times when invisible and material resources were limited and of limited types, one can see why economists are eager to throw out all emotional motivations as having little real impact on calculations other than being the odd bit of crazy data points that crop up now and again in any observation and experiment. With time, emotional rewards in proprietary ownership of access to people in marriage complicated the scene and economic calculations as did many other types of new emotional rewards, mental rewards, and spiritual rewards all geared toward making life better, longer, and more stable.

Try as creative civilization molders might, many people simply would not, or most likely could not move on beyond setting up a secure lifestyle in regard to food, shelter, companionship, and community belongingness. In the early days, even if efficiency did make an early showing rather than having each person prepare their own food after bartering for necessities, many might have easily decided to keep a certain amount of generated food back for themselves, just in case. Survival resources and pleasantness of community interactions would not be so assured that some people would not choose to provide this bit of mental relaxation through keeping a few extra apples in the pantry.

In fact, if a vertical hierarchy organization accompanied the efforts at community efficiency, a smart person low on the totem pole would readily be able to foresee the need for having a few extra food stuffs lying about when that same low on the totem pole person is the first to go without food in times of shortage. Not to say that in a horizontal organization that everyone might refrain from keeping back a few mouthfuls here and there, but I doubt the amount of food hoarded in a horizontal arrangement is more than in a vertical one.

Vertical hierarchy supporters might suppose those highly placed in the hierarchy could forego any need to hoard resources, but chances are they would help themselves as well, just because they would not want to publically be seen to eat while others were refused, creating some amount of moral doubt in onlookers about the nature and necessity of the vertical hierarchy. Also, the possibility of running out of the resources which allow for additional safety, protection from predation, and elevated physical and mental health would be an enormous concern, just as it is today creating huge gaps in resource access.

In any event, some amount of food stayed in the home, never making it to community feasts, allowing for individual access to artistic talents in preparation of food, as well as any other individually manufactured items for creating a modest lifestyle. I suppose in some fortunate cases a person or family would be in a position to make all their own needed supplies. They would build their own cabin, farm their own food, cotton and tobacco, dig their own well, make their own clothes from animal skins and spun cotton, and develop their own utensils to support their needs.

Enjoying the pioneer spirit which permits all this freedom of action, many might choose not to delve into the types of emotional, mental and spiritual rewards found in conspicuous consumption, careful recordkeeping for various community purposes, development of an automated plow or axe to grow much more food than is needed by one family becoming a generous supplier to the community cafeteria, departure from the family farm to work at mass production of the utensils made previously by hand at home, preparation of especially tasty food dishes, a feast of especially tasty food dishes at the elite cafeteria or creation of a work of art designed to make viewers feel privileged to be a small part in the larger whole. It seems to me these are the types of enhanced rewards which got us into modern times.

To some degree the pioneer spirit is making a return in survival and prepping communities anticipating dire events such as wars, governments and large corporations run amuck, ongoing weather disasters, epidemic disease waves and other destructive horrors which have become regularly prophesized. Like the Puritans departing from England for newly discovered America, some people are settling into small communities in off the beaten track areas hoping to avoid the abuses of the entrenched system and to make a better tomorrow starting from scratch, relatively speaking. However, most of the world has been charted and mapped and there is not too much room for competing forms of lifestyles to set up and show up the modern day lifestyle as full of senseless frills and fluff.

If survivalists and preppers are permitted to set up communities I suppose it is due to the fact that there are so many more people than jobs at present, and with the ongoing forward march of technology, the situation only promises to get worse. If some group of people remove themselves from leadership's responsibility and take care of their own needs off in the wilds of Montana somewhere, then leadership may well decide to just let them do so until like the American Indians, oil or some other valuable commodity is discovered on their property.

For the most part all the rest of us accustomed to working for larger companies of some type are not used to taking the reins and providing for all life necessities for the indefinite future, and the higher level hierarchy people in these organizations would be dismayed to find a mass exit of their organizations by people setting up to homestead on their own, returning to pioneer roots. After all, if we all returned to pioneer roots, would the executive, administrative, creative and other professional positions still be needed?

They too would have to return to pioneer roots, and because for any number of reasons largely centering on competitive edge, they do not want to. The professionals might not be particularly good at pioneering and even if they were the absolute best, no one else would care because everyone would be minding their own business, looking out for their own needs. Charles and Miranda may have produced twice as many cherry tomatoes and asparagus as they need using innovative techniques, but unless they want to give their excess away, no one who has been down the road of abusive dependence on a job provider wants to run the risk of transferring a working pioneer production situation into another possible abusive dependence situation again.

Obviously it would be difficult for everyone to return to pioneer roots without land which allows the upper class professionals to heave a huge "Phew!!!" The various enormous financial crises, one of which involved mortgages on residential and some commercial properties, have had a large toll on individual resources in regards to landed property and savings which might allow a person some amount of freedom to take the initiative in planning life supports. Reading about these financial crises of late, it is clear that some very fancy calculations on property and commodities was taking place after the government deregulated assorted industries.

Why did government not have the foresight to anticipate these colossal messes? When they set up the regulation years ago they acted on the knowledge that some safeguards were necessary in any type of competitive situation to keep people competing for survival resources from destabilizing the rest of the environment. The sports people still understand the need for referees. What changed? Well lots of things have changed, but essentially it all boils down to changes in population numbers and changes in types of lifestyle rewards requiring changes in cultural goals.

In the earliest times the human race started out with barter. Then as our lot prospered, we traded using seashells or other ornaments. We got very fancy with the ability to melt metal and coined money, done by an organized central government. As we became a more organized species we used special metals of especially pleasing color and hardness. On and on the exchange of goods was shifted from one type of medium to another. Population growth was largely responsible for the changes until finally, we use specially treated pieces of paper to act as official legal currency, allowing for enough material money to circulate to permit buying and selling of daily survival resources by a world population numbering in the billions.

Money is nice. It allows a person to feel secure and dream hopeful reveries for the future. It even allows a person to take steps, misguided or otherwise, toward achieving dream visions. Dream fulfillment over and above acquiring survival resources which is complete, partial, or misguided, falls into the realms of emotional, mental, and spiritual rewards. Bungee jumping, piano playing, reading about a make believe planet, or building a model motorcycle all have the same type of additional rewards as dreams and may in fact serve some portion of dream fulfillment.

When a person takes those first shaky steps on the road to investing in the rewards provided by dreams or simply decides to live life more fully and gather additional life experience, they are, consciously or unconsciously, boosting their emotional, mental, and spiritual rewards. Whether they intend to be competitors or not, the presence of additional rewards in an experienced lifestyle makes the experiencer, whether they are successful dreamers or not, have an element of additional competitive edge which they did not previously have.

When competition is designed into the environment as a mechanism to structure civilization, it automatically destabilizes the very civilization it is hoping to help cement into a solid foundation for ongoing cultural richness. Remember to think for yourself gentle reader, and of course, you have only my word for my personal recounting of my life experience, but rest assured, that every time I picked up a book, even on the most harmless of subjects for religious comfort, I was improving my mental wellbeing which improved my physical wellbeing, which in turn made me a better more competent competitor to maintain my lifetime advantages, whether I intended to make the world a more boiling cauldron of strife and deceit or not. Frankly, I feel it is kind of sad the absolute presence of winners and losers in the environment leads to this eventuality making the most benign and pleasant of relaxing jaunts through a springtime meadow a commodity to be craftily bought and sold on the market to the highest bidder wanting to corner the market on all competitive edge enrichments.

Put another way, the more a person enjoys their life, even in the most non-materialistic of manners, the more attached to that life and enjoyed life experience a person becomes. When speaking of non-material enjoyments I am speaking of things one cannot own, carry home, and store in the garage. For instance, enjoying the communal trail up Mount Fuji, enjoying the masterpieces of Renaissance Italy in various large museums throughout the world, enjoying a series of lectures on geology or any topic, enjoying a night of dancing and passion at a fancy hotel with the love of your life, taking the whole family to Disney World and so forth, you get the picture.

Very often these non-material rewards which are lived experiences cost quite a bit of material cash, or in this day and age, get tallied up on a credit card balance paid at the end of the month. The use of credit/debit cards means paper money may well be going the way of the gold standard as well. Anyhow, in an effort to support the spiritual non-materialistic ideology occupying modern day ethics and philosophy, those who have enough salary try to express their compliance with conservation of resources by consuming these experiences, rather than a sports car, a large flat screen TV and sound system, or fine jewelry mined from South Africa.

Of course, some people consume both types of products and these are the highest paid people for their services to the community. In order to motivate people into competition for any type of resources which will eventually be viewed as life enhancing and hence competitive edge enhancing resources, some kind of restrictive price tag must be attached to resources which are supposed to act as motivators. If a person can just run down to the store and pick up a ticket for the most exclusive dance club in town with a piece of bubble gum, the dance club's exclusivity will not work well to discriminate competitors (players) from non-competitors (loooooooosers).

If government absolutely had to, in order to bolster appearances and faith in the currency, it could print enough money to cover most or maybe even all of the money that is supposedly out there in the airwaves acting as resource support for the general populace. However, most people will not be cashing out all their various financial accounts so they can hide their money in a safer place than volatile markets, banks, savings and loan associations, and other financial intermediaries, that is, the mattress.

Tempted as I have been with all of my reading of late to go for the mattress of financial security, I personally have decided against it, and I caution the gentle reader to think carefully himself before cashing out entirely also. The ugly instrument of financial mayhem which is invoked as necessary to keep people from utilizing the family mattress, couch, trunk in the cellar and so on in these days of financial uncertainty is inflation. Although the government has massively deregulated here and there wantonly, they still have a few tools of the trade for impacting the economy, fiscal policy and monetary policy.

Fiscal policy!!! Monetary policy!!! What the @#$%%^ are those??? They sound like the same thing. If clear communication were important at all they would be the same thing. Why aren't they the same thing? Please why??????? Well, whatever they are exactly, creating low cost credit on the one hand, forcing banks to buy government securities and raising taxes on the other hand to make credit more expensive, the main point is to control how much actual money is available, in cold hard cash or on the cyber computer waves, for spending on any type of commodity by any type of entity or person.

If I were to take all of my money out of the bank, and believe me I have been sorely tempted to do so, then when the government takes steps to flood the amount of money available generally for spending I will be in serious trouble. By government reducing taxes or arranging for lower interest loans making the loan easier to pay back, any stable amount of cash sandwiched lovingly into a mattress is not worth as much as it was before when it was at least making a small amount of interest offsetting government money swamping. With these aids businesses can invest in making more products and rehire laid off people. More employed people with money to spend means prices go up, inflation, and any money stashed in a mattress will lose buying power and value. BOO HOO!!!!

Cyber money could perhaps equal paper money if government were to exert themselves to go on a printing spree to make it so, but why bother when the amount could change in a nanosecond. However, more importantly to the point is that cyber money represents both material and non-material goods which people can buy or sell to make the economy work and for the world to continue to spin peacefully.

Whatever else may be true about financial calculations, there are a wide variety of them like religions, they are essentially all expressing a theory through the use of the mathematical language and are therefore not required to actually work in real life. At this point the equations are dealing with essentially invisible entities taking the place of a wide range of material and non-material goods it is impossible to quantify in down to earth comparative terms other than someone thinks they are indispensable to quality of lived experience while some are actually genuine survival resources fuelling the body or keeping it safe.

If at any moment billions of dollars materialize or dematerialize, it is because the games of the superrich require enormous stakes to keep their jaded interests from turning to destructive outlets. For the most part, labeled safe investments are still safe, while anyone riding along on one of these excitement pleasure cruises with the superrich is taking their own life in their hands if they do not have a vast store of resources to support such diversions. Life styles for the rich and famous are just that, for the rich and famous. Yes, the rich are different, in more ways than one.

Another important influence on the movement of total counting money out there in cyber space is globalization. Terrorist attacks on the United States and other high standard of living countries by seriously materially deprived groups originating in poorer nations raises the issue of world poverty for consideration. The goal for improving overall standard of living helps make the overall environment richer in shared access to positive life experience. The terrorist mind, ordinarily short on positive life experiences will not have a healthy incubation environment when there are plenty of better alternatives to terrorism that hope can be reasonably invested in.

Why do certain people lose hope or become so utterly filled with hate and negative emotions that they consider terrorist activities and others to be worthy recipients of terrorist attacks? Vocal speakers declaring the evil of other nations while using technology to demonstrate the evil nation's material excesses is a tool in the creation of hostilities. If the declared evil nation achieved their material success using technology fueled by the material resources of poorer nations, than the perceived resentment will be all the greater.

Divvying up moral accountability where governments and large corporations make the decisions on buying and selling of commodities is at best unclear. Adding to the cloudy mists is the accountability of everyday decisions about the running of work places overpopulated with ready and willing workers handled by managerial pickers and choosers and their group of helpers. By the time accountability siphons down through all the levels in the hierarchy leaving the lowest with the least material resources for survival, the scene is set for confusion and reckless laying of blame at the door of any plausible person or persons a good emotionally biased story can be attached to with little consequence to the manipulative storyteller.

In an effort to avoid these caustic tales creating angry suicide bombers and angry incited mobs bent on some amount of destruction to the corrupt, the removal of resources in communities deemed to be well padded in survival resource access in underway. Those interested in protecting their padding are wisely hiding their access to wealth by wearing average everyday clothing, nothing of opulence which stands out or might create envy and jealousy. Still, since in general the American population has enjoyed quite a bit of industrial success, in spite of all careful camouflaging, jobs are being shipped overseas to nations under economic development.

The equalizing of reserved resources for the American people, for example, takes the form of burst bubbles in the housing, stock, technologic and other markets. Initially all the economic principles are put in place to allow the country to function under capitalism, but as the ongoing march of time unveils the holes and imbalances in the system, accommodations to provide survival resources elsewhere must take place.

Essentially, the people in charge must ask themselves how they can arrange to diminish the amount of jealousy and envy creating assets in one nation and arrange for more assets to be available to other nations in need. Deregulating government monitored financial industries on the one hand allows for all types of fancy calculations which will not have any sound practical foundation. The resource reduction of cyber space dollars accomplishes the vanishing in the twinkling of an eye of billions of dollars in assets leaving nothing behind except cyber-memories on eventually written over back up.

The huge financial losses leave corporations looking for means to saving manufacturing costs and one of the largest costs in any production facility is labor. So, labor is shipped to countries where the cost of human time and energy is deemed more affordable, or is at least apparently more affordable to all witnessing out of work Americans. The competition and hard scrabble fight to keep a job, any job, will become part of the general American experience reducing the labels of soft, lazy, spoiled Americans which incite terrorist and angry mob activity. To a degree these same phenomenon have been taking place in all the higher standard of living nations.

Gentle reader, I remind you this is all my opinion and speculation derived from my recent readings in economics books. I personally like to think that before the overall padding of American resources becomes too thin, that jobs and access to resources will reappear in this nation. After enough adjustments are achieved to keep the worst terrorist tales of American waste and excess from being an undeniable reality fueling harmful action, a more restrained yet enjoyable, relaxed lifestyle will be generally available again. Call me a dreamer, but I do not see any point in living without hope.

The alternatives to hope of which I have recently been reminded is the Armageddon, which all who anticipate going to heaven perceive as a hopeful joyful experience. Other alternatives to hope are a huge reduction in world population on the order of 1 survivor in every 10,000 persons, or if reality mimicking Biblical prophecy prevails 144,000 out of the current 7 billion (1 survivor in every 50,000) or an even larger future population number depending on how far out the ultimate population winnowing is deemed finished.

Doing the math, the survivor numbers run between 144,000 and 700,000, as of today. I don't know about you, but I am pretty certain I will not survive a contest with 10,000 to 50,000 other participants. I suppose being a regular lottery player may help a person to weather the enormity of those odds. The 1 survivor in every 10,000 statistic is a fact reaped and remembered from reading over the years the number of humans necessary to ensure species survival while not having the human species overrunning and destroying the planet through uncontrolled activity in unmanageable numbers. Who knows how the people who do these types of calculations come up with their numbers, but, for species other than humans who are moved about on and off the protected extinction list the species survival number is more like 10,000.

I don't want to use the word "lying". "Lying" is such an ugly word. After all, humans can be reasoned with and managed through persuasion, hence the allowance for 690,000 more people than would ordinarily be allowed for other species. The extra 690,000 might be the padding deemed necessary for social engineering mistakes which render some people useless in a vertical hierarchy.

As a minor point of interest, $(10,000/7,000,000,000)$ X 100, the formula for percentage of humans remaining using the traditional species formula, is .00014% of the people alive today would be deemed necessary for species survival if the terms applied to other animal species were applied to humans. In terms of winning the world lottery, very roughly, a person has one chance in 700,000 of being one of the 10,000 humans allowed to remain for species survival if we subject ourselves to same harsh criteria we have selected for other wild animals. Hmmmphf! Something to think about.

Granted, not too many important movers and shakers right now are talking about seriously reducing population numbers. If anything, the publically acknowledged plan is business as usual and economic growth all around which also seems to require population growth. Unless more people can get behind an even distribution of material survival resources which will allow those currently unable to make the step into higher emotional, mental and spiritual rewards to do so, economic growth will have to depend on material production growth.

Instead of love and joyful shared experiences with long time acquaintances one can look forward to more sky scraper penthouses a person may or may not have enough free time to live in outside of work. Instead of regularly shared tasty meals with family, friends and beloved pets, a person can have one deluxe meal at an elite restaurant after performing 6 months of 80 hour work weeks. Additionally, you can expect the work time to be largely wasted as a bottomless time sink so that even though people have plenty of money on record in the cyber bank, they cannot reasonably expect to spend it on anything other than hugely overpriced merchandise reflecting the superior status of long term employment.

Instead of maintaining your own lovely patio flower garden, you will be allowed to visit community parks occasionally, in your lunch hour, if you have time. Rather than making your own interesting apparel and accessories in your spare time as a hobby, you can play video games which allow you to accessorize impossibly long legged models making you personally feel a little ugly.

Making a comparison with an equality structure, a person could perform their community service cheerfully and diligently for 4 or less hours a day, while choosing peaceful pastime activities in an equality environment, OR, a person could compete in an escalating environment of vertical hierarchy being required to make life destroying sacrifices for no reason other than providing some amount of twisted emotional, mental, or spiritual reward to some other person. For example, the sacrifice of the ability to think clearly will be deemed necessary to turn the actual ability to access clear calm thinking into a motivating reward for those willing to compete for this experience. The loss of clear thought processes for the general populace will simultaneously give those declaring the willingness to engage in unregulated competition an enormous edge.

Globalization can mean equality internationally for all peoples now linked via trade and the common shared environment of planetary atmosphere on the one hand. On the other hand, globalization can mean an ongoing separation of vertical classes standardized throughout the world where each class utilizes their own religion and economic theory to justify their ongoing daily activities. Personally, I am not sure how great that is going to work out for the lower classes, of which I am at the moment a member and have an abiding interest in the planned outcome.

If policy makers are having trouble deciding on a course of action, or in achieving success after choosing a course of action, for example tax increases, it is due to the lack of real substance behind money numbers floating about in the air waves and cyber space. Unlike matter, money can appear and disappear in the blink of an eye when various commodity bubbles burst.

Although one of the laws of natural physics states that matter is a constant and cannot be created or destroyed, it seems the amount of money on the planet is open to interpretation as to actual amount. When, for example, lots of celebrities are vying for a house on the beach at Lake Wastefill the cost of a studio apartment may be $1 million dollars. After the discovery of massive amounts of toxic waste disposal from an industrial plant upstream, the same studio apartment is $8000. What happened to the extra $992,000? The loss in land values at Lake Wastefill were recouped at whatever new spot was the new recipient of celebrity interest, maybe.

Given the history of money as starting at barter for material goods, moving onto carved shells and the like, becoming more standardized by centralized government in smelted metals, receiving further support from government in gold and silver standards, enjoying a liberation from physical gold limitations in printed paper money, and finally, shedding all limitations in time and space via computer accounting, it is not surprising that people unfamiliar with the monetary system are flummoxed by the whole works which seem as magic when a person receives a check which they cash and spend. Still, flummoxed or not, they can feel the loss of life experience the economic crises has inflicted on their short allotted life span.

The previous portion of this book primarily explained my understanding, interpretation and conclusions from economics books I have been reading recently. In a nutshell, economic systems have more in common than not. The loudest proclaimers of the virtues of any particular system are of course the people who in practical terms have managed to get the most out of the presence of the economic system through crafty corruption, or ability to forecast the inevitable outcomes of the system crashing with the wall of human realities.

Like religion, economics has commandments, however, the commandments are not clearly communicated, subjected to ongoing public scrutiny and discussion, and most importantly, the keeping of these commandments is not a matter of free will. For the most part the majority of people are kept on the edge of survival resource access so that free will has nothing to do with their day to day decision making. In order to survive, a person will perform any requested action from a blackmailing presence regardless of ethical considerations. In a vertical hierarchy,

142

blackmailing presences are everywhere as a matter or course and actual planning.

To me the solution is plain, and I am not the only person who can see it. A horizontal equality arrangement which permits everyone equal access to material resources via performed community service or a safety net will allow the specter and ability of blackmail to be ineffective. The civilization structure throughout the various communities in the world does not need an enormous overhaul other than the recognition of everyone's inherent worthiness to participate in their gift of life, and making access to resources possible where necessary.

We can still produce cars, luxury yachts, airplanes, scientific tools of accurate measurement and beautiful works of art of all types. Like the spread of new scientific facts, popular media stories, new ways of preparing foods, or new health practices, what will be required is the spread of an equality and tolerance ethic to help smooth the way for those who will feel they are being stripped of their material advantages which afford access to emotional, mental, and spiritual rewards.

Also this equality and tolerance ethic will help those who have unwillingly sacrificed a portion of their lived experience understand the sacrifices others have made which are not evident within the current vertical walls containing life perceptions and blocking comprehension of other's experience. Lastly, an equality and tolerance ethic will serve to encourage each and every one of us to take the time to examine another person's life experience if we are feeling pressured to do so through felt anger, jealousy, and envy prompting antisocial actions and unhealthy internal feelings. Most likely, material security will also make the necessity for such reflections much less prevalent.

Personally I like to think that the world embrace of an equality and tolerance ethic may be accepted as a possible symbolic alternative meaning to the second coming of Christ or the Jewish anticipation of the arrival of the Messiah. Rather than having the whole world destroyed in a conflagration prior to some tiny portion of humanity ascending to the city of heaven, the second coming of Christ could represent the end of senseless sacrifices by humans to create artificial meanings for other members of their community.

The original crucifixion could represent God trying to communicate to man the senseless nature of sacrifices by having Jesus executed alongside of criminals subjected to the relentless labeling of the vertical hierarchy, while a murderer is actually pardoned during the whole process demonstrating the arbitrary foolishness of the whole vertical blackmailing arrangement. In the story of poor Jesus stuck on the cross to make a visual lesson which men to date have misinterpreted, the very misreading of the situation all the more highlights the senselessness of empty sacrifices.

In this religious story, God sent his only son to earth so that men could understand the absurdity of empty sacrifice, to allow men to enjoy their gift of life, rather than falling into the sin of judging and holding down their brethren, and hence holding down themselves. Instead of suffering, the cross could symbolize a person with a healthy balance of priorities able to live with the full use of his abilities and outstretched arms to gather needed information and resources while also taking corrective balancing actions. The lower portion of the cross shows man moving thoughtfully with one foot in front of the other to make progress forward slowly and carefully, for all mankind.

Well, so far lightening has not struck me down yet. I suppose, given this encouragement, I will continue on with the next portion of this book which is an interpretation of the Ten Commandments, which make a showing in three of the world's most popular religions, Judaism, Christianity, and Islam. The substance of the Ten Commandments appears as well in Confucianism. When examining the Ten Commandments I will rely heavily on the Golden Rule as stated by Jesus to "do unto others as you would have done unto you". I believe the overall kindness ethic makes a showing in almost all the religions out there, with perhaps the exception of Satanism.

Because I feel economics and religion both attempt to guide human behavior one way or another, I will try to incorporate some of the economic precepts which govern desirable economic behavior into the discussion. By removing the possibility for confusion which arises when a person tries to dovetail two theoretical disciplines into one code of human conduct on the spur of the moment, in this case combining for example the Christian religion with Capitalism economics, a more consistent honor code for daily decision making will be achieved in advance, making for better decisions, hopefully.

A New Age Look at the Ten Commandments and Economics

Gentle reader, as in my other two books my interpretations and speculations are a result of my lived experience and information gathering. I encourage everyone to do their own interpretations and speculations informed by your very own personal situation circumstances. However, I hope my example serves as a useful, entertaining demonstration of how to go about your own investigations, or as a jumping off point for further ruminating of your own. Don't be scared. Half of the thoughts which pop into my head are not particularly useful, but very many are. Be patient with yourself and in time you can develop a synthesizing thought process for yourself. Good Luck.

Most popular religions have a long and ancient history. Now a days there is some new age stuff available, but very much of the new age values are right in line with the values expressed in the older religions such as hope for the future, patience, community celebration, truth, honesty, peace, healing, forgiveness, harmony, love, kindness, wisdom, cleansing and purification. The new age philosophies however, also bring some new values to the table which might not be greeted with much enthusiasm in the ancient religions, for example, intellect, inspiration, creativity, psychic ability, clairvoyance, past life recall, astral projections, inner power, channeling abilities, spirit guardians, and transformation.

Reconciling all these various new values is a little easier than one might first think. When writing the Bible, many of the authors used all types of symbolic language, parables and other obfuscating devices to protect themselves from the authorities when conveying helpful but perhaps not at the moment popular messages. Similarly, many of the new values mask more practical realities which the new age writers are not comfortable with owning in outright plain English.

For instance, astral projections which is being able to know the specifics of a location visited in a dream, could just as easily be a way of dressing up Internet research, gossip from friends, deductions from entertainment media or some other more grounded knowledge source. By clouding the source of information, the source of information will still be available to the astral projector making edgy, unpopular conclusions or drawing contrary lessons from dream experiences should some empowered entity become sufficiently concerned to take some kind of controlling action. Keep all this in mind as we stroll through our examination of the Ten Commandments.

In addition to addressing the Ten Commandments of the ancients, I will in spirit with the new age trend bringing spiritual guidance up to date, try to address some of the more recent developments in modern times as they impact the Ten Commandments. I think it is wise to remember that the Biblical Ten Commandments which still have a steadfast ongoing sway in three popular religions lasting for the last few millennium or so do indeed address very pressing human concerns. For this reason the commandments have had a timeless quality of being of current interest even many years after their first inception. How many legislated laws have fared as long or had a worldwide audience of accord?

Lastly, although the Ten Commandments cover a lot of ground aided by the presence of the Golden Rule, I would suggest in the spirit of tolerance and equality a new guideline consideration for personal honor codes which goes along the lines of the old prayer of supplication for being able to know what you can change and what you cannot with the wisdom to know the difference. Obviously gentle reader you can change many things about yourself, but do not feel that you have to, if the change involves a serious diminishment in quality of life.

A person could choose to make themselves available 24/7 on an on call basis for work allowing his coworkers the freedom to come and go as they please. While this generous individual would be curtailing his personal life at the expense of the expanded freedom of his coworkers he might feel the tradeoff was acceptable due to his love for the work and work environment. It is a personal decision. Others would grievously feel the loss of their ability to have a personal life and personal interests. There is no one rule. Each must make their own decision aided by their own consultations within themselves with themselves, god, Mother Nature, or the cosmic order of light, laughter and rainbow sunshine.

Just so we know what exact Ten Commandments I will be referring to I am getting the information from Exodus 20:1-17 of The Book, a special edition of the Holy Bible which is supposed to be an easier to understand translation. Essentially the list is as follows with a few odd paraphrasings, editorializings and other embellishments of my own. I am pretty sure you will be able to tell where scripture leaves off and I begin.

ONE: I am the Lord your God/ I made you so I know everything there is to know about you and the environment I created in 6 short days. Don't be an ass and think you know better than I do. If I am telling you I have granted you the gift of life to enjoy, I mean it.

TWO: Do not worship any other gods besides me/ Besides wasting time flat of your face uncomfortably revering incorrectly, it might just piss me off witnessing such foolhardiness. Since I am reported as jealous, you can assume I am jealous of the precious gift of life I have generously bestowed on your lucky person, so please do not waste it with onerous adoration unless such activity is inherently pleasing to yourself for some more earthly practical reason.

THREE: Do not make idols of any kind and worship them instead of me/ Again, for those without enough imagination to get beyond the immense distracting beauties which I populated the earth with for human pleasure, I, your God, cannot be defined or sculpted into definite solid, tangible, human defined shapes. I am the Lord your God, not the other way around.

146

FOUR: Do not misuse the name of the Lord your God/ I, the Lord, your God, do not endorse personal hygiene products, sports cars, palaces, restaurants, movies, or any other human creation, no matter how inspired in heart, soul and spirit. Please try and remember I made a vast creation populated by many beings who all want their opportunity to enjoy the expression of the odd flight of fancy here and there, regardless of popular critical acclaim, advertising savvy, or societal usefulness.

FIVE: Remember to observe the Sabbath day by keeping it holy/ All work and no play makes Jack a dull boy even to the most forgiving suffering God. Please do not throw away your granted gift of life by not taking regular intervals to bask in and to contemplate the wondrous glory of my creation and it's multitude of life enhancing diversions. Go out and play.

SIX: Honor your father and your mother/ Appreciate the people who take care of you and teach you about the world when they could just as easily kill, injure or consciously misguide you into injury. Assume, if for no other reason than that you have spent loads of time together and their reputation hinges on your reputation, that your parents love and care about you and want an ongoing lifetime of experience as your companion. Naturally if they do attempt to kill, injure or consciously misguide you into injury, you had better find someone else to honor with your lifetime companionship.

SEVEN: Do not murder/ I, the Lord, your God have granted all people a gift of life for personal use and it is not for fellow humans to decide who gets to delight in their gift and who will not. Kill joys may be allowed into heaven, but boy are you going to feel remorseful when you get there. Eternity is a long time to feel like and be remembered as primarily a toadstool, even if forgiveness and forgetfulness help soften the remorse with eons of time.

EIGHT: Do not commit adultery/ Do not dishonor your vows of any kind, to me, the Lord, your God, or to your spouse, lovers, parents, friends, or pets. Love is a treasure that I, the Almighty, frown upon the earthly folding, bending or spindling thereof. When the earthly time for earthly vows has run its course, let whoever is relying on the substance of said vows be aware of your change of spirit so they can adjust their gift of life accordingly with as little loss as possible.

NINE: Do not steal/ Do not deprive another person of their God given gift of life experiences, their survival support materials for experiences, their emotional health to engage fully in experiences, their spiritual meaning to understand experiences, and mental abilities to gather experiences.

TEN: Do not testify falsely against your neighbor/ Do not speak garbage, rubbish, or lies. For starters, these tales are almost invariably boring to all the people studiously following my directive to enjoy their gift of life. The people who are interested or seem to be interested may use your lies in a manner you may not approve of. Most importantly, any prayers for clear understanding from me, the Lord, your God, may be answered only after a stern lecture detailing all the falsehoods recently fobbed off as truth. Think how big a chunk of your God given gift of life experiences that could eat up.

ELEVEN: Do not covet your neighbor's spouse, house or other possession/ Again, enjoy your God given gift of life. Yearning for things which belong to others when you have equally supportive, life enhancing materials, acquaintances, and life experiences of your very own and of your very own choosing is wasteful, not to mention societally destructive and inefficient. Believe it or not, I, the Lord, your God, do look into such things. If, for instance, you have not settled on a person to share intimacy and life experiences with, try to find someone who is not already happily attached elsewhere and will consider your attentions impertinent and uncomfortable, wasting your gift of life and theirs.

Hmm. I think I got a little carried away there with my summarizing and also, somehow, I came up with eleven commandments instead of ten. Whoops. Eh. No matter. You get the gist, and of course further explanation is forthcoming. Before I go full blown interpolating of the Ten Commandments, I will give a brief explanation of my process for the gentle reader to use in his adventures in thinking for himself.

Since I want to reconcile two disciplines which have already, with varying degrees of clarity, stated their theory and principles, I need to reverse engineer them both. Put another way, I am going to try and see why certain principles or commandments are deemed useful to a society structured by an artificial vertical hierarchy. In my opinion, at least on a survival subconscious level, the people who choose to honor various disciplines or create them, do so many times out of a need to find a healthy, comfortable mental space to occupy within the larger dominating surrounding social environment.

Most individuals mentally occupy the dominating surrounding social environment using perceptions gathered through their five senses. Perceptions of overall environment vary due to career type, family atmosphere, and the prevailing environment surrounding other participated in activities. This dependence on the five senses gathering information which is processed within the brain leads to the popular magical testimonies of mind being more important than matter or "mind over matter".

Mind over matter allows for questionable explanations of the movement of chairs, pencils, paper clips, and the presence of unlocked doors and flickering lights. Aside from unconfirmed telekinesis, if a person persuaded of the truth in spiritual disciplines determines life is better unencumbered of any material baggage, then this persuaded person will be much happier in their brain/mind, where happiness registers, than another person equally bereft of material possessions who desperately wants a Hummer, penthouse, and swimming pool. The person not persuaded by spiritual teachings will not have the benefit of "mind over matter" in regard to enjoying his gift of life free of material burdens and may in fact be better equipped to perform cleverly staged acts of telekinesis for large paying audiences.

Others choose to enhance the comfort of their mental space through the use of alcohol and other mind altering drugs. Although not personally recommended by me, nonetheless many still choose this course due to minimal options for improving mental perceptions. Some manage to improve mental perceptions through an active fantasy life which is pursued at all times where an actual intersection with reality is not needed to perform a job or healthily interact with the outside environment, like when operating a car or walking in crowded streets.

Still others may have some kind of fantasy life foisted upon them due to the nature of the work place, family members or other influential life impacting personalities exercising their power over subjected lives. This segment of the population may grow quite large with time as the defenses supporting the artificial vertical hierarchy get more and more theoretical without an actual supporting presence in physical nature's reality.

Although there are plenty of people who will assert that a large audience of believers in God, the paranormal, or the presence of superior DNA makes these items a certainty regardless of physical evidence, flawed logic, or uncovering of devious schemes, Freud and other psychological professionals label these popular systems of erroneous thinking as mass delusion complexes. I remind the Gentle reader that depending on the surrounding details, the passionate assertion of these various fictions almost invariably creates the setting for some type of artificial hierarchy with all the problems such social structure brings in its wake.

New Age Spiritualism, Ancient Religions and Economics are all theoretical models for understanding the surrounding environment which affects a person's ability to access a positive, calm, healthy mental state.

When a person contemplates the presence of a creator, a unifying cosmic force or the utter lack thereof, the conclusion or lack of conclusion leaves them joyously happy, calm, quite sad, or somewhere in between, mentally. For those spared such musings there is the uplifting presence of faith, or the certitude that humans are adrift on an earthly cosmic raft which may sink momentarily, for some also an uplifting state of mind negating any sense of responsibility regarding others.

Although human beings are composed primarily of a physical body which houses a physical brain in the head, the brain with its electrical impulses, nerves and memories is responsible for interpreting information from the five senses and creating the individual personality which interprets daily experiences. As any observer in the animal kingdom will tell you, animals register pleasurable experiences as important life time events. Even those creatures supposed to engage in minimal amounts of conscious thinking, optimize their survival security, creating relaxation and pleasure. Keeping the importance of survival security in mind, we come to commandment number one.

ONE: I am the Lord your God

I personally conclude that if there is a God responsible for this wondrous experience here on the planet earth than he is an incredible being the essence of which is well beyond my limited understanding. The only conclusion I feel safe in embracing regarding this all generous being, if they are there, is that my life is a gift to be enjoyed and experienced as completely as possible without disrupting someone else's similar journey.

Risking the error of using my limited mental equipment to fathom the depths of God, still, I do feel the support from using my own life experiences is not completely irrelevant. I could not imagine giving my cat a toy mouse and then telling him he can't play with it, he must wait until he has died, and then his spirit can play with a golden toy mouse in heaven. Foolishness. The mental state of a cat stripped of all stimulations and toys except perhaps the frustration of seeing inaccessible toys would not be conducive to admiring the lovely household full of kitty cat diversions I have provided for the sole purpose of having happy cats. Wouldn't a possible God do as much or more?

So, using good catechism logic, starting with the FACT that God wants man to milk his personal gift of life for every morsel of pleasure he can find (tenuously supported by actual physical evidence, you say; I say perhaps, but this is how these exercises are done) the human mind looking for a fuller understanding of God's wishes must fill in the many remaining blanks. Does God care about the other humans a person sees wandering

150

about sharing his planet? Does God expect these other humans wandering about to have equal access to pleasures? Does each person need to worry about whether some other human person is having enough fun? How does anyone go about answering such questions?

I am sure many will accuse me of going well beyond my limited earlier conclusion, but that is what sorting out these matters is about. Answering the above types of questions is done by determining the impact these situations will have on your personal mental state upon perception via the five physical senses of the raised question's enactment. When formulating conclusions the state of sensitivity of the physical senses must be considered as well as the state of survival security which dampens mental and emotional sensitivity to perceived events.

I personally find it impossible to witness violence in movies directed at animals. I know that in the making of the movie no animals were hurt, still, I cannot watch. Fortunately, I have been spared witnessing much animal violence in person. Occasionally I see some poor dog being dragged around by children or trying to keep up with people on bikes and want to take some kind of helpful action, but mostly, there is very little I can do about it.

What I can do about upsetting situations does not matter at the moment. Naturally if I could fix all the problems I see I would, but as important, I recognize that suffering is taking place and I don't like it. I am not remotely comfortable with witnessing these events, and I try not to. Otherwise, when I see a dog happily dancing about its owner who is making a big fuss over Rufus, frankly, I can't get enough of the happy spectacle.

Much like being proud, or even just satisfied with a career and family life, getting to meet fun physical challenges, solving mental puzzles, or connecting with spiritual truths, watching the pleasurable experiences of other beings one has a fellow feeling for improves your felt and perceived quality of life and mental state. Not meeting challenges of various types and witnessing distressing events disrupts a person's survival equilibrium until the person manages to heal the wound by desensitizing himself, solving challenges, or helping where possible a distressed creature.

Whether or not God cares, I am delighted to find out that I do. Since I am using myself as a starting point for a God which has provided this breathtaking planet, similarly to my previous conclusions regarding the Almighty granting a gift of life, I am going to say God also cares. For the moment, questions answered, albeit somewhat briefly for a catechism.

Given the various sorts of physical, emotional, mental, and spiritual gymnastics available to a person to improve their life experience voluntarily or as a response to a blackmailing presence which nonetheless affords

151

some mental support for taken actions, trying to economically reduce the granted gift of life to some kind of equal measure of inner and outer experiences is impossible as well as an absurd ridiculous goal. The crafty calculations of all physical, emotional, mental, and spiritual rewards affecting mental state are perhaps the very essence of evil portrayed in almost all spiritual messages.

When I speak of equality for everyone, I am referring to equal access to physical, emotional, mental, and spiritual rewards. Some people may not choose to participate in any spiritual rewards, for example. Currently, all the ruthless competitors bypassing spiritual rewards and moral compasses are helping themselves to extra helpings of material substances such as houses, cars, yachts and the like. Although a person might suppose this greedy hoarding of material goods was responsible for others going without, this is not the case. If anything, the avaricious desire for material goods supporting a person's mental space puts many people to work with access to survival resources.

The problem created by greed may be too much work with some overworked. I imagine that once a wealthy person has enough boats, for instance, that the arrival of the next boat will not be an imperative deadline matter in most cases, affording the workers on luxury crafts the ability to enjoy job security from long lists of waiting customers. Lucky them.

Some spiritual groups as stated earlier go as far as possible to not utilize any physical supports to their spiritual pursuits. These same spiritualists may also choose to bypass conscious mental rewards for trance states achieved through drugs or extreme physical experiences. It is their granted gift of life and if these seekers want to connect with some experience outside of themselves which is essentially undefinable yet highly personal and rewarding, as far as I am concerned, they are free to do so.

There is a group of people who emphasize mental exercises above all else. Food, friends, physical surroundings and stimulations of all types take a far second to keeping the mind primed to be able to respond to mental challenges at a moment's notice. For some living life in this manner is a preference while for others it is a survival necessity making the determinations of experienced rewards impossible.

Clearly a person who finds pleasure in problem solving is having a good time. Another person who feels that access to survival resources would be diminished or absent if they did not engage in problem solving professions may get some amount of relaxation rewards every time he feels his job security reinforced, but he is also forgoing other pleasures, which the person does really miss, to keep a keen sharp edge.

At some point the person who has foregone certain types of pleasures may find he can no longer muster any enthusiasm for postponed delights which he was perhaps hoping to enjoy at some point when things got less competitive and more relaxed. The act of problem solving will still provide some amount of job security, but not more than before, and this person will have suffered a loss in pleasure resources if certain types of simple pleasures are no longer accessible due to disuse for one reason or another. Additionally, when the importance of job security increases due to other rewards no longer working as rewards, competition in the work place is jacked up a notch or two, destroying pleasures for others.

In my experience the reward calculators make no allowances for the nature of rewards and give equal amounts of rewards under the most dissimilar of situations. Adding in the earthly reward calculators own perverse pleasure in misidentifying everything or absolute sense of guilt and powerlessness in being unable to improve the system somehow, I would have to say these economic calculations of rewards are grossly in error, a fact which given everything I have learned on the subject, I should not find all that surprising.

Although I have serious doubts about assigning this accounting task to God due to his general mysteriousness, still, if the choice has to be made between God maybe, just perhaps performing this chore, or having perception inhibited humans managing this enormous feat of recordkeeping, I am with the inspired Biblical writers who suggest leaving these reckonings to the Almighty and minding your own business. The choice boils down to perfection by God in the invisible reward distribution of emotional, mental and spiritual rewards, if He is actually doing the math, or inevitable human error when trying to evaluate these invisible quantities, creating rapacious waste in an era recognizing the need for conservation of resources.

The previous is a definite case of having the wisdom to know what can be accomplished by humans and what cannot. Since money in economic terms has turned out to be fairly intangible, what is describable are concrete survival resources and other luxury stuffs of life which make it worth living. A person could live in a studio apartment, or they could live in a one bedroom house with yard and swimming pool. I am really quite uncertain that God has an abiding or even any interest whatsoever in such matters, but that does not mean that human interest in these matters is wrong on the one hand, or absolutely necessary to be declared a functioning human on the other.

In new age spiritualism when a person is recounting their past lives they invariably have lead lives fuller of sexual partners, better housing, more glamorous careers as kings and queens, more laden with powers as oracles or some other improved lifestyle which makes for a better story for listeners at the least, and improved day and night dream foundations for the person accessing previous lives. To date I have not heard anyone recount their previous life as a priest for a fundamentalist church, as a bank teller, as a night time office cleaner, as a cafeteria server, as a high school secretary, as a journalist for a small town paper, as an unemployable writer and so forth.

Do the people happily employed in the above types of jobs ever find themselves wondering about their previous life experiences and try to channel their earlier selves? Speaking for myself as a member of the list, the answer is no. If, however, the people are unhappy members of the above professions seeking some kind of an outlet and do not find reality too constraining, they can engage in full fantasy mode to conjure up all types of previous life histories for their own enrichment and the enrichment of any others entertained by the weaver of these tales as long as listeners are not taken too great advantage of.

Personally, I see these tales of past lives as a wish to enjoy life more fully. Something is missing for the night janitor, so casting about for fulfillment elsewhere they opt for some of the new age flavored experiences which allow the individual to fill in the substance of healing beliefs on his own. The individual is not limited by the outline of ancient texts and scrolls for material to improve his mental state. If he/she likes, they can imagine themselves a highly desired and sought after societal figure attending all the most fashionable parties and creating a stir wherever they go. In this manner a person may choose to be both a Christian leading a life guided by good Christian behavior, while also indulging in some healing past life recall on the side. Why not? Does God condemn past life recall? I am the Lord your God and there will be no past life recall?

Yes and no. One of the other types of books which came to hand as I was writing this book was a book on "The Other Bible". This bible has pages and pages of Ancient alternative scriptures. Looking through these leaves of ancient wisdom was quite an eye opener. I suggest gentle reader you should take a look yourself. Anyway, according to the traditional Bible, for example the King James Version, past life recall does not jibe with dying and waiting in your grave asleep for the Second Coming of Christ.

As far as I can tell there are no accounts of Jezel who was a middle school teacher in the current life, but Queen of the Orient previously, preceded by being an accomplished Greek musician, preceded by being a temple priestess providing sexual relief for those needing a sanctified outlet, and so on. We do not all get to live a variety of lives hoping to accrue enough holy points to make heaven. We get the one chance before the book of who gets in and who does not is closed.

It may be the inspired writers, satisfied with the importance of their current contribution to mankind did not feel the overwhelming pull to embellish their current life in this manner, also, Jesus was probably silent on this subject. Looking through the alternative Bible there is room for all kinds of creative interpretation of the Old Testament and large amounts of this interpretation takes place in these gospels and scrolls. Given the conflicting version of events with those portrayed in the traditional popular bible, it is not surprising that the presence of the other source materials for the Bible have not been broadcast far and wide.

However, creative interpretation does not have to stop with the writers of the Dead Sea scrolls and other less well known gospels. Within these ancient texts the essential message is that the defining of reality by man, that is men generally taking authority over life and others, is the first corrupting evil which creates death on the planet, not eating the apple suggested by the devilish serpent in the Garden of Eden. In fact, in some cases the serpent is equated with Jesus himself because accessing knowledge is the redeeming action a person can take to ensure his stay on the planet is awakened and joyful, rather than the sleep of slavery.

In Gnosticism Heaven is already here on earth. Humans, however, have blinded themselves to the earthly heavenly experience by creating the sin filled social environment and placing consuming importance on living within this manufactured physical, emotional, mental, and spiritual space. Even where humans have attempted to decipher and implement God's divine will for earthly experience, they have failed due to human limitations and imperfections.

Sadly, in this spirit of self-loathing of human capacities, much of Gnosticism's literature is spent condemning physical experience of the corrupted body and the emptiness of all the rest of life experience. The Gnostics view martyrdom as not a real sacrifice when the martyrs are depicted as wanting to sacrifice their lives, which are worthless anyway, to help others see the truth of the martyr's belief system.

In the spirit of reviling the physical body, engaging in self-destructive activity or in promiscuous sexual habits further demonstrates a Gnostic believer's indifference to living any type of quality life on earth. Also, some Gnostic sects go so far as to proclaim the creation of earth as not an act of the Divine God of Light, but as an act of the Evil God of Darkness, in other words Lucifer, making the quality of lived human experience on earth that much more a question of definite suffering.

Well, that is quite a differing of interpretation opinions there, and to some degree I am throwing in my additional embellishments to interpretations when I feel further explanation is needed in making the language plain and accessible to the ordinary person. These buried gospels surfaced recently in archaeological projects and have been attributed to a group called the Gnostics, who like any religion have several churches and furthering branching of beliefs.

Interestingly, one of the primary tenets of the Gnostic belief system is that the world has a dual nature, light and dark, good and evil, and so forth. The very presence of an exact opposite interpretation allows for an ongoing battle between traditional Christianity and Gnosticism, permitting the constant stir of survival strife to create other types of more practical confusion, playing a part in keeping everyone slightly off balance.

If gentle reader you have read my other two books, then you know I fall somewhere in between. I believe in the possibility of a benevolent God it is difficult to say much more about. I do not go so far as to label all the others who have gone quite far indeed in defining God through inspired writing as evil or authoritarian, but I gather that is how the Gnostics feel about the matter via sifting their mystical symbolism, similarly to sifting the more traditional Christian symbolism which I have done in all three of my books. In turn the traditional Christians have labeled all who declare it is impossible for the human frame to know God and thus dismissing the Bible as inspired literature, as evil and damned.

Economically, authoritarianism is often a product of totalitarian governments. In the earliest of ancient times when human kind was first thinking about their environment which supported their gift of life, wherever it came from, it is not surprising that inspired writings would mimic and lend survival support to an environment heavily influenced by dictatorial mankind in small groups. Equally, it is not surprising that early on the texts more supportive of authoritarian power were preserved while texts arguing against the authoritarian structure's wisdom were suppressed. It is the nature of authoritarianism, similar to Communism, to squash dissent outright in an effort to preserve harmony.

I will add that I find it interesting that these contrary texts should surface now, almost as a final blow to teetering Christianity, while also adding in the opportunity for further divisions and weakening of the Christian doctrine from a source other than rapacious modern scientific hands. The coast is almost clear for the more scientifically supported oriental religions of spontaneous living to catch hold, and if these oriental doctrines still cannot find a solid home, the Gnostic doctrines may do just as well for condemning the presence of all manmade rules.

Personally, I do not have a problem with rules which help to smooth societal waters, like the Golden Rule: to do unto others as you would have done unto you. Authoritarian rules which support the presence of the artificial vertical hierarchy I am less crazy about. People do need to know the outlines of civilization, but perhaps the outline should be less exclusionary and more inclusionary. If a person is different, it does not mean they are abhorrent to man and God, it just means that they have structured their life meaning differently, which is okay as long as meaning is not derived by inflicting damage, pain, and chronic suffering on others.

Not all Gnostic inspired writings agree on the doomed nature of earthly existence. Some writings point to the human ability to gain knowledge to improve and deliver earthly existence from the errors of manmade society on the one hand and the vain, ignorant God of Darkness on the other, no doubt one in the same thing once a person wades through all the symbolism.

Personally, I construe this gift of knowledge to be identifying the artificial vertical hierarchy civilization structure as the source of general unhappiness and violent actions. Once this truth becomes generally accepted, the methods for humanely restructuring the social environment into a horizontal equality structure will take time and effort, but improvements to the less tangible and visible emotional, mental, and spiritual atmospheres will go quite a ways in smoothing the physical transition.

As I never tire of saying, physical things will not have to change all that much, see my second book. Most people will be able to keep what they have, perhaps in rare over the top cases a wealthy person may be asked to downsize to 10 mansions instead of 20. Otherwise, people will be granted access to material resources of food and housing which there is actually an abundance of on the planet. The change will be in the group presently serving as the negatively labeled without access to money to pay for basic necessities. This group will be permitted access to resources, when and if they want them.

Getting the food and housing where it is needed may present some logistical problems, but from what I can see, there are plenty of administrative logistical planners and clerks out of work ready to help move the planet in a joyful, loving direction. In the small town I currently live in there are quite a few empty buildings which have been empty since they were built. The current talk is of tearing these buildings down and building something else which may or may not be used.

Surely, these buildings could be refashioned into housing as easily as they could be torn down and rebuilt into slightly different structures which might again remain empty indefinitely. If I were a construction worker, I would feel better about repurposing an empty building into housing for the currently homeless rather than simply engaging in empty use of construction skills to no identifiable end. My guess is that some of the present homeless population may have construction skills they would be more than happy to employ in upgrading old buildings that they could live in.

I must remind the gentle reader that in order to enjoy an equality lifestyle, part of the agenda will have to be some kind of voluntary population control. Population control is what will allow for conservation of limited planetary resources while also permitting quality problem solving because the problems can be clearly defined and not constantly shifting like sand in the wind. The items on the planet which man can control are him and his structuring of society.

There may be some amount of weather control available by now, but the desirability of man monkeying with the weather is questionable. More to the present point, man cannot make the earth the size of Jupiter with lush forests and new oil wells to provide new land and material resources to support exponentially growing populations. Maybe in science fiction and fantasy novels these events can take place, but here in reality on earth, definite physical limitations are present.

In conclusion, God, Mother Nature, the Cosmic Universe, or Dumb Luck somehow threw together the material elements available and came up with our Solar System, Galaxy, and Universe. Learning more about the physical rules of this creation helps mankind live in accord within the boundaries of his material surroundings, allowing man to enjoy material security and benefit from emotional, mental, and spiritual wellbeing. Further, understanding the chemical, emotional, mental, and spiritual workings specifically of the human body allows man to create an amount of felt security where necessary to make up for material shortcomings and lack of understanding until these deficiencies can be remedied in the near future, hopefully.

TWO: Do not worship any other gods besides me
The second commandment sounds full of violent jealousy and vengeance, on the face of it. However, as with any of the inspired texts, a lot has to do with how a person chooses to go about interpreting things. Naturally, in terms of societal popularity and security, going along with one of the most widespread interpretations in current usage seems to be the best choice, provided a person is willing to forego many of the mental and

spiritual rewards of thinking for yourself and being in conscious full agreement with an adopted belief system.

My personal belief system, while not enjoying the benefits of security in popularity, does provide an opportunity for liking yourself personally, examining your beliefs for yourself personally, and reaping all the benefits such abilities and actions yield as well as participating pleasantly in the life experience. Obviously gentle reader you will want to do your own mentally and spiritually improving homework on these matters, but I suspect the more you look into this subject, the more you will come to see the opportunity to inhabit this planet as a gift of life of some sort, to be loved, appreciated, and relished, peacefully and noncompetitively.

If you have spent any time at all awake and open to the vast parade of experiences marching past the windows to the brain of your very own viewing eyes, you know that there are many ways to define the life experience. Suffering is one of the more popular explanations and descriptions of life experience, especially in lands where material resources are short due to poor technology and no curbs of any kind on population growth. Suffering for God or Christ also makes a significant showing in many Christian churches and in highlighted doctrines.

While I am completely in favor of cooperative compliance with performing some amount of public service activity to keep the vast logistical works of producing and distributing survival resources of all kinds, physical, emotional, mental and spiritual, I personally feel it is less than desirable, what I would almost call a sin except for the fact that I do not like calling anyone sinful, or evil, to engage in any public service activity to the point of irreversible sacrifice of health, limbs, and life. Having said that, I do realize that many people make these sacrifices prompted in most cases by blackmail and coercion, so more correctly, the label of sin and evil belongs to the nefarious blackmailers, blackmailed themselves by the sin creating artificial vertical hierarchy.

So when a jealous God is telling you to revere him correctly, I choose to interpret this instruction as not allowing your associates to blackmail you into sacrifices which are essentially meaningless and not actually pleasing to God. Even God interpreted symbolically as social leadership, which I often do in many cases to help me understand what is happening in the surrounding environment, does not want laborers and producers of the quality environment enjoyed by all earthly participants to senselessly injure themselves or otherwise disable their abilities through addictions just to make the utilization of a machine work force seem like the most desirable choice.

159

Some people may choose to injure themselves because they are counting on an improved life experience due to relief from the black mailers making injury suggestions and also a relief from expected levels of responsibility. Sadly, it is only after the injury is incurred that the victim realizes that black mailers do not stop black mailing once a demand has been achieved, they follow success with more demands. As for diminished expectations of responsibility, many do not appreciate that responsibility in control over your own life is one of the good, life improving experiences in the toy chest of life.

Much like describing labor as drudgery and boring so that a machine work force can replace the human work force subjected to the emotional roller coaster ride of the artificial vertical hierarchy, responsibility gets negative descriptions which make the outline of responsibility seem almost impossible. The fact is all that can be reasonably expected of a person is being responsible for your own actions which include communicating effectively information where it is needed. A person has no control over another person who takes clear communication and information and uses it to muddle the works. Much of the muddling results from the nature of the artificial vertical hierarchy causing many to try and level the playing field.

Naturally responsibility may also include having to let go of people purposely ignoring clear communication, but a lot of this responsibility can be lightened by making sure the obfuscator is aware that continued neglect of clear guidelines will result in job loss, and knowing that even after a person has lost one job in particular, tolerance and a safety net of survival resources will be in place within an equality environment. However, a lot of pressure can be brought to bear in a vertical hierarchy on people who might not participate properly in black mailing networks placed in pivotal positions by making the non-networkers feel responsible for the people who refuse to do a job correctly, while also not at least moving the person not performing their job into some other more suitable position in which their disregard for the rules will not matter as much.

Management cannot be held responsible for a person brought up to believe that it is the duty of all general labor to create as much trouble and impediments as possible. Similarly, anyone who follows a church doctrine, which states it is the responsibility of men on earth to punish others not deemed in compliance with God's wishes, may well be far beyond managerial control. Instead of assuming the managerial responsibility of communication and education of the work force, unfortunately, in many cases management adopts other less clear manners of sending messages which serve to waste time and resources further while never creating any progress in establishing a cooperative, persuasion oriented environment of harmony and peace.

It may not be possible to re-educate a person brought up with counterproductive instructions from family, church and associates, but a company should at least try for a while. It is part of a company's social responsibility to not make matters worse for a person unfortunately informed by earlier companions. By not accurately informing this person when the opportunity presents itself the company personnel are reinforcing the prior mischief instead of giving a person a foundation from which to build faith in the social fabric if he himself participates in accordance with reasonable expectations.

With the widespread use of these practices I must suppose that it serves some specific practical purpose unrelated to efficient production and achievement of goals. As stated previously in both of my earlier books, the purpose is to create the artificial vertical hierarchy through the use of the appearance game. In these cases management is banking on utilizing pickers and choosers, the appearance game and the blackmailing, shaming nature of the artificial vertical hierarchy to perform quite a bit of managerial duties, shoring up the managerial position's security even more.

By destroying the foundation for cooperative, tolerant, peaceful harmony which is the use of a minimal amount of clear rules applied compassionately, the removal of company education and communication leaves everyone not in the protected network confused, off balance, and fearful. Yes, by using the violence of miscommunication, no communication, and arbitrary rules, a blackmailing networked manager can assume responsibility for his department, but this amount of responsibility could just as easily be achieved using clear communication, clear rules, and clear compassionate application of rules.

Why has such a shift taken place? Overpopulation is the primary cause. With excess population looking for jobs that have disappeared due to technological advances, the spreading of the job market overseas, and the natural tendency of people to improve in their job given the freedom and encouragement to do so, many perfectly adequate employees are out of work and secure access to survival resources.

Not surprisingly the arbitrary violent practices of management cause employees to engage in their own arbitrary violence making leadership feel out of control of all production and distribution of survival resources. What is a person to do? One option is to go ahead and enjoy your gift of life peacefully by doing a good job, communicating as clearly and honestly as possible, and through the natural exercise of mental enjoyment of your gift of life grow in job performance and emotional attachment to your career gathering some amount of survival security and certainty.

Personally, given my background, the above outline is the most desirable way of enjoying a gift of life, but not everyone starts from exactly the same point of physical, emotional, mental, and spiritual experiences, so conclusions may differ. Given my conclusion that God is essentially benevolent, but mysterious, I am not sure how far his interest or power extends into judging each individual's unique conclusion to go about enjoying a gift of life within the current overwhelming environment of artificial vertical hierarchy.

Given the ongoing state of affairs with the general absence of popular educating literary texts of a nature such as this one, I am going to go with God's granting of free will in these types of decisions. A person can choose to opt for allowing everyone general access to survival resources across the board, or a person can engage in fierce competition or benefit from the presence of fierce competition without uttering a contradictory word to the presence of the hierarchy civilization structure. Whatever a person chooses, in agreement with my own benevolence conclusion, God will forgive everyone. Forgiveness will naturally be all the easier if in fact God has lost interest, but God's ongoing interest is irrelevant in the presence of free will.

If things worked in reverse, one might almost sympathetically grant God the freedom to look about the Universe elsewhere for a while, taking a break from the wasteful spectacle of those choosing not to enjoy themselves or depriving others of the security to fully enjoy their gift of life. As it happens one other large difference between the Gnostic belief system and the traditional Christian belief system is that everyone, absolutely everyone is forgiven and gets to go to heaven within the Gnostic framework. As mentioned earlier, in the Christian framework, a miniscule percentage of the human race gets to participate in the eternal afterlife.

In Communist lands where the economic/government system takes the place of religion, the second commandment receives actual earthly support in that no spoken word or traditional religious activity is tolerated which would interfere with the outward appearance of perfection for the current organizing ethic for society. The free will and freedom to speak out is denied, or has been until very recently with globalization impacting the environment of all nations. As mentioned earlier, the freedom within Capitalism is still apparently present, but there are enough ardent supporters of the artificial hierarchy who step in to sort out matters of dissent on their own using networked activity which carefully skirts the line of legality.

Having pointed out all the practical matters which center about the injunction not to worship any other God than a benevolent creator, the angry and consumed with jealousy chief of the artificial hierarchy, or some other popular or personal alternative, a person can still choose not to worship a supreme being at all. The main point in not adoring any being is not to worship a lesser being than the actual Supreme one. In practical terms, this mistake would lead to all types of life hardship not eased by satisfying personal choices and activities, nor eased by achieving some level of survival comfort, but complicated by the error of living life constantly backing a losing horse at the races expecting to win. Loss would be ongoing, inevitable, and without any helpful personal inner rewards, a recipe for a wretched short life if ever there was one.

THREE: Do not make idols of any kind and worship them instead of me

The third commandment looks a lot like the second one, except I suppose the caution here centers on mistaking the Christian, Jewish, or Moslem God for money and power, for instance. If a person chooses the path of total practicality making the artificial hierarchy the God of choice, as in unfettered Capitalism, then this same person must be honest enough with himself to acknowledge the fact that he is essentially divorcing himself from most types of traditional religious morality. Theoretically, mind you, if a person were to choose the God of unfettered Capitalism and pursue this ideal with a fanatic absolutism, then the presence of the type of harsh competition outlined earlier would be acceptable to the selecting person and he would be at ease with all competitive actions including coercion of others into his ideal, just as happens in religious crusades.

Problems arise for this absolute Capitalist however when he to decides to temper the Capitalist ideal with networking between like companies or individuals to soften the hard going on the competitive path. Additionally a caving in Capitalist might decide to enjoy a certain amount of supportive noncompetitive parasites to populate a life improving entourage. The compromising Capitalist would be exchanging his pure God of perfect competition for the corrupted idol of cooperation among friends, and let others compete and foot the escalating bill. If others have opted for some other God ideal, they may be unaware of their designed and planned role and fail to take the proper actions to correct for perfect competition transformed into labor unions, monopolies and healthy relationships with friends for only a select few.

Equally, if a person adopts a modified Christian ideal emphasizing equality rather than a more vertical organization, he still is expected to embrace the sacrifices demanded by society speaking for God. When society assumes the role of God but does not actually deliver the balanced equality attributed to God when opting for an artificial vertical hierarchy, all kinds of confusion as to the real nature of sacrifices takes place. As in the Capitalism situation, a cherry picking of Christian ideals takes place between the various branches and sects of a religion, accounting for the vigorous insistence on there being only one right religion, or economic system.

Having said all of that several times in this volume, I am not saying that a form of popular manmade idealism executed in action to the fanatical letter of perfection is the actual ticket to happiness in the third commandment. All manmade theorizing and inspiration is flawed by wishful thinking, vanity, desperation to please authoritarian powers, and other veiled survival instincts. The ticket is not to worship the theoretical or inspired cooperative thinking of another highly acclaimed flawed human being who does not really know a whole lot better than you do what life is all about. You must permit yourself plenty of personal forgiveness on the road to thinking for yourself and getting to know God personally for yourself, rather than accepting as an idol a pre-packaged interpretation.

Remember, God is essentially unknowable to the human mind, and he may not even be there to be known and understood. When pursuing an understanding of the Almighty for yourself, consider your personal gifts from the universe which are supported by society. If you are indifferent to freedom within manmade society, you can consider all possible gifts. In any event, try to find a life path which allows you full satisfying access to the physical, emotional, mental, and spiritual rewards you find most compelling and follow it. Change when rewards become compromised and try to find an equally or at any rate acceptable alternative path. Good Luck. No blind admiration for someone else's idol.

FOUR: Do not misuse the name of the Lord your God

In much earlier times I would have been running a larger risk than I am in this modern period of scientific enlightenment, still, with ongoing risk to my fading popularity, God does not pick sides in wars, for example. Neither does God endorse certain corporate products while condemning other products to criticisms of evil and the like. God does not have favorite sports teams no matter how creative or inspiring coaching prayers are, and God does not prefer blondes.

God or the Cosmic Universe did at the very least give humans an amazing brain which allows for all types of environmental improvements and the creation of items of beauty, aid and interest. Not being an animal it is hard for me to describe the extent of their mental processes, but if observation of my cats is any indicator, I would say they are very intelligent beings. Animals may be even more intelligent in some manners than humans since my cats often have to outwit me without my knowledge to achieve personal goals. My cats may simply use in great abundance the most intelligent mental product of all, the emotion of love, because I can refuse them nothing unless the request is damaging.

Being that there is a vast assortment of popular religions, with new versions achieving some amount of acceptance all the time, I am also going to maintain that God does not favor any one religion over another. Neither does God favor science or economics over religions. Naturally, inspired writers could not write with the confidence and excellence which they accomplish without feeling they are indeed chosen vessels of communication, but, even if the writers have forgotten, out of necessity to produce their literary products, it is wise for the larger reading population to remember that much of the inspired text gets filtered through the human being squarely surrounded by a vertical hierarchy environment. In other words, feet of clay are still attached and also inspiring those hands and spirit of vision.

There are no shortage of people who think I am bit crazed in regards to animals, but humans do share this planet with all types of flora and fauna which enrich our daily experience just by being here, and, also by being ALIVE. God may or may not have put all these others types of life on the planet for the sole disposal of meeting human needs, but, I suspect the mysterious, complicated God who created this bountiful and rich environment had a more widespread plan in place in which some kind of meaningful life experience was intended for all his life forms. It just makes the most sense to me.

We as humans, granted tremendous mental capacities, can either move in a direction of intensifying competition, or in a direction of emotional love which would allow us to provide reservations of land for other species to inhabit according to the Ultimate Creator's will. Of course, to have untainted forests, jungles, meadows, swamps, and the like, we must start controlling population numbers now. Frankly, I see the challenges of providing and caring for the diverse environments this planet naturally creates to be as interesting and inspiring as winning productivity challenges, or simply having construction workers build empty buildings.

Economically growth will have to shift from improved technology, property values, luxury goods, entertainment goods, and so forth to include improving shared conservation lands which will cause no one undue alarm or bitterness if people themselves are secure via a safety net of resources, tolerance and other aspects of an equality environment for mankind. For example, in addition to reaping the mental fantasy rewards of placing yourself in the star role of a favorite TV series, a person could also enjoy virtual tours of beautiful landscapes inhabited by real animals provided by unmanned drones. As a bonus, new jobs would be created in the oversight of these reserves. The necessity for absolute economic growth itself could be slowly phased into an equality environment not requiring continuing population and economic growth as emotional spurs and motivators.

Consider that usefulness can expand to embrace usefulness to other species which God, the Ultimate Creator, or the Cosmic Flower Arranger included as travelling companions within the Milky Way Galaxy for human enjoyment. Obviously, human enjoyment can also be expanded to include the visual experience of other life form's journey on the planet rather than eating meat for dinner or wearing leather and seal coats in harsh climates. In my opinion, it is this peaceful, life affirming option for mankind which will help the species get past globalization and the financial crisis shaking the foundations of current societal arrangements.

Mother Nature, God or the Almighty may still not be willing to lend the use of their name to this man made societal approach any more than this being would put his name onto Fascism, for example, but the emotional growth in love does not require additional personnel on the planet, using up Rain Forests, polluting the oceans or allowing totalitarian organization of the lower classes and animal species. I can't help but feel God would be grateful for sparing his creation these traumas.

FIVE: Remember to observe the Sabbath day by keeping it holy

Whether a person believes in a Supreme Being or not, they should for their own personal benefit think about the surrounding environment - natural, social, and universal - in order to knowledgeably engage in fruitful enjoyment of their gift of life. Bask in the beauties the planet earth has to offer, ask why the social environment works a certain way, and ask "What are the various types of spiritual belief systems out there and how will the choice of one over another impact my ability to live?" Although God may have granted free will, the political organizations in various nations may attempt to short circuit this gift by strong persuasion of citizens into one type of belief system over another.

According to the literal interpretation of the fifth commandment, there is one day a week set aside for considering the above types of questions or, if one has already made up their mind, worshiping the God of their choice which may turn out to be the Capitalist or Communist economic system. Personally, I find myself posing questions all the time, and then I answer them if possible, or wait until the answer eventually comes to me, if it comes to me.

Some Gnostics pursue transcendent truths by turning inwards. Discarding all the surrounding influences of the social environment which can blind the individual to the real nature of the Almighty, the seeker spends his holy day in prayers of supplication for wisdom. The prayer addresses the Almighty as the Beloved and expresses an intense longing for greater understanding of the Creator's ways of love and wisdom which in due course come to the patient prayer in bursts of vision and understanding.

Personally, I cannot speak to how helpful this manner of contemplating these issues is, but there are plenty of people who swear by it. I suppose this experience parallels on a much smaller scale the way my kitties might feel about me as the provider of food, shelter, clean litter boxes, toys and other kitty cat life enhancements. I do feel my cats must spend some amount of time trying to figure me out since they are aces at giving me pretty much what I want and need.

Since kitties do not have to worry about blocking out a surrounding kitty cat society, they have a real advantage of a life time of experience spared damaging exposure to artificial arrangements mimicking nature inconsistently and poorly. Conclusions for cats, and no doubt humans will vary depending on bodily health, and the daily experiences which although blocked out in the human case, will leave a person with an overall predisposition toward a manner of thinking and feeling about the life experience.

If a person is still looking to make a decision he will have to determine whether he believes in an Ultimate entity or not, if there is just one god or several, if the Ultimate is good or evil, and what the Ultimate wants for the human experience – joy, happiness, suffering, pain. In the absence of an Ultimate Being or the presence of a being beyond definition in bountiful detail, a person will also need to consider whether the individual is going to be onboard with the earthly ideal of the society he inhabits, whether he is going to define his life as playing the social appearance game or whether the individual will work to replace the hierarchy and appearance game with an equality safety net of tolerance and love peacefully, or some other more personally regarded social ideal.

In my opinion these issues can get pretty complicated very quickly so if a person chooses to devote more time to resolution efforts initially, it may pay off in the long run in less needed time later on. However, the fifth commandment does implore the individual to keep his mind focused on these issues at least one day a week, probably to help a person keep mentally aware of their choices so they can make continuous, spontaneous decisions which will be in accord with their life code and not leave the individual, surrounded by many needs to take unrehearsed actions, feeling bad due to forgetfulness when one does not keep taking updating refresher courses, in a manner of speaking.

For many fortunately placed within the vertical hierarchy these decisions follow naturally from a life time of education from parents and supportive surroundings which do not raise questions for a person who has never had any other experience than being a lucky recipient of societies munificence via technology. In some cases a wise advisor may help the privileged to an understanding of the realities beyond their sheltering palace walls, or, it may just be a question of time before someone crawls through an unguarded hole in societal fabric shielding a fortunate, wreaking havoc and creating a newly disillusioned person who will need to start spending time reflecting rather than simply worshipping on the Sabbath.

Whatever the case may be, life time Catholic priest, vacillating religious enthusiast, world traveler, hardened businessman, or retiring moral cat lover, having a strong awareness of who you are and where you stand will help with everyday decisions in surprising manners, keeping happiness and calm security available health aids close by or on the visible horizon of hope. Having said all that, as stated earlier, once a certain point of reflection and confidence in moral code has been achieved, be sure to support your choice of code with supportive actions which make your feel good and confirmed in your choice, once again strengthening your coping abilities generally. Go ahead, have fun, you have already done all the thinking leg work supporting your fun choices.

Before leaving the fifth commandment, I notice that one of the main stumbling blocks for myself, and I believe also for others, for making an unequivocal stance in favor of a definite Good Creator by Design sort of God is the presence of suffering. At present I choose the option of a Good Creator because I feel it is the best choice given the other alternatives as outlined previously in my other two books. The all important question is "How can a good God allow so much suffering on the planet due to human actions?"

One validation for suffering put forward by the Gnostics states that suffering is not truly experienced as suffering. Instead, a person who suffers as a result of being different and cast out of regular society is in a position to laugh at all those blinded by authorities, and the smart ones do laugh while those who do not laugh deserve to suffer. Yikes. All sounds a bit harsh to me, and in my experience suffering is no fun. To date I have been unable to locate the humor in having missed out on many life experiences, but perhaps that is my personal problem.

In the vein of elaborate doctrines, the Gnostics, in their creative variety opposing vehemently traditional Christianity, also came up with a group of 365 heavens, one for each day of the year which earthly people travel through to get to the topmost heaven. This vast assortment of heavens is a slightly different take on Buddhist reincarnation. With such a complex set of heavens, I suppose it is possible that man is not the most advanced creature in God's zoo, for lack of a better term.

Man may be so far removed from God in fact as to be comparable to a flea or ant to human forms here on earth. If man is the equivalent of a flea or ant inhabiting the very bottom heaven to God, than perhaps this might offer some misty cloud to scarcely see through to an explanation for the allowance for human suffering on earth.

The tiers of heaven are arranged by the idea of God needing someone to keep him company or to appreciate the journey plan he has in store for mankind. Evidently Buddhists are appalled by this possibility of the creation of bedlam and misery to ensure God has worthy companionship, or receives the appreciation to help soothe his lonesome inferiority complex. Perhaps God himself suffered quite a bit at the hands of the God just one heaven above him, so He wants to create the trials and tribulations which will ensure, to his mind, that the heaven he rules is populated by sympathetic souls who are rich in suffering experience.

In some Gnostic belief systems God the Creator is somewhere between ignorant to outright evil, but, still at some point, this flawed God produces a son which helps beings in his heaven into the next heaven, or beings on the planet earth into the beginning of the heavenly journey. In this manner the wiser son and his rising followers also help the flawed God to heal his ignorance and evil. With the passage of time and growth in wisdom, earth and all the heavens become filled with the beauty and wonder of light and love.

Here on earth psychologically, children of ignorant, overbearing parents can sometimes move beyond the inculcated education of ignorance received from parental authority, and utilizing sensitive empathy skills can break a hurting destructive cycle of interaction. Making the break out of a cycle is a big step, and must be done again and again to improve the humane quality of the social environment. Thus the Gnostics come up with 365 heavens, but as you gentle reader can see, you can come up with the number and types of heavens you personally require to achieve a sunny disposition for most of the time.

Yes, suffering is an enormously difficult question, which I am not sure I can answer better than any of the other inspired or otherwise writers, but I guess, I'll give it a try. For starters, suffering in the world may not be solely due to human actions. No doubt mankind must take the bulk of responsibility for wars, poverty, pollution, and other manmade disasters, but in an effort to be complete, no doubt the occasional animal may play or tease a prey animal unmercifully, hunt a particular delicious prey animal into extinction and thoughtlessly pollute the drinking pond with animal waste products. Admittedly these other instances of suffering are pretty small potatoes in comparison, but if some other animal were to become the dominant super predator, than they might destroy the forest by eating all the leaves off the trees, as some scientists suggest as one possibility for the failure of dinosaurs.

However, unlike the ravenous dinosaurs of old, I like to believe, on my hopeful days, that God has built in a fail-safe for mankind which will prevent utter devastation to the planet and also provides some amount of comfort to the suffering humans. I am talking about the wonderful feats of invention and imagination which the human brain can muster as survival resources, real or imagined, when necessary. Personally, I do not like the fact that some portion of the human population is driven to imaginary fantasy material to make it through the day with or without the added benefit of mind altering drugs, but at the moment no one is consulting my wishes for a loving equality environment with a tolerance safety net.

Additionally, I am a firm believer that human beings granted access to physical, emotional, mental, and spiritual survival resources can be in themselves the Good Creator by Design for the environment on the planet earth, taking care of the humans and other species. Call me a dreamer, but I do feel this environmental possibility for structuring civilization is a tangible, achievable possibility. Given this possibility, which on my hopeful days is not too far into the future, I like to think that maybe, just maybe, a Supreme Being arranged for this amazing journey for mankind if man will only see the sense in pursuing love instead of competition.

It is right about now that I suspect people will start circling their index finger next to their ear whispering "loon" to one another, and perhaps one or two will search about helplessly for a strait jacket or the means to getting as far away as possible from my deluded self, but as long as I am trying to answer a to date impossible question, I will further assert that all the animals as well as humans have been granted access to heaven or the "good" after life already as compensation for having to wait for man to get his act together and get on the right page. God has forgiven everyone resorting to medicated lifestyles to mentally handle reality, and he has also forgiven the hyper competitive who make the environment so stressful and resource deprived, as well as everyone in between.

God is waiting and we will get there. Well, it is a bit thin, and no better than any other inspired material which asks believers to wait for the Second Coming or some other cheerful future event. Still, I hope, but I also caution the good gentle reader to enjoy his gift of life as much as possible and avoid senseless suffering. As stated earlier, I really do have trouble investing in an afterlife, but I suppose if you are going to have a benevolent Creator who undeniably has permitted all kinds of suffering to date, than I do not see any way around the solace and compensation of a remarkable afterlife as an explanation and encouragement.

Further, with the tremendously powerful God who is so vast in scope as to be unknowable, of course it really is impossible for me to assert my version of heaven with any serious conviction. Just as likely, there is some kind of plan which may or may not include an afterlife put in place by this Good Creator God, and I, along with everyone else, will simply have to take it on FAITH that God intends to ease my and everyone else's suffering in due course. Another stretch of the mental imagination I know, but I prefer a Good God to an evil or indifferent one.

I will add that embracing a benevolent Creator who supports love, tolerance, equality and a safety net, whether that entity is really there or not, will improve the atmosphere on the planet overall through stress reduction for the wealthy and poverty stricken alike. Given the alternatives, why not opt for a harmless nod of thanks to the human brain's ability to organize faith in human nature into a better society for all? You have at least one day a week to think about it.

SIX: Honor your father and your mother

Up until now with the sixth commandment, God's instructions have addressed the individual's relationship with God, the Universe, and to a degree society. The remaining commandments address the individual in ongoing relationships with others of a more personal, intimate nature. In consideration of these last commands the Golden Rule to "Do unto others as you would have done unto you" may prove useful.

The Golden Rule works best in regard to other people who you know from experience share a lot of like values and concluded wisdom.

171

This guideline can still be of use in other cases of diverse personalities, but in these instances a supplication for wisdom to know the difference between things within your abilities and those beyond is also applicable. Lastly, when you are considering events and interactions between yourself and almost total strangers, than a generous nod toward tolerance of enormous differences in outlook will be necessary.

One example which may come up fairly regularly is the interactions between large grocery/department store personnel and professional classes of doctors, lawyers, accountants and the like. Due to the vast differences in ongoing daily experiences these people are going to prefer different manners of handling situations. When professionals are interacting with other professionals within their same calling, the opportunity for misunderstandings to arise from misapplication of the Golden Rule are less likely than would occur between professionals from different fields. Innocent misunderstandings are still more likely between professionals and store clerks, manufacturing personnel, farm laborers and so forth.

Although I notice the modern tendency to label as a grave sin polite, mechanical interactions between various members of society with vastly differing backgrounds, nonetheless, the polite forms and etiquette do have a place in smoothing the waters when time to sit about ruminating and reflecting on others is unavailable due to pressing work demands. I suppose that if a person valued their interpersonal interactions as a means of networking or just enjoyed the artistry of a pleasant conversation with others from varying walks of life, after work one would take the time to think about the interaction events of the day and improve the quality if possible, or try to heal hurt wounds from perceived insensitivity.

The pursuit of power in networks, artistic pleasure, or healing would be the stimulator of contemplation of the outlook of others. Many try to tap into psychic abilities and forecast the directions others are headed in either consciously or unconsciously, determining that action which started out as artistic pleasure or healing may eventually morph into networking for power. I suspect most motivated artists of preparation realize early on that spontaneous human interaction is highly unsatisfactory material for crafting into what turns out to be fleeting and scarcely appreciated works of art, hence choosing to focus energies elsewhere.

As for healing, a person can improve their self-esteem and general understanding to the point where they fully grasp that the manner of chance acquaintances and total strangers has almost nothing to do with them personally. Having healed, they may feel they have to continue their pursuit of truth found in human interactions and discover the vast array of other possible motivations for continuing rude disruptive behavior found in coworkers.

This person engaged in a personal enlightenment journey, may conclude that networking in his current circumstances of harassment from coworkers is indeed a smart, survival oriented decision. These choices are naturally quite personal, but I imagine having a vast assortment of personal obligations in the form of wife, children, house and car payments have an impact on the final outcomes.

Making decisions guided by personal obligations rather than principles surrounding a solid work ethic supporting the much larger society, admittedly composed of nonexistent relationships which do not impact the individual to affect conscious decision making, damages the general work atmosphere. Eventually the work force reaches a point of production uncertainty and inefficiency, requiring more personnel, creating larger networks and more confusion. The cycle continues until the only way to return to a place without the power networks means jobs must be given to machines, staff totally replaced, and jobs shipped overseas or given to immigrants.

When trying to determine whether a healing journey will turn into networking for power, a look at the person in question's career and lifestyle choices will provide insight. Given the networking tendency which creates population growth, it is not altogether surprising that such a push toward the use of machinery to provide survival resources was initiated. Additionally, with the realization of the shared atmosphere on the planet, globalization has received an unsuspected aid via networking run amuck. People need food and shelter whether or not a group of people feel they are receiving a competitive wage.

Let us return to our busy professional who has never entertained the idea of not acting according to principle during work hours due to his career serving many people which brings consciously home every day the reason why principles are in place. This hungry professional arrives at the deli counter of the grocery store looking for a fresh vegetarian hoagie and right away, he/she is wondering where the menu is. Off in the near distance physically, but in terms of mental calculations the staff might as well be miles away, a group of deli counter personnel are having a discussion.

Remember, these very same deli counter workers feel in competition with the professional for obtaining equal treatment of their children at school, for providing massively advertised toys to their children who are influenced by other school fellows, for nice housing to provide a stimulating and healthy environment for their children, for medical care and attention for their children and an array of other incidentals some of which may be more selfish, but which will allow the parent to interact in a loving manner regularly with their children. You would not think competition would have such far reaching consequences throwing everyone into the competitive whirlpool together, but there you have it, they are all doing it for their children's respect and love.

Long ago via networking the deli counter workers have come to a mutual understanding to create a certain amount of necessary work and to always remember where important loyalties lie. One might suppose the nature of providing sandwiches on demand would require a level of excellence in service, but in the grocery store sandwiches are made for the cold display case, salads likewise are bundled up into containers, cakes chopped into single servings and soups divided into bowls serving two to four people. Only when a sandwich which does not appear in the display case is requested does the need for a menu and service of the moment arise.

If an industrious, or even a moderately motivated focused worker were to apply himself at the deli counter, it might be the case that during a shift comprised of this worker and others, only 3 people would be needed instead of 4. By a careful apportionment of interruptions, breaks, mishaps, and social discussion, an extra shift can be generated always, when not really necessary, compelling some amount of shiftlessness in workers whether they are comfortable with it or not.

Part of the difficulty lies in the management coming by creating the necessity for appearing gainfully and honestly fruitfully employed at all times. It is in fact part of management's fault, in that they can be unwilling to treat the workforce as individuals recognizing the differences various compositions of personnel might bring to any given shift which creates the zeal to produce the appearance veil of busyness.

Whatever the case, our crowd of socializing deli staff stand about in their discussion, perhaps they are drawing straws for who has to serve that stuck up professional so and so, and the hungry professional watches their mini party with distaste. When the decision is made about who will continue slicing cake, who will ladle soup, who will fill cold salad containers, and who will have to engage in a polite interaction with the person who looks like a professional snob, the losing deli worker walks up to the waiting starved professional and looks expectantly for some verbal directions. The professional is expecting some amount of courtesy, "Hello, how can I help you?" would be enough, but as I have mentioned in my other books, courtesy has been a modern day casualty of improving the environment in society. Hmm, go figure.

The survival instinct not to piss off someone higher in the hierarchy than you may have been supposed to buffer all social interactions by early social engineers. Survival instinct would be supposed to create social courtesy between those granted better access to resources, while fellow feeling and sympathy would provision the social courtesies in the cases of equal or lesser access to resources interactions. To some degree professionals are discouraged via the appearances of pettiness and felt shame against complaining about the less fortunate, unless extreme provocation is involved. Naturally creating justifying provocation is to be avoided and done so by testing the limits of rules and manners to determine the safety zone.

If the professional demonstrates an ease with not having to engage in fussy interaction with a service person, the service person is now free to feel insulted. If the professional tries to introduce social niceties into the interaction by starting with "Hello, how are you?" he is forcing his values on the service person and the service person is now free to feel insulted. Either way, since the professional is perceived as competition and the enemy, naturally, he cannot win or receive comfortable service, departing the store to some degree disgruntled. How much easier would even the smallest of chores be if all this competition could be bypassed with a tolerant, loving safety net of equality?

Applications of the Golden Rule in this instance would require the professional to have experience understanding of the deli clerk, waiting for the group to agree service is now due, and accepting the attitude and tone of interaction which is offered so as to get on with the matter. Otherwise, using mental reflection the professional concludes the wait for sandwich service might be revenge for clients of professionals waiting in crowded reception areas. Further he might decide that the deli workers prefer to stock the case with no interpersonal interactions with others creating interruptions, which professionals personally dislike. This result would lead to less need for deli personnel, a cut in hours and wages, and the need for even more disorder of work processes.

On the other hand, the deli clerk's application of the Golden Rule means they put their competitive feelings aside and provide helpful, friendly service, as they would like to receive after getting off a long shift on their feet all day. All the better if deli workers can understand that professionals must constantly respond to the changing environment of laws and knowledge, that since clients can grossly outnumber the professional, the professional winds up working longer hours than many

175

other types of workers, and for these reasons and perhaps others, really deserves in terms of inputted hours the pay he receives.

It may be the case that various classes of workers, deli and professional alike, recognize each other and hence the deli worker would offer a speed and quality of interaction to a fellow deli toiler otherwise not generally available. Once again unofficial choosing of teams to some degree heals competitive strife between people able to discern and act on differences, while creating larger rifts between various career niches. Bigoted mind you, but also still supportive of the mighty God of competition. How about the mighty God of equality? Any takers yet?

Professionals would argue that even competition has rules and using children as an excuse for ruining a personally labeled competitor's day is not sporting. Professionals, by their very nature, can be quite competitive because professional associations may limit the amount of professionals within any career niche and to attract the right kind of high paying clientele. If they feel competition is being introduced where it does not socially belong according to their ideas of good sportsmanship, then they can always choose to get dinner elsewhere altogether, bypassing the premade cold sandwiches, salads and soups.

Additionally they might inwardly fume that if they treated their clients to silent, unhelpful service after lingering in the waiting room for hours; they would be thus punished, feeling very righteous in their removal of business. Rarely do the professionals entertain the possibility of how the overwhelming environment of competition creating overpopulation is destroying social manners.

It is not possible for everyone to have experience understanding of each other's situations, and it is a little unreasonable to ask for this amount of ongoing reflection on a daily basis along with providing a solid work performance. To return to the point of everyone having the same experiences naturally, most technology would have to be discarded and we would have to return to a much simpler lifestyle. Out of the most intense necessity, populations would be winnowed due to the deficit in survival resources which a return to nature would certainly cause.

Wouldn't it be better to have some basic interaction guidelines and etiquette in place and let warm good feelings do the rest? Rather than bespattering courtesy with negative labels of generating mechanical, cold, impersonal interactions, dispose of the competitive vertical hierarchy. The arrival of a loving equality social environment would afford many warm sunny dispositions without requiring everyone be under each other's skin, leading to a diversity and spontaneity in available social interactions quite naturally and pleasantly.

Basically in applying the Golden Rule, a person must put aside all competitiveness, resentments, favoritism and other damage promoting emotions arising in yourself or which you imagine may arise in others. Embrace and encourage any tendency or circumstance which creates generous fellow feeling for helping others whose needs actually permit the professional service provider or other type of service provider access to survival resources and a higher quality of life.

Worries about creating resentments in others can lead social interactions astray as well, causing confusion and distance. I suppose some would prefer this confusion and distance to warm but fairly orchestrated interactions, but I expect many of these creators of isolation are social predators whose needs are served by having some portion of the population confused, distanced, and weakened by loss of human contacts in their life.

Otherwise, a man may not be sure whether he should open the door graciously for a lady because she may be too liberated to appreciate the gesture. What should he do? Open the door anyway and let the lady inform him that she would prefer to get the door herself. In the future a man can then, with more complete information, properly apply the Golden Rule. Of course, opening the door for several chance ladies who travel the same route as our gracious gentleman, he may forget when one tells him to treat her like a man, but, our lady can always arrange to open the door for him on occasion if she is concerned being helped by a man on a daily basis in the most simple of manners will impact her continuing independence.

I wonder if a liberated woman were to find herself exiting the Post Office or Grocery store with many packages otherwise busying her hands and perhaps blocking her vision, if she would not appreciate a helping hand? Would this liberated woman only want help from another woman? Would she expect the men duly chastised and educated with the previous male insensitivity to female independence to somehow recognize when a real need is present and yield up the help when a clear neediness was in evidence? Would it perhaps be better to limit the liberation movement to where it belongs, in the career market and job place, rather than expecting the whole of social etiquette to be reformed in the correcting of this specific situation?

It seems to me the mechanical interactions are being moved and changed in this instance rather than disposed of altogether. Instead of opening the door as a matter of course, men must not open the door as a matter of course. Only if a woman is demonstrating a clear situation of requiring help, may a man risk offering a gracious gesture, which will actually be more in the vein of a helping hand rather than a polite nod of social manners, and I guess, not so infected with the virus of mechanical coldness. As you can see gentle reader, it takes time and effort to sort the possibilities out.

If a man fails to recognize the need for door opening when in the midst of a more vital situation, he is now guilty of not being in the moment, being mechanically shut off, or in his own little world of private musings and considerations. Since the fellow is not getting little injections of warm fuzzies into his day via the mechanical social niceties often infused with genuine kindness, he may choose to follow the modern directives to be less impersonal, insincere and mechanical by enjoying the odd day dream along the path to get coffee or whatever. Using some part of consciousness for a day dream he fails to open the door for a package laden woman or even a man simply because he is no longer on the alert for little opportunities to provide help and enjoy the positive vibes which come from good fellow feelings.

I find the new arrangement a little queenly or kingly if someone prefers. The new expectation is for men, and I suppose women, to be on the alert in every moment to provide the right type of social interaction to any chance encounter by assessing needs and delivering the right comments and actions. It is absurd and bordering on the impossible. Personally, I find it offensive, and I do not want everyone trying to get too personal with me and then experiencing some amount of insult when I choose not to behave as an open book in an otherwise hyped up competitive hierarchy environment.

More likely, what starts out on the surface as a call to making interactions more personal and rewarding is actually a means of balancing the completely unbalanced vertical hierarchy with a cheap band aid. Social engineers constantly surveying the health of the social environment within the health destroying vertical hierarchy noted the lower classes are suffering from a sense of powerlessness, so removing expected social courtesies from the lower class rule book will give them a sense of power, meaningless power mind you, but a sense of power which will not create problems for the social engineers by giving the lower class any real power, which alarms leadership already grossly undermined by advancing technology.

While enjoying the power to be rude and offended by anyone placed higher in the hierarchy, the new lower class little kings and queens, like men being shorn of the niceties of polite gestures to ladies, will be robbing themselves of opportunities to gather small warm fuzzies. In a service providing day, these fuzzies can accrue to a nice little nest egg, as any embezzling accountant of pennies can tell you.

On the other hand, in response, professionals are doing their part to isolate themselves from offensive interaction, creating the environment for removal of survival resources and shortening of stress induced rigidified lower class lives. Like the sociopathology in Capitalist economics, cracking a few eggs to make an omelet is okay, as is the sacrificing of life span for the lower class which is desirable from the social engineers point of view to always have an environment nimble and open to necessary change.

Somewhere along the line a person gets exposed to these ideas, necessarily comes up with them on their own, or suffers in helpless anger and rage even if a person is extremely wealthy, although the presence of abundant material goods allows some amount of helpful healing in most cases. Parents, educators, siblings, and good friends are supposed in the many tales of creative storytelling to be the shapers of personalities, always sifted through the individuals very own unique set of attributes which are no doubt also a product of these influences, perhaps on a more subconscious level. I would like to add in the effects of loving animal relationships also as influencing a person's ability to get in touch with their gentle, sympathetic nature.

In summary, people crossing your path on a daily basis may be interested in pleasant social exchanges for the sake of creating a pleasant social environment generally, or as likely, given the overwhelming emphasis on competition and the presence of growing numbers of population, are competitors searching for an edge or a prize to take back to an interested competitor or population winnower. The people who do bestow real help and wisdom into your life are to be treasured, no matter who they are. Given the need for two parents in the work place in modern times, or in the earliest times death in child birth and general early mortality, the people historically who do offer support to the individual may be parents, or could easily be other persons.

Usually those people who consistently seek you out in preference to others and other activity actually like and enjoy your company. Desiring the continuation of the relationship, these people will take steps to insure your continued survival in a real, practical manner. At some point ongoing associations do impact reputations, creating some amount of shared interest in maintaining the upstanding public character of those who regularly populate a daily routine. Unless other pressing factors of creating an image for the competitive appearance game make a showing, most people do try and behave sincerely when approaching others in an ongoing manner to establish friendships. Still, be sensible enough to realize that anyone can retract their companionship if they feel threatened by association with another person who has suffered negative labeling; it is simply a fact of life.

SEVEN: Do not murder

Well, it seems pretty simple. In real life few have actually seen a real dead body although everyone has witnessed countless staged murders in TV shows, movies, video games, books and other media. On the one hand the human race in high standard of living nations is somewhat desensitized to pretend death without actually witnessing real death, or real horrifying situations. As stated in my earlier books, it is these fascinations with extreme events which do not come up in most people's everyday experience which, in my opinion, prevents these same consumers of this type of fascination from seeing the smaller, but no less deadly mini-deaths/murders which do skate through their existence on a regular basis.

Creating the toxic work environment which forces the productive non-networkers to feel unwanted or to outright lose the appearance game due to crafty manipulation of work performances by others may not be quick, swift murder, however, it can begin the rusting process and destruction of this productive person's reputation. Others at new work places can take advantage of previous mayhem to a reputation in supporting all erroneous labeling efforts to a solid productive work ethic oriented employee. Given enough of these craftily executed brandings, and a person's reputation is effectively destroyed in order to support entrenched network inefficiency.

Those with destroyed reputations may not be the victims of vicious serial killers who wipe out their victims in a matter of hours or days, but the time frame and number of people involved is the only difference. It is only a matter of time before the person begins to succumb to the health impacts of stress at being negatively labeled to create superiority motivation, fear motivation, cruelty relief motivation, and other motivations in the competitive hierarchy work environment. It may take several pickers and choosers in various work places to destroy a person's good appearances and reputation, but in time, the repetition of a lie, any lie, begins to take on a life and assumed truth all its own.

Since most people occupy neutral territory, being the solid pillars of stone supporting society, they have no idea about the appearance game enacted by the pickers and choosers for management officially, or unofficial leadership and networks within the working environment. If through some misfortune they begin to see through the appearance game veil, the observant run the risk of betraying their new knowledge through their actions if they do not wisely attempt to mask the presence of this new wisdom. Otherwise, those with no experience to contradict the lessons taught by parents of good people vs. bad people readily believe that some people are naturally good, while others are naturally bad. See my first and second books for further elaboration of this phenomenon.

Thus, when the Bible speaks of murder, I believe the Bible is addressing all manners of consciously dealing health damage for individual gain, in support of networked favorites, or in support of networked power. Eventually the unnecessary stresses to health lead to physical, mental, emotional, and spiritual impairment and the impairment's consequences, shortened life, less enjoyable life experience, and in the worst cases, the hastening by the individual himself of his own death by injurious behavior to gather limited rewards in destructive abundance which are still available for the socially damaged, but living person to collect.

As I have stated on numerous occasions, I do believe that the best manner to go about life is to share the enjoyment of the gift of life equally among the planet population. By controlling population numbers via birth rate where necessary, humans will keep survival resources in abundance preventing all types of murder. Obviously the presence of the seventh commandment's continued popularity and its presence in one form or another in the majority of popular religions means I am not entirely alone in this belief.

Due to the history of the planet riddled with instances of wars, population relocations leading to genocides, concentration and internment camps and other atrocities carried out by leadership, leadership supporters, and the citizenry benefitting from these actions, the smaller telltale events leading up to these massive executions get lost in the panic and sensory overload from attention diverting spectacles.

The work place injustices previously outlined are a portion of the indicating events. As any good student of the Bible will tell you, the book of Revelations is filled with many other warning signs. Whatever does happen in terms of further atrocities may or may not be available for public consumption in the future due to better control of appearances, just as work place mislabeling can now take place rather easily with few any the wiser to the underlying chain of calculated events.

Future purges may not be carried out according to race, religion, sexual orientation or mental health status, but according to who has the least skill in networking, that is the least interest in power over others. Admittedly, these grossly unfortunate events are not a result of human evil, but a result of humans failing to accurately describe the problem of overpopulation. The solution is biting the bullet, and informing everyone that for the sake of the world, the sake of the human race, the sake of the ability to enjoy a love filled environment, limit offspring to at most one child. If possible, substitute in some other activity to fulfill emotional, mental, and spiritual rewards.

As for heaven, I personally like to think that even the most poisonous of evil toadstools whose mental apparatus has rotted due to stressful competition within the artificial vertical hierarchy will be forgiven. This attitude may not be particularly glamorous, and there are few portraits of the forgivers walking lightly and breezily on their toes while gracefully carrying a bouquet of flowers rather than a machine gun, but still, perhaps this popular imagery can be replaced by the flower tenders and happily dancing couples enjoying the opportunity to cooperatively enjoy their sensitivity to each other and background music.

In my opinion it is up to humans to exercise their free will to mold the atmosphere on the planet to realistically allow an individually wonderful experience. Flights of imagination can come up with all types of divisions and excuses for placing some in vertical slots of preference, but I suggest skipping these particular flights of imagination and plumping for equality, love, and a tolerance safety net which includes absolutely everyone. No murder supported by imaginary criteria.

EIGHT: Do not commit adultery

We all make promises of undying friendship, continued attraction, permanent employment, employment with growth potential, unswerving devotion or constant fellowship. For those who are very young without much guidance and protection from the larger social networked environment, a person might look like a flighty butterfly unable to make up their mind as to long term lifestyle decisions. In reality, this person might be quite happy with any job that lands on their plate, for instance, except their network associates are not powerful enough to allow this person to attain the status which permits a permanent spot, and the person themselves does not want to step over moral lines, though many are not asked to participate in the job duty of dirty work to attain a more permanent standing.

Likewise, a person might flit about from church to church trying to find a place which feels comfortable, without requiring too great a leap of faith into clearly defined dogma which makes little true to life sense. Additionally, a person filled with the romantic visions available in media entertainment may bite off considerably more than they can chew in a young moment of passion, only later to find what a big mistake they have made and the extent of bad of advice to be followed in media material.

Lastly, some people following questionable advice from others make bad decisions about the type of long term friendships which will suit them by using networking criteria rather than shared temperament and interests.

The eighth commandment is pleading for people to be careful with each other's self-image and public image. In the presence of confusing advice which is not fully explained or fully digested through reflection by the consumer, association mishaps take place. These mishaps can simply mean beginning an acquaintanceship and moving too fast so as to miss the overall incompatibility of the parties participating in the budding bond. Mistakes are human however, and must be tolerated and even encouraged since learning usually takes place.

Although I have included additional types of relationships to the marriage relationship usually the sole focus of the eighth commandment, I feel that all public social connections are important and have some bearing on social happiness. When a person accepts a job offer, the hiring manager and new employee may not exchange vows of willingness to work exhaustively to make the employment contract last, but, ideally, both parties should do their best. When a person moves from job to job, he must present a list of all his past jobs plus references. Is the romantic searcher so encumbered?

Imagine a man handing a list of his past romantic attachments to a possible woman who is free to and perhaps even expected to check up on the references for the last few encounters. There may be fodder for a rollicking romantic comedy there, but taken seriously, well, it could get rather messy rather fast. This practice has not received consideration to help with the blossoming divorce rate because of the possibility for absolute social mayhem.

A man calls up his new lady friend's last three lovers, gets the low down on the important stuff, will she cheerfully engage in his favorite sexual acts, and then proceeds to find out why they left her, gathering the ready justification of why he can break up with her at some future date. This line of questioning is taken by cads in the romantic department and equally, by cads in the work place. In the workplace the questions during job reference checks are will this person tow networking lines, do dirty work, and the excuses for previous dismissals.

Legally, hiring managers cannot ask the above types of questions, but like many laws requiring the weaker party feel sufficiently empowered and enraged to initiate the application process, the laws are generally ignored because managers do not feel threatened with being caught and subjected to due process in the current age of much graver offences needing attendance, not to mention the difficulty of proof. Romantically, there is no impediment to background checks of all kinds, some of which do actually take place.

The feared social mayhem is not so much the background checks leading to cunning seductions, so much as the background checks leading to fewer trial liaisons. Given the bell curve and the appearance game, the more people with romantic failure notches on their belt, the easier for pickers and choosers in the environment to come up with a satisfactory label and apply it where needed.

If women knew in advance that their prospective sweetie would be demanding non-mutually satisfying sexual activity regularly while orchestrating the exact same type of departure as her previous marriage hopefuls, she would likely forego the experience altogether. The severely curtailed sexual pool for the men would make them destructive and unhappy while making negative labels for the discriminating ladies more difficult to apply.

Strictly in terms of the marriage contract, men and women are not to take sexual partners after they have exchanged vows with each other not to before God. In my experience, however, many choose the open marriage contract and others engage in a satisfying game of apology and forgiveness allowing the forgiving partner to experience an amount of relationship security due to their willingness to permit dalliances other partners might frown upon heavily. Whatever the case, if the partner being cheated upon does not feel the need to be enormously disturbed by partner's infidelities, then, in my opinion the only other person with any say in the matter is the third wheel, consulting made agreements with the married flirt.

Starting from God wanting everyone to enjoy their gift of life, the first fact impacting the sexual market is there are always more women than men, meaning that not everyone can smartly partner off into acceptable little boy/girl units. If the "misery loves company thing" is supposed to and does offer enough companionable solace to the ladies who will never be allowed sexual access to a man unless she marries one, than I suppose the social engineers via religion might have had a workable plan.

Long ago, however, this plan was doomed to failure for many reasons, not the least of which was extra women are still hungry for food, shelter, and emotional, mental, and spiritual experiences of some kind which must somehow be addressed and fulfilled outside of the marriage bond. All kinds of things were attempted, convents, brothels, professions like secretary, sales girl, nurse, teacher, and so forth which gave women a place by their own efforts of employment rather than dependence on the man they snared in the race to marriage.

Naturally when the options for single ladies were less attractive than being married, women bickered and brawled over the available men like women in the basement sales at Filenes and other department stores. However, with time and the gleanings of the preventable tragedies from overpopulation on the horizon, new possibilities were opened for women through advancing technology so jobs would not necessarily have to be taken from men, allowing women to decide if the necessity of marriage to any man who would take them was absolutely necessary after all. In addition to avoiding population increases by the most ill-suited of couples simply trying to avoid the worst social stigmas, these new job positions humanely allowed both men and women to opt for a more tolerable single status when they could not find themselves paired with a person they were actually physically comfortable with.

The granter of the gift of life and leadership, in their best most secure moments do want everyone adequately taken care of and happily supportive of the works provisioning for everyone. The ladies permitted careers with occasional liaisons may feel as rewarded as those who choose a man they like, respect, and feel physically comfortable with to support via domestic engineering. It is a matter of personal choice, but the error to be avoided is misleading others as to intentions in any market, marriage, job, friendship, or otherwise.

Betrayals of any kind destroy trust and love in the social environment. If God is watching I am sure he recognizes the losses taking place regularly by those trying to cheat others or simply gather a rare moment of bliss in an otherwise empty life experience. As with any type of misguided behavior or toadstool the Almighty is no doubt forgiving due to the incredibly stupid error of the artificial vertical hierarchy overwhelming the social environment which He personally had nothing to do with, and which otherwise is everyone's fault, whether they know it or not.

In regard to betrayals, always remember not to betray yourself. Much like learning to love yourself, it is the first step in being able to treat others with kindness, honesty, and sympathetic understanding. Many religions belittle self-love as being a person's main obstacle to spiritual communion with the entities in the great beyond, whatever they turn out to be. Again, accuracy in describing and defining the problem is more at issue in this case.

Whether an individual man or mankind ever gets in touch with the enormous power and intelligence behind this great Cosmos, in my opinion, has nothing to do with whether a given individual senselessly sacrifices his health in a wasteful manner to make the presence of the artificial vertical hierarchy appear credible. What does happen when a person sacrifices some portion of health in a personal betrayal is this person now expects others to make the same foolhardy mistake and personal betrayal. It is a destructive cycle which only serves to reinforce the misleading appearance of natural competitive vertical hierarchy, the destroyer of equality, tolerance, love, a safety net and most importantly, enjoying life, the reason for being here.

Humans have been given an amazing brain which allowed our species to move beyond absolute competitive survival demands fairly early on. In order to enjoy the easing of this burden we must choose not to continue betraying ourselves through self-inflicted sacrifices, creating the pain and mental blocks to higher truths and clear thinking. We can unwisely turn our backs on the wonderful granted gift of life, trading it in for power over others as a weak substitute for personal control, but like the directive not to turn your back on an all-powerful God, turning your back on the generous gift of life wherever it came from, amounts to about the same thing, reduced quality of life experience on all fronts, physical, emotional, mental, and spiritual.

NINE: Do not steal

Stealing is to take away without right or permission according to the first definition in The American Heritage Dictionary. Traditionally stealing refers to property, a pair of sunglasses, a car, an intellectual design for computer technology, the characters and plot of a copyrighted story, and other materials which amount to actual survival resources or access to survival resources.

Less traditionally, isolation of an individual through limited resources can also amount to some amount of theft when robbing them of enhancing life experiences. Of course, if a person does not notice that they have been robbed of a particular lifetime experience, for example killing another person, has this person been robbed of life experience? What if the person would not want to participate in that experience even if the opportunity was handed to them on a silver platter, has this person been robbed?

Materially speaking, some people have 20 houses, 50 cars, a couple of boats, planes and other assorted travelling devices. If a bicycle were to disappear from such a person's stable of vehicles without the owner actually noticing, has a theft taken place? Is this act comparable to a tree falling in the woods in the absence of a listening ear?

Technically, if the police do not get informed by a wronged citizen, the theft does not receive official recognition. Consulting some of the teachings by Jesus in the Bible, a man or woman has committed adultery if they have looked upon another member of the opposite sex with lustful thoughts, so, no doubt the religious view is that a theft has taken place even if the person is only thinking about how nice it would be to cover 10 miles on a bike rather than on foot, prompted by a bike rack full of unused and unlocked bicycles.

If someone were to come into my house and help themselves to a few of my hats, would I consider the act a theft or a THEFT? Naturally, the hats I handmade personally putting in over 30 hours of focused crafting skill are more valuable than a hat I picked up for .50¢ at the thrift store, or so I think at this particular moment of musing on the issue. Further musing might reveal that through regular use and many compliments I am actually rather attached to my thrift store special and would feel equally aggrieved on both occasions.

There is a lot of psychological speak out there about violation of territory being the worst trauma in such an experience, leaving the victim feeling insecure, utterly unsafe and deprived of his sense of things being right in the world in his previously tranquil little retreat from encroaching outside intrusions. Given the ongoing invasion of privacy I have been subjected to by every person, organization or company availing themselves of the excuse of responsibility for others under their protective umbrella, where does this privacy loss leave the theft issue?

I suppose I am not meant to know that my privacy has been utterly compromised and continues being compromised on a regular basis. Perhaps the fact that quite a lot of people are reported as being privacy deprived is anticipated to provide the "misery loves company" thing, or that realizing the dangers from terrorist madmen would make me feel even a larger security loss/theft from the media loving terrorists if no one was doing anything about the heavily reported acts. Seems like a simple commandment, but clearly, it is quite complicated.

Looking at theft as an economic act, a person steals a loaf of bread to eat when starving, a person in drought ridden Africa tries to steal money via an internet scam to pay for food reportedly available for purchase by anyone with the funds, a person does a dine and dash at a fancy restaurant when they have enough cash for regular simple fare such as beans and rice, or a person hijacks a truck of frozen meals to sell himself at cut rate prices to all takers. These acts do not all look the same, but in the strictest black and white terms, they are all theft, and in the earliest of times, treated as such.

Nowadays soup kitchens and food banks leave very few people with the limited option of stealing to eat. Additionally, most areas have some kind of Food Stamp program where funds are provided by the State or Federal Government. We have come a long way baby from the times when the theft of bread meant life imprisonment, but reading the paper and the internet it is easy to see we could slip back into cruelty ignorance via artificially induced survival resource shortages at any time.

Given these helping organizations, the theft of bread by a homeless person is still looked on very negatively and unsympathetically. Although many in the United States of America have access to food, the quality of food banks and free meals varies considerably with talk of reductions in services to bologna sandwiches. Food Stamps have exclusionary loop holes as well as the ongoing threat of being discontinued all the time. The addition of these realities blurs the commandments black and white lines considerably.

There are many helping organizations for people in nations short of food, creating similar parallels to the above outline, but also additional difficulties. The situation in a country separated by land masses and oceans is complicated by the fact that often donated goods become goods for sale once again in corrupt hands or hands trying to keep the benevolent cloud of philanthropy donor over the leading heads in receiving nations, rather than the actual original nation of production, confusing the whole theft issue once more. Leadership in any nation wants to appear effective and the source of survival resources for their peoples in one manner or another.

It is hard to justify a dine and dash. A person who has enough to eat with the opportunity to enjoy some amount of variety if he applies himself to acquiring culinary skill should not feel the need to resort to stealing food from a fancy restaurant, right? With the proper care a person can apply himself to making adequate substitutions for the more expensive ingredients, and check helpful books and videos out of the library. Admittedly dinner in a fancy restaurant is a luxury good designed to create competition for the emotional and physical rewards which accompany this exclusive indulgence.

The people in attendance at that fancy restaurant have the expectation of being surrounded by other people with equal easy access to monetary resources, feeling safe and relaxed in an environment unlikely to reveal predators hiding behind the ice bucket or sitting at the next table. Although the presence of the artificial vertical hierarchy does a pretty good job of masking the nature of the situation involving various sorts of restaurants, the presence of restrictive resources is comparable to segregation of people into what is imagined to be separate but equal resorts of culinary delight.

In most cases the personal choice to go to an all-night breakfast and pancake spot is not considered improved by the average "breakfast all day" fan by thoughts of rich, unusual European Food to be had elsewhere at more expense. However, every so often a person with the same amount of resources as the "breakfast all day" folks comes along and wants to see what all the fuss is about.

Add in the folks who just want to get out of the house, and why not go somewhere unusual to spice up an otherwise unchanging landscape, and the population of dine and dashers starts to take shape not as absolute low down cheaters, but as civil rights protesters wanting an opportunity to enjoy enriching culinary and cultural experiences like other attendees. Obviously there are cheaters looking to get a free meal as well, but I caution the gentle reader to consult my first and second book regarding the bell curve, the appearance game, and blackmailing coercion before shutting the book on the lives of the perceived cheaters absolutely.

Then, there are the people who pull off enormous capers, taking incredible risks, and thus, achieving incredible profits. Sounds like I am talking about innovative Capitalists, but I am actually talking about my last theft example where a bandit steals a truck of delicious frozen meals. Like Robin Hood of old, perhaps our reckless bandit is stealing frozen meals from what he imagines is a large company who can use the theft as a tax write off, and selling the food at heavily reduced prices to people with little disposable income making for himself a modest profit. Win, win, win. Well, who can argue with that? Social engineers in favor of their system of arranging the civilization environment which clearly states in law and commandment, do not steal, that's who.

Somehow or other, a means of distribution of survival resources which keeps people satisfied with the civilization structure has to be conceived and executed. If at some point the structure breaks down and a small number of relatively useless individuals goes without, creating some minor private innovations and small discrepancies to anticipated allotments of resources, as long as things basically seem to be humming along, the design and plan are effective. Any morale loss felt by witnesses can be dealt with in media entertainment by remaking a modern version of Robin Hood which helps people address the lack of official interest in crime and other seemingly unfair events.

Who knows for sure? I do know that economics and religion are all about motivating people to participate in a society which departed from overall equality quite some time ago by having a person compete for his rewards outright or via cooperative competition. Practically, to keep the works from blowing up, the person's desires match up with the point at which he no longer feels too great a sting at not getting the higher level of anticipated reward from won competitions because the individual starts losing. The individual's desire to keep himself at a certain level of desirable comfort keeps him in continued striving to achieve whatever goal completion is his allotment at his level of competitive skill.

Not surprisingly, a person who does feel he has been cheated in societal rewards may resort to stealing, at least, the meaningful life experience of others and the mental clarity and calmness which allows solid good judgment, keeping the content of theft within the law, while achieving a set of substitute rewards to the lost anticipated ones for the unhappy loser. Again, in terms of practicality within the artificial vertical hierarchy, this person, to improve his perceived deficient rewards will feel the need to reduce the happiness of those below him on the hierarchy ladder, a safer proposition than attempting further losing competition with those above.

Destroying the emotional, mental and spiritual value of rewards for those below makes the disgruntled failure's position appear and feel better. I am pretty sure economists ignore this issue, and the religious people probably address it with the ninth commandment, do not steal; in this case, do not steal other people's meaningful explanations for life events and calm mental state.

Given the vertical competitive nature of Capitalist economics, a strict interpretation of the ninth commandment is not my favorite tool for making decisions. I prefer the Golden Rule, doing unto others as you would have done unto you. How would I feel if my apartment was regularly used as an unofficial supply store justified by my being otherwise deemed generally useless? Granted I have a lot of hats, clothes, jewelry, books, and craft supplies.

If someone in the National Security Association or some other lesser protective body official or unofficial checking to make sure I have not finally turned the mental bend by amassing guns and bombs, searching through my apartment finds some craft supplies that I seem too busy to use and rehomes them, how would that make me feel? Not great I can tell you. Sure I have plenty of stuff and most likely no one thought I would miss a small scrap of material I picked up at a thrift store for .50¢, but I do.

I did have plans for that piece of cloth and I am annoyed it is gone. Am I going to go about planning the destabilization of the western world via horrific mayhem because of this loss? No. Does that make the theft okay? Economists might classify this loss as within acceptable bounds since no consequences to people who might actually get quite upset with economists for oversights has occurred. Is the theft within the Golden

Rule? Perhaps the person that took that cloth thought it would not or did not bother them when a similar disappearance took place amongst their goods in bountiful supply.

Since there is a call by some religions and civic engineers to make others conform to the prevailing ethic in society which bestows benefits on all peoples living under the umbrella of that ethic rather than out in the middle of a beast ridden jungle, the apartment surveyor might also consider it a duty to perform the odd lesson teaching moment here and there prompted by personal convenience temptations. Forgetting that for many the nature of the artificial competitive hierarchy still means a jungle atmosphere, beasts and all, for the poorer members of civilization, the surveyor completes his self-appointed instruction errand smugly.

The problem with this course of action is that since the apartment surveyor cannot be on hand to teach the lesson personally, or leave a little study guide, both of which would provide actual proof of privacy invasion, the lesson which I actually draw from having some of my material pilfered is not the lesson intended for the teaching moment along the lines of being overall less materially oriented and sharing surplus materials I am not going to use. Instead, I gather the information that privacy invasion has escalated to the occasional small theft of property, probably in the hopes of going undetected.

At the risk of destroying some personal meaning which will not be balanced out by mood improvements from my version of a teaching moment I would say that since this security person has chosen to be available for security work and feels an amount of support from their employment which engages the majority of their action time, their crafting activity does not mean as much to them as it means to me, making their ability to apply the Golden Rule from a personal viewpoint uncertain. Additionally, the creation of elaborate justifications for destructive behavior to others does not provide a meaning protection shield from disillusionment by the ill-used furious.

A more helpful way to apply the Golden Rule is for a person considering lifting an item not belonging to them, no matter the value or whether the loss will be detected or not, to ask himself how he would feel if an important personal item of their very own were to be callously removed? Even with a prayerful request for an infusion of wisdom, a person cannot know how the value of any particular item in a personal collection of lifetime acquisitions will be construed, best to be on the safe side and assign it a very high value, leaving it alone.

If you want something which belongs to someone else, ask them. It may well be the case they will give you a part or that entire .50¢ piece of cloth. Using this time honored practice you will get what you want, you will get to thank the giving person, both parties will benefit from the interaction, and the actual goal of supporting the fabric of civilization will be achieved. Win, win, win.

Gentle reader you are no doubt shaking your head about my obsessive focus on crafting material. It was after all a .50¢ piece of cloth in an acquired stash. Why haven't I moved on? Was it the escalating loss of security and privacy invasion, or was it something more? Was it the future meaning of the completed craft once I had finished my project? In other words, was it the dreams I had attached to that piece of cloth? Would it be wise for humans to start judging the content of supportive dreams which allow for enormous screw ups in the economic plans of survival resource distribution to pass through the goal posts, scraping a win out of the Capitalist economic system, for example?

Strictly in terms of stabilizing society, generally we cannot go around ripping dreams apart even if the dreams erroneously support an economic system which has apparent resounding success due to the frauds of the appearance game. Too many people would be reduced to confusion, uncertainty, and unwitting destructive behavior caused by the loss of their personal social compass, adding in more damage to the already ailing social environment. Even though some destroyers are unable to manufacture any satisfactory dream material of their own short of derailing other people's hopes, a more peaceful solution will work while still allowing for progress.

The peaceful solution which I am advocating is a move toward an equality environment regarding access to survival resources emphasizing tolerance, love and a safety net. You have heard it all before, but I would add this solution will continue to allow technological progress which is of such great importance to those whose self-esteem is tied to mental challenges.

It is the case that the mental challenges people feel insecure rather easily unless things are changing all the time or problems are arising requiring their particular strengths and skill sets. In an effort to improve society, we do not want them to feel robbed of their future, dreams, and positive life experiences. It wouldn't be fair, just as it would be unfair to expect the continued loss of these items for others deemed less valuable during the current times of uncertainty, technological expansion reducing human jobs, and overall expansion of employee pool to embrace all people in the world.

Over the long years of human development, the march of history and changes has created a social environment which now requires all serious mental challenges to impact more than just one person looking for something fun to do. In terms of expense, these challenges involve precise, complicated measuring instruments which perform ongoing scientific inquiries or the challenges require the creation of computer circuit boards. The economic question of cost in resources is daunting indeed.

Admittedly, the hobbyist at home can build a home computer or telescope, but for a mental challenges person to be integrated into the larger social environment, his mental challenges have to be guided by and provide for society in some manner, just as everyone else's employment generally does. However, when the mental challenges people set to work, their finished production efforts overhaul the social environment through the new inventions wide spread deployment and capacity to perform feats of manufacture and study. Clearly society benefits, but some might argue that quite a lot of meaning is lost, or perhaps stolen, when technology is assimilated into the environment in such a manner as to create further steepening inclines in the artificial vertical competitive hierarchy.

How can we prevent this meaning theft to those adjusting to the implementation of new technology? To the degree that technological advancement has meant the generation of security, interest, purpose and meaning by superiority and ego feelings at being mentally gifted, how can those losses to meaning be preserved and not stolen? Through the recognition that all exercise of skillfully acquired gifts of any type is a gift to society deserving reward, meanings of all types can be preserved.

Society infused with an equality ethic will allow all to enjoy optimally their gift of life. Perhaps minor thefts from others in rare moments of unspecified spontaneous need may occur. For example, a .50¢ piece of cloth destined to play a rather small part in a person's dreamscape when they are otherwise able to participate fully in a gift of life right here in the moment, may disappear from a collected stash. My guess is, more likely, surveillance personnel will be generally less tempted, if the need for this type of employment diffused throughout society is still necessary when people feel like vital, included members in their culture they have a definite interest in preserving.

Most people should not steal when taken care of via secure survival resources and I would be surprised to find that any of these people chose to do so without some prompting mental imbalance or coercion from an outside source. Given the presence of the hierarchy, some people are actually expected to go without and eventually will give into the temptations of theft simply to get a meal in some cases, providing the visible set of bad guys needed to lend the hierarchy credibility. As stated before, equality and secure provision of resources would make all the difference.

TEN: Do not testify falsely against your neighbor

Okay, I admit, my summary explanation of the tenth commandment gets a little carried away and I put quite a few words into God's mouth. Sorry. However, regarding the words I did not put into God's mouth, I stand by those as being basically true.

It is unwise to speak all manner of garbage, rubbish, and lies, but that does not stop most people from going ahead and doing just that, at least to the people located below them in the vertical competitive hierarchy. Lies, unfortunately, are everywhere, like the atmosphere, you take a step you land in listening range of ten lies. What can a person do?

Besides the lies from obvious competitors for the same resources in stocking a desirable appearance appealing to others, there are the abundant lies informing consumers about the benefits of products, behaviors, attitudes, and mental reasoning practices. Indeed, perhaps, I am not being completely fair.

All lies do have a grain or two of truth. Gentle reader, it is for the consumer of spoken and written words to sift the proclamations and determine just what truth is to be found in the presented material. Generally the buried truth is not the obvious statement of information which most people are expected to make as their spontaneous immediate conclusion.

Are the lies of advertising and marketing the "false testimony against your neighbor" of the tenth commandment? Most advertisers and marketers calculatingly refrain from any mention of competitors lest a busy, addled consumer trying to multitask unnaturally get the message garbled and identify some other cereal producer as having the best breakfast food. What a waste of advertising dollars that would be!

No doubt a particular brand of breakfast cereal is highly desirable and perhaps the best overall food for a certain segment of the population, but it may also be the case that the laudatory statement is edited not to include qualifiers such as the best breakfast cereal made from the flaking process using a recipe for 40% corn, 40% wheat and 20% rice. In addition to being the best cereal of this type, it may be the only cereal since the recipe is patented. Who knows? The advertising second is expensive and consumer attention spans are short the manufacturing company would argue in defense of their promotional statements.

Technically, the letter of the tenth commandment refers to running around gossiping about your neighbors and acquaintances to others, ruining their reputation and perhaps creating official trouble for them as well. In much earlier times, before everyone's life experience content radically departed from being very similar overall, this spirit of do not lie was all that was needed to be specified in the actual letters of the commandment.

Now a day, a more broad encompassing statement of "Do not lie" is needed to cover the vast number of ways mischief can be created through rubbish communication in the social environment. Simply stated, as with betrayals, murder and theft, lies destroy the portions of the social environment supportive to love, trust, and sympathetic understanding of each other which would allow a cooperative, equality social environment to function as effectively, more effectively even, than the current vertical hierarchy rife with waste.

Since lies are often calculated to act as precursors to slow murder, betrayals, and thefts of the types already discussed throughout this book and my other two volumes, I am not going to rehash that material here. I am just going to make two more short points regarding the destructive nature of lies.

I have noticed in my travels that many people engage in ongoing, lengthy, almost stream of conscious like lying behavior in the work place which I have concluded is a substitute for actual substantive communication. Most of the time this type of lying communication occurs in medical settings or medical manufacturing companies, although it crops up elsewhere when mining for personal information is underway. In my experience medical professionals are very big on transparency and the expectation that people will share everything, absolutely everything in the furtherance of a cooperative society.

There may be the occasional no nonsense medical professional who wants to focus on the matter at hand due to their personal version of professional behavior, but the opposing viewpoint is definitely out there, creating the setting for opposing points of view and battle even within the healing medical community. In any event, the stream of consciousness babblers of whatever comes to mind except actual truth are attempting to comply with the enforced sociability of the work place without actually losing their privacy. The option of comforting silence is not permitted as I learned since that road leads to job loss.

Therefore I would caution the gentle reader to be aware of the various underlying motives of lies and the expectations for the consumer in terms of anticipated action. The coerced workplace babblers do not care for the most part what you do with their manufactured fairy tales most of which they do not remember themselves, repeating them in various versions throughout the week to keep up the required stream of sociable chatter. The overseeing managers do expect fellow employees to contribute their own stories and entertaining verbal prattle. Apparently singing and humming also is unacceptable leading to the same outcomes as silence.

Verbal monologues outside of the workplace can and do occur and are of a similar nature to the workplace speeches, although other goals are present on the agenda. Someone is mining for information, and the lecturing questioner is actually trying to extend the process of information gathering for as long as possible in an attempt to emphasize their usefulness and possible anticipated rewards. Maybe they are just trying to relax their victim. It may be the case that these bungling interrogators do not actually want to achieve success because they inwardly disagree with the whole process while being forced to participate in a small way in aiding social enterprises.

The above is speculation on my part to explain occurrences which take place during the day, but I feel the conclusions make sense within the context of my life and daily experiences. The topics for discussion or lecture are usually always about some topic of personal revelation I am expected to chime in on, or react to in a revealing manner. I try to be forthcoming, but sometimes, I do keep my own consul. Given that I am not allowed to have real friends and social interactions, it is quite tiresome at times. Naturally gentle reader having this information to hand will help you to recognize the same phenomenon in your life, if you have not already.

Remember, I am not particularly persecuted. I am simply a member of the class of generally useless people now utilized as sounding boards for information on perceptions and motivations, and also queried just in case I become more toxic via head injury, drug ingestion, tumor, or blood clot. For any number of reasons, you too gentle reader may be needed as a revealer of perceptions and motivations or as a sounding board without any real genuine acquaintanceship and warmth being expressed by socializing parties taking a charming initiative on one occasion but never to be seen or heard from again.

Which brings me to my last comments on lying. Although lying is prevalent in the environment, most people when being honest with themselves and others, will admit that it is not enjoyable to be subjected to a steady diet of lies, or to have to spend some portion of the day constantly sifting through communications for truth spoken by a group of daily peers one hoped in youth would be more companionable, if silent more often than not.

Despite the literature to the contrary on man being a voluble outspoken character, I suspect that like other animals, man uses speech practically as a means of relaying information and otherwise remains relatively quiet. Unless a person is crafting a joke, having to come up with something to say which won't make the speaker feel idiotic is hard work. First you have to figure out what others might want to hear, and then you have to scan your brain to see if you have any relevant insights and then try to milk a few fun facts to know and tell for as long as possible, until inevitably, there is simply no more to be said.

Who are the people who insist on filling the airways with some kind of noise when there is actually no shared experience, information, or helpful substance available? Well besides musicians, storytellers and other entertainers who might also prefer silence until they had perfected their show, you have the propaganda folks who want to convince others of questionable truths and flat out errors. Right now I am sure there are a few people pointing accusing fingers at me in regard to my repetitious call for equality, love, tolerance and a safety net.

Personally, I do not feel my writing is propaganda. I feel it is the sharing of conclusions from life experience in some amount of detail to help the gentle reader learn how to mold conclusions for himself and to demonstrate my internal thinking process of asking questions and answering them. Propaganda usually is very brief so as to leave out details which would unmask the slogans and pithy sentiments the propagandist is trying to instill in consumers. Like other books of persuasion I provide the information and process by which conclusions are reached, with which the reader is free to disagree and argue to the content since there is no force, compulsion or blackmail demanding mental compliance.

Right near all the economics books in the library are also books on Totalitarianism, which is why I bring up propaganda in this discussion of the Tenth commandment of lies and bearing false witness. Between fellow citizens naturally some amount of misinformation takes place dictated by the competitive zeal of the participants wanting a position in society. Over and above the squabbling between neighbors in the earnest endeavor to provide for children, spouses, and themselves, you have the group of people charged with creating the appearances necessary to provide the required social environment of the moment.

When a nation is experiencing a period of armed conflict, suffering from negotiated treaties and embargos, or otherwise at the mercy of more powerful world forces, there is more emphasis than in peaceful times on the sacrifices the military and others must make to protect and provide survival resources. Real sacrifices are made prompted by the movements

197

of nations. The content of life experiences gets curtailed. Suddenly more secrecy is necessary. More invasion of privacy and other civil rights encroachments are tolerated in situations of crisis. Since nations in crisis develop enmity with other nations, terrorism is more prevalent providing the pragmatic backdrop for all types of incursions into home sanctuaries by all types of organizations.

Crisis caused by natural disasters in the form of storms, earthquakes, tornados, tsunamis, droughts, and other visitations by Mother Nature elicit national responses to remedy the crisis situations and remove discomfort. As if the vagaries of climate were not enough, human strife is usually prevalent due to the lack of survival resources which are destroyed during the storm events.

Witnessing nations to these acts of God and nature expect lessons to be learned and plans put in place to prevent future catastrophes which may or may not materialize for the victim nation. If the victim nations in question rely on religion predominantly as a unifying force for the people where science and technology play a small role in unifying the people through employment and helpful hygiene and medicine, one can expect the poverty stricken nations to continue on much the same path as before, directed by an unchanging God who will do as He sees fit and man must await his fate.

Needless to say the leadership in these nations supported by primitive religion may be willing to accept generous gifts of aid in times of distress, but otherwise, wish to leave the technological situation unchanged since technology brings in its wake a complete overhaul to society structures based on some type of vertical hierarchy. However, the ready availability of water can be quite a persuader ultimately, as is ready food, and basic medical care, moving the poorest of nations into a higher standard of living than previously.

To achieve these types of changes in this type of environment I would say pretty much no propaganda was necessary except by leadership in the nation wanting to assume some amount of credit for positive changes and propaganda assurances to this same leadership who does not want to experience deadly egg on the face when the water well dissolves into the ground in the next storm. Although some amount of exchanged "It was nice while it lasted" would provide minimal comfort, it might turn out to be no comfort if populations had expanded based on the ready availability of water supplies. Five people scrabbling for water are bad, fifty is much worse.

So the problem is finding the right technology for any climate site on the planet, supported by the knowledge base of the current population.

Since the least expensive and technologically complex aids to improve the environment are employed, members of the poorer nation are able to step up and learn the needed skills and information to maintain the new machine technology, the new medical helpers, or other new innovations. New deployments of technology can take place when needed or when the new technicians feel ready and able to take the next step in water provision technology, for example.

At some point, water, food, shelter, basic medical care and other necessities have been acquired and assimilated to act as permanent survival resources under reasonably expected natural crisis events. The occupants of poorer nations could continue to consume invented technology of the Western world, or guided by their still highly influential religious spiritual beliefs which encouraged them in the first place to make all the changes and learn a whole new set of information, they could take a day of rest sort of speak, and leave well enough alone for the moment.

That is the funny thing about religion. It can work both ways, as the encourager of effort and hard work in gaining knowledge to help the community, or as the condemner of knowledge in good and evil. The proper labeling of knowledge is the trick, and perhaps where propaganda starts making its first appearance after survival security has been basically attained.

After all, what exactly is knowledge? Knowledge as often as not is power in understanding, granting a person power to act with good judgment regarding his own life, and the power to understand the workings of the surrounding environment. When does knowledge, reasoning abilities and predictions of future outcomes change from good to bad? Originally mental acuity helped provision the community, but at some point the continued sophistication of technology unintentionally allowed for misuse in personal gain and advantage.

The complexities of technology which require a large time investment for acquiring specialized skills and knowledge permitted the propaganda of "more intelligent people designed by nature" to pass the general consumption goal posts. It takes time, concentration, patience, and a willingness to interact with technological material, but with rare exceptions, anybody can do it. You will not be a pro tomorrow, next year, or even in three years in some cases requiring an enormous knowledge and experience base. Remember it takes time, determination, and the willingness to stick with it, but it does not take a special set of DNA genes or a particular color of skin and hair.

When does the refusal to gain knowledge change from bad to good? Clearly a person should resist knowledge acquisition of the nature

199

that the world is flat, the moon is a perfect geometric globe, eating broccoli will make your head explode, and men are from Mars while women are from Venus. There is no limit to the cranks and virally infected information out there, figuratively speaking.

Given the amount of wistful calls for simpler times and a more natural approach to life, it is not surprising that some group of people are choosing to ignore science and technological advances altogether. I personally might be guilty of a minor technological brain melt down due mostly to my inability to afford financially to keep up. It may also be the case that I do not want to deal with the fussy confusing contracts which surround all new technology. My problem is less of technological brain impairment and more a fear of misunderstanding twenty pages of legally fine-tuned rules and regulations the infraction of which may cause me severe personal distress.

I suspect that others are not so much uninterested, or scared of new technology so much as they are concerned about the impact to their lives, jobs, and personal power in the social environment. They feel it was only a few years ago that the office got a new computer network involving several job losses, and now they are going to upgrade the whole works again.

Who is going to be the next to go? It is with these kinds of changes and losses that people begin to simply refuse to upgrade skills and use new programs and new technology efficiently. It is not that learning is not actually kind of fun and interesting. The problem is that these changes are usually accompanied by losses of valued job security and personnel in the environment. Hence the propaganda emanating from those in administrative professions is a lack of computer savvy, only making their intelligence position worse and adding more misinformation to the gradations of intelligence hogwash.

At this moment, as far as I can tell, the economic ideal across the board is still for growth in economic returns of money so that the expanding population will be able to use that extra money to support their habit of breathing, food consumption, sleeping in safe shelters, and other basic necessities. Populations in underdeveloped countries are also providing an outlet for new materials and technologies developed specifically for their climate and so forth, keeping others busy, but not exactly remunerated in the conventional sense. Hence the need for computer generated dollars at the least, but also the export of actual jobs giving the underdeveloped populace funds to be taxed so the government can make the appearance of paying for the new technological improvements.

Globalization is well underway, providing a quality of life and standard of living across the board for everyone, which is hard to label as anything other than a good thing, propaganda or no propaganda. However, propaganda can still be utilized to label those bereft of useful, meaningful employment as lazy slackers. Add into the unemployment mix caused by improving technology the question of whether the nations slower in technology utilization can be counted on to always want the latest new gadgets in order to keep up, and you have a genuine negative propaganda program floating the airwaves.

What if the developing nations decide they want to stop? Adequate food, clothes, shelter and medicine is basically good enough; they want to play more in the abundant desert sun, and limit population growth. Who can blame them? I am not sure I want to insist they have to learn more and work harder at more complex technological endeavors so that I can in turn learn more and work harder.

I said learning was fun, but what I suppose I really meant was that learning is fun at a reasonable pace. Also, some of the dry subjects for learning need a truly meaningful goal present on the horizon, or some type of encouraging meaning backdrop to help a person engage fully all their faculties. Learning may be fun for learning's sake for some, but these may be the insecure mental challenges people not sure they will be appreciated and liked once everyone catches up to them. More accurately, the mental challenges people are not learning for learning's sake, they are learning to insure a secure and healthy survival atmosphere for them personally.

When technological advance and learning new knowledge comes down to insuring psychological security and power for the best learners and reasoners because they feel threatened, I personally believe the pursuit of knowledge needs to take a new direction toward sympathetic understanding. Creating a more loving and tolerant atmosphere, and provisioning everyone with a safety net will prevent the "generated through ongoing study" smart people's imagination from feeling a threat created by some group of people returning to violent jungle survival behavior.

Otherwise, propaganda cleverly devising arguments for some people being superior to others will be permanent environmentally accepted lies. The presence of these lies coupled with blossoming population growth and the egos created by superiority are the foundation of brutal, freedom destroying totalitarian regimes.

According to the books and some people I have met along the path of life, apparently an environment of equality is part of the recipe for totalitarian regimes. Really? Well that is a tough pill for me to swallow.

Frankly, I don't buy it. In my opinion the books and the hierarchy supporters determined to change my mind about a horizontal civilization structure were trying to create an amount of propaganda against equality so that people would be frightened by the prospect.

I have already related my personal experiences in which fellow workers tried to use deceit and clever sequences of events to blame me for mistakes I did not make so I would finally admit I was wrong and a subpar person myself, accepting always being the person moved about from workplace to workplace to preserve motivations for witnessing solid pillars of stone. For me, all those machinations supported by the vertical hierarchy structure are the recipe for totalitarian regimes, where arbitrary leadership makes decisions according to criteria of the moment to experience unfettered freedom for leadership and the inner circle of support personnel.

Perhaps quite of few other people by luck of being in the right place at the right time may also manage to eek out some quality of life for a while. Frankly, it all depends on the success of human engineering experiments in concentration camps, the onward march of technology doing jobs previously done by humans, and the final number decided on as necessary humans on the planet to maintain the species.

Just as emotional, mental, and spiritual rewards can take on a survival imperative in a competitive hierarchical society, so does the freedom to make all the rules at a moment's notice, apparently the regular practice of both Stalin and Hitler, the totalitarian mass murderers of recent history. Reading the books, apparently the use of constant replacement terror kept supporters in check while propaganda kept the general population basically at ease with events.

In both Russia and Germany duplication or even multiplication of official organizations and job positions kept everyone in constant jeopardy of losing their valued spot. The conclusion is although a hierarchy was present from the elite down to the citizen sympathizers, the replacement dynamic rendered everyone essentially equal, making equality the culprit. REEEAAAALLY!?!?!?! Oh please. I am not sure that even qualifies as equally as plausible as "the cat ate my homework".

I am just guessing here, I wasn't there, but the presence of death squads, concentration work camps, extermination camps, purges, and regularly unexplained disappearances I would say was more responsible for keeping people in constant jeopardy of losing their "spot". If the equality present in the regular issuance of the threat of death is the type of equality to be avoided, than okay, let's not plump for the equality in death dynamic as the tone for our equality civilization structure. As I never tire of saying, the equality I personally am advocating is the one supported by enjoying the gift of life, love, tolerance and a safety net of survival resources for everyone. Equality in life versus equality in death, pick one.

As you can see gentle reader, it is all in how you tell it. Keep your eyes wide open for lies, false witness and propaganda, and try not to participate in these activities yourself or you can see what you have to look forward to. It may not be a lecture from God shortening your gift of life, but it could easily get shortened.

ELEVEN: Do not covet your neighbor's spouse, house or other possession

Finally, we made it to the last commandment not to covet. It may be the case that once again I got a wee bit carried away and put a few words into the Almighty's mouth. We'll see. Still, concentrate on enjoying your gift of life and do not allow others, or the promptings of your competitive survival instinct to diminish experiences, people and material resources which are perfectly adequate and fully capable of shouldering emotional, mental, and spiritual meanings.

If God, leadership, or leadership's pickers and choosers are watching, and I assure you that the latter two are in many cases, than the spirit of your ongoing dissatisfaction with security in a nice house, spouse, family and career may land you sooner or later in quicksand. When choices have to be made to satisfy the demands of an artificial vertical hierarchy, some kind of criteria must be used to place a person on the bad guy side to balance the overall motivational equation of good people vs. bad people.

The criteria can range from a person's downward spiral impacting the fewest attached dependents and pillar of stone social acquaintances to a person wanting to maintain the comfortable standard of living they are used to sharing with lifetime acquaintances and friends, all of who are somewhat or completely negatively labeled already. Naturally if a person has become addicted to constant change or has somehow gotten sold on travel and constant change by witnessing an appealing media tale, this person may become negatively labeled also.

Being on the run in a socially acceptable manner, a person may not fully understand the nature or even the presence of his negative label. Whether the person knows it completely or not the unstable/negative label is there preventing any hope of permanent employment, while still allowing for being the rolling head whenever a workplace scapegoat is needed. It is not exactly a win-win situation, but for social engineers and economists, it is close enough.

In the absence of highly visible social detractions, pickers and choosers, who have made up their mind that in order to fulfill quotas a certain person is the most desirable candidate, must find a way to visibly destabilize the choice candidate, derailing uncomfortable questions about why such a nice person got the axe. If all else fails, outright erroneous propaganda can be used, but if possible, getting a person to declare public dissatisfaction with their job is better.

For chosen single women/men, a failed romantic encounter can be utilized to erode the quality of the workplace while helpful picking and choosing cohorts simultaneously present other career alternatives as being easily gathered for the taking, like extra fruit otherwise going to waste and disuse on the ground. The other careers need never actually materialize after the scorned and shamed person leaves their job.

If the scorned and shamed person musters some resiliency and pluck, they may emotionally survive the failed romance, but the presence of the event for all solid pillars of stone witnesses will support any accusations of oversights and mistakes. Given enough time and doubt creation in the atmosphere, any chosen individual can be shown the door with a minimum of collateral damage to productive personnel kept out of the loop of the appearance game.

This career ending chain of events does not always begin with a failed romance, simply accusing a chosen person over and over again is enough, and without any disputes from the chosen employee can create the desired dismissal almost as efficiently as with the failed romance. Use of the failed romance allows for the gathering of information which will make the ability to design an accusatory story that much better and harder to detect.

The lessons in covetousness here are several. Although the epitome of romantic thought is not to exclude any possibility for romance guided by the practical concerns of the artificial competitive vertical hierarchy, still, it is best to avoid forming intimate attachments at the workplace while the competitive ethic is still so prevalent. If restraint cannot be mustered, do your level best to prevent destruction to your career satisfaction when and if the romance goes south.

Avoid the conclusion of thinking a change of scenery will heal the wounds only time can really take care of prompted by coveting an unblemished job environment. Opting for the short term solution of coveting another career position over healing yourself and the reputation damage in the current environment can lead to repeat episodes of the same event once networked management gets the word out. Remember, scapegoats are needed and used everywhere. The popularity of the Bible is based in part on this environmental psychological fact.

As with any type of serial killer, once your number is up, your number is up, but it is also possible that several people will be chosen as the possible scapegoats in a redundancy plan to get the labeling accomplished sooner than later. It may also happen that like a pardon from the governor of the state for those in jail, you too may benefit from the dumb luck which brings extra work to your company right before the axe falls of your thin neck. Lastly, even though pickers, choosers and management have the outright solid advantages of more freedom to act and better information to act on, still, even the best laid plans can go awry, giving any chosen blame taker a second lease on career life, for a while anyway.

Hang in there at your job for as long as you can before the inevitable takes place, and then, do not blame yourself or call yourself a loser. Learn the lesson of not coveting a new environment prompted by unpleasant events at your current job coupled with sly encouragements to leave. Your job was fine before you met that manipulative lout currying favor and establishing competitive advantage. You may very well wind up having to leave anyway, but leave on your own schedule or make it difficult for the propaganda appearance game to easily blind others through your professions of disagreement with the labels others are so anxious to match with your name.

One last word of caution, I have noticed in my employment travels that some group of people choose to accept or embrace their role of scapegoat, taking the blame and dismissal at work places whenever the demand for actual severed heads is made. I believe their calculation is that it will be easier to get new employment as an eventual blame taker than as an equally dedicated hard working employee as the other insecure employees and management, creating some amount of distress in anticipated fears of replacement before a person even gets picked for hire.

Obviously there are countless scenarios out there for consideration and which are applied in assuring the chosen personnel remain in a workplace with untainted motivation. Gentle reader it is up to you to sort the events in your personal work environment and to succeed as best you can. Clearly success is most readily assured when a person is satisfied with their career choice and not coveting a position elsewhere. Coveting the job you actually have places your name on the list of anticipated removals as close to the bottom as possible given your other competitive social assets.

One of the other noteworthy characteristics about totalitarianism is the lack of rational behavior as defined by the material profit motive.

Since totalitarians want to take over the world, survival resources come in handy for conquering other nations when provisioning the armed forces, but otherwise, these survival resources might wind up generating freedom for actions not dictated by the regime and could create obstacles to the immediate domination of the occupied territory and peoples.

Clearly totalitarians take a dim view of the types of actions which are supported by relaxation from survival stress, creative artistic endeavors of beauty for instance, which their regimes may support only through carefully supervised work projects. Otherwise, the odd peasant producing art will have to find odds and ends to fuel his desire to create something lovely.

More likely what the totalitarians are concerned about, or any system designed to limit resources to some group, is the creation of good feelings between happy secure people which tend to generate even more emotional support and security seemingly out of thin air and the good chemicals produced in the brain through beneficial social interaction. Naturally shared trust, belongingness and joy in all its forms reduce the efficiency effects of terror. In order for the terror to work, all the joy and so forth has to be erased and replaced with panic. It takes time for this substitution to take place, impairing the freedom of movement and achievement of desirable outcomes for terrorizing leadership.

The profit motive to produce efficiently as many goods as possible for sharing amongst everyone is an ideal profit motive I am not sure appears as such in so many words in any modern economic system. Most economic systems to survive the hierarchy environment they were born into also have to present some version of civilization structure founded in a hierarchy of some kind, and therefore distribute all produced profit unevenly.

The Communist use of hereditary leadership and the constant need to use extra resources to continue expansion of their ideal in the world prevents too much excess to fall into individual hands creating unpredictable events and impaired domination. Similarly, the networked capitalist ideal assures that resources remain in the hands of those successfully networked and properly onboard with how resource disposal is to take place within the various levels of unevenly rewarded careers.

The totalitarians seem to incorporate both the use of all excess materials for expansion, keeping the poor in concentration camps entirely on the survival edge, while providing better resources to the upper levels in the hierarchy for as long as the members of these levels avoid a purge. With globalization, all these lines and differences are getting blurred somewhat so that a person in the Capitalist career system who loses sight of being a distinguished and superior professional might find they are purged into unemployment, not a fun place to be, but not a concentration camp either, … yet. Given enough time, increased population, concern for the environment, and restricted resources in some regions and all excess materials may have to be used to combat terrorism and globalize the planet without killing the planet.

Like everyone else, the totalitarians want to create a predictable environment so leadership can feel secure in their positions and ongoing decisions, while also creating a level of confusion for enemies in times of wars reducing easy anticipation of planned actions in the totalitarian territories. Historians note that this is upsetting to the opponents of totalitarian regimes, not being able to use the self interest in the profit motive to politically predict the climate of a renegade nation.

It almost seems as if these other countries are saying the totalitarian nations are not playing the game of war fairly. Is it possible to play the game of war fairly? War is a game? Is it a war when a country armed with machine guns attacks lesser developed nations? Is the profit outcome of the conquered peoples in nations given due material consideration in all aftermath? Well, I digress, but it does make you wonder.

Barring unassimilated conquered peoples, in general the outcomes of lust for power and survival resources which are used to manipulate the population into competitive zeal and frenzied productivity gives leadership in a nation material military advantage to protect national territory and hopefully, lots of goodies for the preferred population to consume creating a rewarding lifestyle. The reverse of this efficiency and provisioning of the populace with as large an allotment of survival resources as can be reasonably maintained is not caring about the physical wellbeing of the populace, or only caring to the point of providing the bare minimum of survival resources to sustain life.

The totalitarian regime supporters count on, I am guessing, the presence of absolute freedom to engage in activities which the other profit motive civilization structures frown on right from the beginning, i.e. freedom to murder, steal, rape, bear false witness, and other violence. Eventually a person might expect his number to come up for execution, but at least he will have lived a life full of domination through extreme inhumane experiences visited on others, which some might judge as preferable to having lived a life right from the start as a receiving victim of extreme inhumane experiences.

In a slightly different variation where the totalitarian dynamic is still being masked behind appearances, a person might choose to be a scapegoat for as long as possible and self-medicate until a drug overdose carries him away, or a person can choose to be an official or unofficial picker and chooser in the environment of those who will become scapegoats.

In the totalitarian regime territories there is no moral compass which says a totalitarian person must follow certain rules and leave the atmosphere of the jungle behind. To me, it almost seems as if the cosmic universe is being put in charge by removing all moral man made guidelines in civilization except for the dictates of the moment as determined by the totalitarian regime's leader or leaders.

Does the above outline remind you of anything? It reminds me of the ongoing trend to get rid of all rules and adopt philosophies of the moment as outlined in my second book especially, and to some degree in my first book. When I wrote my first book I was noting internally the similarities between the structure of concentration camps undermining individuality and freedom to behave morally, and some of the happenings in workplaces trying to achieve the same goals with me.

Now reading these other books it almost seems as if some group of people is using the learned lessons from WWII totalitarianism as blueprints and updating the practices for modern times so the presence of this population control mechanism will not be too obvious. At some point enough power and territory will be amassed to once again allow uncontrolled freedom to perform any action. The whole lot from murder to pillaging will once again be permissible while also being easily hidden behind a screen of propaganda and utter control of the entire dominated environment.

Oh my. I sound so paranoid. I do hate sounding paranoid so I must remind myself that the above is just one version of the outcome of mass globalization which is taking place in modern times. As I have said before, I believe in globalization in these times of all nations impacting the shared atmosphere. All human beings and other living organisms must share the planet, polluted atmosphere, ocean and all, to participate in the gift of life.

Given the increase in available people for the job market due to technological advance, actual technological advances removing jobs from the environment to be given to machines, and continuously improving medical and agricultural technology, humans must also engage in voluntary population control to prevent the resource shortages and excesses in population which in World War II set the stage for Hitler's and Stalin's totalitarian regimes. As stated earlier I am speaking about having only one child or no children and structuring life meaning around smaller families or the replacement activities and people to the traditional larger family units. I do not endorse purges of large numbers of population ever.

Also as a quick review, I advocate equality in participation in the enjoyed gift of life, rather than equality in the fear of death arriving at any moment for any person, allowing all manner of horror to march past panic stricken witnesses. I suppose some people are going to suggest that some people will not get to enjoy a rich fulfilled gift of life because they do not have the freedom to murder and so on. Personally, it is hard for me to take this objection seriously since I feel very few people will feel short changed, but then again, I do want to include everyone.

Why does a person opt for murder, for example? According to the totalitarians murder is quite natural and the only obstacle to wholesale human destruction of each other is the bonds of civilization and meted out punishments. It may be the case that in the very earliest of human history before certainty in survival resources was an ongoing shared social memory that murder of an isolated person with food must have been a desperate temptation many acted upon. However, sociable enjoyment of company led to cooperative actions in amassing food, and by happy accident, two food gatherers managed to generate more available food together than each might have done separately.

I suppose the totalitarians are enjoying the sociability in the presence of the preferred companions in the master race, and everyone else is as easily murdered as a miserable flea or ant polluting the beautiful environment. I have got to admit I am scaring myself a bit here, but we shall not dwell on this very depressing subject for much longer. I do want to include everyone in the enjoyment of the gift of life, and I want everyone to be able to enjoy this gift on their own terms as much as possible.

I am supposing that an emphasis on tolerance will help the totalitarian personality overcome their blood lust, when the majority of the surrounding environment aided by the presence of all types of survival resources does not support the blood lust ethic from either below or above. Also, I am concluding that an environment rich in all types of physical, emotional, mental, and spiritual rewards will have enough alternative fodder to make the transition from absolute freedom rewards in an otherwise sparsely populated environment of the other type of rewards seem as an okay exchange.

If I am not mistaken, I believe many facilities of healing use art therapy of some kind to help divert antisocial tendencies, giving a person an alternative source of self-esteem and actual fulfilling activity. In an environment of equality, the ability of the competitive hierarchy to reduce and destroy activity rewards will not be present requiring a person add in some amount of absolute freedom in action/self-esteem rewards into the mix to balance the individual while creating further mental isolation with the use of invisible self-esteem compensations only a very few informed others will have any clue about.

I would also add a note of caution against trying to undermine emotional, mental, and spiritual rewards which help to cover logistical material foul ups in physical resources and help to mend the damages from the competitive vertical hierarchy. In opposition to coveting a neighbor's house, spouse, or automobile, a person using hopeful dream material for an improved future is generating a positive emotional state on invisible rewards he is anticipating securing for himself.

Hope provides quite a bit of motivational energy and even when the specific goal is not achieved, some ball park target will likely do as well. In many cases the dream is actually enough, while helping the person to reach an improved mental state which allows for the setting and achievement of reasonable goals. In this scenario hopeful coveting of material similar to the neighbors, but not the neighbors, is the root of all economic activity.

Actual removal of another person's goods or companions is more aptly labeled revenge fantasy material. Obviously revenge fantasy can still provide a hyped up state which allows a person to function, but overall, diverting the revenge into socially acceptable goals of building one's own lifestyle from unclaimed materials is more societally stabilizing than tearing apart another person's already established lifestyle.

Although some argue the presence of any kind of nonprofit motive rational for actions reduces overall political predictability, leadership still primarily concerns themselves with the provision of bountiful physical survival resources to the populations which leadership serves. Although exceptions exist, politics is mainly the activity of leadership, even in an equality structured civilization. Enraged mobs are also responsible for some small amount of political activity, but by their very nature can predictably be counted on to be unpredictable and publically quite destructive.

The separation of church and state, the romantic freedom to pursue love and affiliations anywhere a person deems fit and the mental freedom to at least be able to think about absolutely anything are still considered the prerogative of the individual, not political leadership in action. In as far as any individual member of leadership engages in these activities in their free time is, as with any ordinary individual, their private affair. Otherwise, when performing their public service, leadership adheres to the profit motive rendering them quite predictable, open and transparent.

As stated more fully in my second book, I believe it is advisable for production and distribution personnel of survival resources in the environment to be primarily focused on efficiency, or the profit motive, to supply enough and more than enough survival resources which will put the population in a place of physical security and calm.

The general populations of laborers are fast losing their jobs to more reliable machines. Working in an environment where everyone is allowed to be happy, productive, cooperative and secure insures the reliability of the human work force which remains. Otherwise being on competitive edge until one loses a competition creates all types of demoralization from not winning. Given that only one person can be the winner, it is more profitable and productive to downplay competition and allow everyone to think and feel themselves a contributing winner within their own self-esteem creating brain.

Using extremes to make my point clear, it is desirable for emotional, mental and spiritual rewards to develop from a place of physical survival security and comfort rather than from the atmosphere of, for example, a concentration camp. Within a well-resourced hierarchy environment those in the top bracket feel most supportive of an environment which has judged them worthy and given them material rewards. Looking about at others who are receiving the basics for survival plus some amount of luxury items, the top feels like people are happy and well provisioned for in the absence of any protests to the contrary.

A person in this happy situation may need to engage in the minor manufacture of invisible rewards, but not too many. No doubt there is a mandatory amount of invisible superiority rewards where the recognition of fortunate circumstances is absent, as must be the individual blind spot for any hierarchy to continue without parading as the nonsense it actually is. As long as overpopulation is not creating angry resource deprived mobs, totalitarian tendencies among leadership need not make a showing to secure the unabated presence of rightful desert invisible rewards for the privileged positions.

In a hierarchy environment where resources are limited to begin with such as a concentration camp you have scrabbling to be on top without any survival certainty which dehumanizes all interactions. Any conversation can essentially turn murderous or murder producing in some fashion as a matter of course in heavily resource restricted environments regardless of hierarchy placement. There is no peaceful harmony to witness; it is all one survival lunge for scarce resources.

211

As for manufacturing of invisible rewards, I have read that many concentration camp survivors used memories of loved ones they hoped to be reunited with to cope with the horror. Some used the anticipation of the situation being corrected soon and returning to life as usual. Others who never had or could no longer muster these anticipations, either promptly died or embraced the possibilities of the moment, becoming the top prisoners in the camps for as long as possible, making the best materially of a losing proposition and being as violent and inhumane as the Nazis themselves, until finally, they too lost all.

The middle section of a well-resourced hierarchy will have some members striving for a superior position. Those who strive without success must accept a label of neutral non-winner at least, and actual loser at worst. Otherwise, in the middle it is safest not to appear too ambitious, but fully satisfied and employed at a career position. Some in the middle may silently amend an assessment of the hierarchy in favor of a more egalitarian ethic. Some will take action through charitable giving to the underprivileged.

Invisible rewards would be along the lines of feeling that essentially things were right with the sufficiently provisioned environment and in order to keep the presence of survival resources easily and readily available, giving excess resources away affords a person the invisible rewards of generosity. There would be some invisible rewards from being able to do a good job and behave in a cheerful manner which releases health giving chemicals in the brain.

Some might even generate some invisible superiority rewards to leadership and the wealthy for being selfish in taking more than their fair share. Further rewards could be generated in superiority to those less fortunate not displaying a sufficiently helpful and hardworking attitude. In the case of superiority rewards for the relatively safely provisioned middle group, silence as to the presence of these insolences on the one hand and arrogances on the other is advised.

I cannot speak from personal concentration camp experience, but I imagine the middle level in a camp hierarchy to be ranked by the amount of hope a person can generate since no fraternization of any kind was permitted allowing for actual interpersonal socializing rewards. Everyone would be utilizing some amount of hope and trying to keep this hope from disintegrating. All hope would clearly be lost if a person found himself a chosen member of an execution party, so all manner of bribes and other crafty abilities would establish rank in keeping a person as far away from peril as possible. Invisible rewards again would be of hope in creating survival distance from devastating recurring events with absolutely no remorse for what that means for anyone else. (Remind you of anything?)

The lowest level in a well-resourced hierarchy will have some members striving to elevate their position with success, and others failing, as with the middle class. In the lower levels these attempts generally mean less loss in terms of social face if a person does not succeed, so some amount of calculations as to impacted society members does come into achieved success stories.

It is wise for a lower level person to take the hint regarding unrealized ambition if this person is not deemed worthy material for advancement, otherwise more vigorous deterrents and harsher labels may be applied to preserve appearances for witnesses of continued failed advancement attempts creating discomfort and questions. Although there is a lot of advice to keep on trying, make sure no one is flagging you down to land, in a manner of speaking.

Invisible rewards for the lower class in some cases are being spared the nagging call of ambition to be perceived internally and externally a legitimate nice person. If resources are fairly plentiful a person can have a solidly materially supported lifestyle and camaraderie amongst others relegated to the same lower class element by blind luck.

A person in the lower level is a little freer to indulge in visible superiority rewards of the selfish hoarding upper level, causing some confusion for those in the middle witnessing such free open condemnation of those more fortunately placed and more strategically and powerfully networked. It is a gamble to say whether or not the confusion will resolve itself into letting the bad example pass to help create openings in the middle level by imitation of the example, or whether the middle level strongly identified with their particular spot in the hierarchy will take networked punitive action.

Naturally one can enjoy an invisible spot of questionable glee from the lower level watching the descent of those placed in higher levels being forced into reduced circumstances to maintain the proper number of visible negative deterrent examples. One can always sink lower, into homelessness, prison, or death, but when the environment is generally well provisioned, these more drastic demonstrations of negative deterrents for the higher levels are not as necessary since losing status, associates, and the standard of living one has become accustomed to are usually enough to keep people in the higher levels in line.

As for the lowest of the low in the concentration camps, these people generally die very quickly. They are not there to set an example; they and everybody else are there to provide experimental social engineering material and are expected to expire sooner or later. Invisible rewards can be harvested by embracing your inner sadist and relishing all pain suffered by others.

In an equality environment where everyone is secure and allowed to enjoy their gift of life, a person can reap rewards on all levels, physical, emotional, mental and spiritual. Given the more uniform provision of security and employment, people will have more in common, being able to access tolerance and compassion that much easier. Invisible rewards? Where do I start? The sky is the limit for everyone.

If a person wants to advance in love he can pick long term companions to share experiences and leave competition for the people who want to experience that emotional and mental reward. Love can also be enjoyed in a more transitory manner by simply enjoying the people one comes across on a daily basis. Do both. The sky is the limit, maybe.

The sky may just be the beginning. Think big, it is a mental reward for the taking and no one will be interested in stopping you to protect personal survival advantages. The only rewards a person would be deprived of are the ones he is least likely to want to exercise in a secure happy environment.

Just looking at these groups, which atmosphere provides the best humane environment? I am going to let the gentle reader consider that question, if necessary, further for himself.

Use of private emotional, mental, and spiritual rewards is fine for people in the privacy of their own individually directed time and activity. Like leadership, management would be badly advised to try and balance individual desires for popularity, puzzle solving, communing with god, swimming pools, art supplies, dance lessons, and other luxury goods enjoyed after community service is performed, by removing all sick days, personal days, holidays, vacations and other previous policy created stress relief valves in the environment. The removal might give management absolute freedom to do as they liked in regards to creating mental states in others, but reduction in these types of benefits reduces happiness and productivity, impairing profits and survival resources.

Individuals within the labor pool can use the mental improvements from the feeling and knowledge that they are supporting their lifestyle, which in an individual lifestyle can range in priorities from popularity to sky diving. The varying priorities will not matter, what matters is the overall positive vibes everyone can access that he is performing his bit, has survival resources to support his priorities, and has a sense of open camaraderie with the persons who regularly populate his day and those who just pass through. Management will have no need to covet the mental state and lifestyle of those burdened with less responsibility because in the equality civilization structure, their felt responsibility will be much lighter and more equally shared.

A Few Last Reflections on the Ten (Eleven?) Commandments

I have spent a lot of time reading books and reflecting to come to the conclusions already structuring my life time experience in accordance with the sage advice of my father to behave as a decent society member through honesty and the Golden Rule. Thinking about all the time and effort spent to comprehend the gist of other people's written word, it seems like an enormous work investment to arrive at the same place I started at, but I am not complaining.

Neither my healthy body nor questioning mind ever prompted me to doubt this wisdom, although the wisdom imparted by work associates to do the opposite certainly caused me to look into the foundation of their wisdom, and hence all the reading. Everyone must make the decision as to personal code for themselves based on their circumstances within the social environment. I will point out however that the moral code in the Ten Commandments, the Golden Rule, and the supplication for wisdom are tremendously popular and have weathered many years of changing governments and economic systems.

Even when people do not live up to the absolute letter or even the spirit of the commandments, many people do to some degree know about and pay respect to this ethic through the desire to perform in accordance with God's commandments of general decency where possible. With the ongoing exponential growth of populations within a steepening vertical hierarchy, more and more people are finding they must throw up their hands and "do what they got to do" when confronted with difficult life choices.

Modern day religions acknowledge these regular compromises and assure followers that heaven is still a possibility when only God can judge and look into a person's heart. Still, the presence of these actions spoils the moral environment for witnesses who do not rely on such assurances, and also for the compromisers who must feel at some point that the many necessary compromised decisions either mean that the person individually surely must be going to hell by now, or the other choice being, that no larger moral God or authority is out there overseeing the works after all.

The impact of going to hell or the loss of an overseeing God leaves some people without a behavior compass until they finally settle on the rule of the jungle within the confines of the civilization pen. For others this same conclusion prompts the decisions already reached by many life optimizing addicts to improve quality of life for the short term of remaining duration.

This description of events sounds like the final days as written in the Bible. Perhaps the inspired writers were able to anticipate these events watching the growth of populations in their lifetimes, and the consequences visited on those deemed least useful. In an attempt to wring some small drop of emotional rewards out of the doomed situation for the lowest of the low, the anticipation of the whole planet falling apart for the wicked to be replaced by the city of God for the righteous was deemed the best alternative within an unsatisfactory group of possibilities. Sort of the "least of all possible evils" if you will.

So, with the world declining into "doing what you got to do" and choosing the "least of all possible evils" where does that put a person trying to find a life code? The moment to moment life style of the jungle? The coping trance of the self-medicated?

One apparently brighter, if definitely more difficult to implement alternative, is the moment to moment lifestyle as influenced by the Ten Commandments, golden rule, and supplication for wisdom. From what I can gather walking around and absorbing various influences in the environment, this is a hoped for outcome for the general populace to stumble upon at most ideally, a very near moment in the future.

Truly, I cannot speak as to how this mental state is to be achieved, which is why I label the alternative as extremely difficult to accomplish. It may just be another one of those impossible logical constructs put out there regularly to give people a point of focus for actions, once again allowing the hierarchy to sneak in all around the edges, like perfect competition in capitalist economics and equality based on conquest ruled by a hereditary hierarchy in communist economics.

If a person cannot live within the Ten Commandments, he cannot live within the Ten Commandments even when he has no idea what the future may hold and has no personal companionship ties with the future. The thing about invisible rewards and hope is that people can and do very easily manufacture this life tonic for themselves in their brain as needed if at all possible.

Mental occupation of fantasy worlds will be an epidemic. There may be absolutely no foundation in reality to support fantasy material, but that fact need not stop anybody, and probably won't. People may not be viciously or even tenaciously for survival breaking the Ten Commandments, but rather taking actions in conformance with their personally, subconsciously created fantasy land. An in depth explanation of

216

Psychology is not within the scope of this book, or even my expertise, but as I understand the subject, the subconscious is primarily concerned with individual survival within the larger group, throwing all kinds of whammies into community organization when a person feels individually threatened but not so absolutely terrified to prevent their own helpful brain functions.

I discovered in my reading that the progression of totalitarian exterminations starts with those deemed mentally impaired, perhaps in the outline explained above. Cleansing campaigns continue with each new conquered territory, and even after the new territory is safely under military occupation and control, the secret police come in right away to ferret out any person whose mental compliance is questionable, and removes them as well.

With these very first sanitizing eliminations that seem to the overburdened populace from resource shortages to be the least harmful and threatening, the mechanism is put in place to continue regular cleansings of anyone deemed unpredictable or simply a needed warm body whose absence will create the necessary terror. Be careful what you condemn others to because you may be condemning yourself as well in a jungle environment.

It takes a totalitarian regime removing all freedoms and personal rewards, and replacing these with terror to achieve some semblance of the Ten Commandments guidelines within a lifestyle lived moment to moment to accommodate unabated population growth. In this case, the government/ruling leadership group replaces God and tailors the interpretation of the Ten Commandments to support their needs of the moment. The general populace does not engage in interpretation for themselves, but are merely the awaiting terrified open vessels of the interpretation from leadership.

The totalitarians do engage in some amount of advertising and marketing for their world view. In keeping with their overall mission to take over the world they are using movies about assassins/spies who manage to outwit the corrupted elements in the surrounding networked bureaucracy due to their exceptional mental and physical skills, and the intense training they received. The consuming populace is being assured that just as before, even in the new ethic of no rules, things still turn out for the best.

For sexually frustrated ladies such as me the movies star heart throbs such as Matt Damon and Daniel Craig fall in love with flat chested brunettes in many cases. These sorts of plot devices make it hard for a woman like me to want to see through the surface story, but, if I want to live an enjoyable life, I had better. Employing highly gifted, skilled and trained young people to dispose of a wealthy crazed businessman no other civilization device can reach is a problem created by the steep vertical hierarchy and grossly uneven rewards.

Just as with the drug problem, once one drug kingpin is removed, others step right up to take his place. The rewards for attempting this type of gamble for position are enormously enticing when contrasted with being a loser within the criminal community, the other alternative for those choosing to make these gambles. The businessman desensitized by playing for high stakes may behave in the same manner.

Fixing the actual problem instead of one person here and one person there could be done within the rules out in the open by a civilization structure emphasizing equality and distributing resources to all. It might be the case that the overall equality structure would serve as the antidote to this social dysfunction, not requiring any further remedy.

Although I get the feeling that the removal of rules and planned lifestyle suggested by the moment to moment philosophies is the preferred alternative for some portion of civilization, I cannot help but favor the lifestyle which allows a person to plan, build and invest in a gift of life, and I personally suspect some amount of lifestyle continuity will create the most peaceful, harmonious world for all. When people are allowed to be invested in their community, they are not going to want to tear it apart or replace it consciously or subconsciously. The community structure which allows for the most community support and individual freedoms to create this community support will be, in my opinion, the hope for the future globalized world.

Totalitarianism offers a return to the jungle ethic for those who have become completely disillusioned with the peaceful civilization dynamic of working, building a family and friend circle, and developing others elements in a settled leisure lifestyle. Likewise, anyone who feels their physical and mental gifts are superior to all other people and can fuel energetic lifestyle support from the feelings and actions of superiority also has an inclination for the totalitarian organization. Justification for this lifestyle is found in following the Orders of the Universe, following a natural progression of events or living as nature intended in a survival of the fittest, might makes right dynamic.

As with defining God in detail, defining the Order of the Universe, defining exactly what constitutes progress and exactly who is the fittest on the planet, man or the cockroach, these are impossible questions to answer. These questions are interesting to some and perhaps aid in accessing survival resources for those absorbed in these deliberations. If like dancing or eating a good meal stimulates the physical body, the consideration of these questions mentally stimulates and satisfies those who engage in their deliberation, than certainly these luxury hobby interests should be tolerated and shared with all others who take some interest, whatever amount, themselves.

Instead of using the observed jungle dynamic within the organized structure of civilization, I would suggest the use and promotion of behaviors which are known to healthily stabilize the individual within organized society. After all, society is made up ideally of more or less healthy individuals. Once some portion of these individuals starts being seriously poisoned through some manner of deprivation, you are disrupting the whole healthy system.

As stated earlier, the Ten Commandments have endured for quite some time, but by now, given new information from science, need ongoing clarification, interpretation and emphasis for enjoying a gift of life generously bestowed on all. To that end, I would suggest humbly bearing in mind that humans can neither describe nor know beyond a shadow of a doubt the Almighty. If humans must wade into the deep dark unknowable waters of divining the Almighty's will, I would suggest limiting wild speculations to the bestowal of the granted gift of life for the general benefit of perceived experiences. It does not hurt to think about your perceived experiences and even to be grateful if they are predominantly rich in good feelings and other types of lovely rewards.

Remember and treasure the people who help you along the way. Do not take actions which limit another person's ability to benefit from perceived experiences. Try to employ and seek wisdom in the Golden Rule, but always err on the side of allowing each person to make an informed decision about the form of quality experience for himself. Well, those are some guidelines gentle reader, by all means carry on and think up a few for yourself.

Consult how various thoughts and how contemplation of various actions makes you feel. If you feel moved to take a generous giving action, by all means do so without concern for the overall profit motive being disrupted resulting in undesirable impacts on the capitalist economic model of perfect competition. That model does not really work as theorized anyway.

Listen to your joyful dancing body. Listen to your calm thinking mind. They are telling you to share and enjoy life as much as possible in your current circumstances. Use your healthy body and clear mind to gather observations to sift for truth to improve the planetary environment we all have a lifetime stake in. Peaceful informed numeric population control, equality, tolerance, love and a safety net would be a good start.